Blue Pencil Warriors

Censorship and Propaganda in World War II

John Hilvert

University of Queensland Press

First published 1984 by University of Queensland Press
P.O. Box 42, St Lucia, Queensland, Australia

© John Hilvert 1984

This book is copyright. Apart from any fair dealing for the
purposes of private study, research, criticism or review, as
permitted under the Copyright Act, no part may be reproduced
by any process without written permission. Enquiries should
be made to the publisher.

Typeset by University of Queensland Press
Printed in Australia by The Dominion Press-Hedges & Bell,

Distributed in U.K., Europe, the Middle East, Africa, and the
Caribbean by Prentice Hall International, International Book
Distributors Ltd, 66 Wood Lane End, Hemel Hempstead, Herts.,
England

Distributed in the U.S.A. and Canada by Technical Impex
Corporation, 5 South Union Street, Lawrence, Mass. 01843 U.S.A.

Cataloguing in Publication Data

National Library of Australia

Hilvert, John, 1945- .
  Blue Pencil Warriors

  Bibliography.
  Includes index.
  ISBN 0 7022 1953 3.

  1. Australia. Dept. of Information — History.
  2. World War, 1939–1945 — Australia — Propaganda.
  I. Title. (Series: University of Queensland
  Press scholars' library).

940.54'889'94

Library of Congress

Hilvert, John, 1945- .
  Blue Pencil Warriors

Bibliography.
  Includes index.
  1. World War, 1939–1945 — Propaganda. 2. Australia.
Dept. of Information — History. 3. Propaganda, Australian
— History — 20th century. 4. World War, 1939–1945 —
Censorship — Australia. 5. Australia — History —
20th century. I. Title. II. Series.
D810.P7A84   1984   940.54'88   83-12345

Blue Pencil Warriors

Contents

Acknowledgments *vii*
List of Abbreviations *ix*

Introduction *1*
1 Origins *10*
2 The Beginnings *17*
3 The Early Development of the Broadcasting and Censorship Divisions *36*
4 Murdoch's "Department of Expression" *53*
5 Foll's Consolidation *77*
6 The Department under Ashley *96*
7 Bonney and Ball: Expression and Suppression outside the Department *131*
8 Transformation *153*
9 The Censorship Row of April 1944 *174*
Conclusion *197*

Appendix A
  Press and Broadcasting Censorship Order: Publicity Censorship Directions, 31 October 1944 *204*
Appendix B
  Statistics: Censorship Instructions 1940–45 *220*

Appendix C
  Joint Press Statement on Censorship, Sydney,
    17 April 1944   *225*
Bibliography   *237*
Index   *253*

Acknowledgments

This book was based on my MA thesis completed in 1979.

I acknowledge with deep gratitude the assistance received from my supervisor, Mr Murray Goot; to Dr Cameron Hazelhurst for his comments and suggestions on an earlier draft; and to Professor Don Aitkin for his encouragement and support throughout the study. I am especially grateful to Emeritus Professor W. MacMahon Ball, Professor Geoffrey Sawer, Ms Helen Ferber, Mr Lionel Wigmore, the late Mr C.E. Sayers, Mr Ian Hamilton, Mr Robert Horne, the late Mr Tom Hoey, and the late Mr Hattil Foll for sharing with me their recollections of the Department of Information.

I would like to thank also Jack Waterford and Linda Bruce for their encouragement and assistance. Any faults remaining, however, are mine alone.

And special thanks to Chris.

John Hilvert
Canberra
September 1982

List of Abbreviations

A.A.	Australian Archives
AAP	Australian Associated Press
ABC	Australian Broadcasting Commission
AFCB	Australian Federation of Commercial Broadcasters
AIF	Australian Imperial Force
AJA	Australian Journalists Association
ALP	Australian Labor Party
ANL	Australian National Library
AWA	Amalgamated Wireless (Australasia) Ltd
BBC	British Broadcasting Corporation
CPC	Chief Publicity Censor
CPD(HR)	*Commonwealth Parliamentary Debates* (House of Representatives)
GHQSWPA	General Headquarters South-West Pacific Area
MUP	Melbourne University Press
NEI	Netherlands East Indies
OWI	Office of War Information
SPC	State Publicity Censor
s.w.	shortwave broadcasting
UAP	United Australia Party
WPB	War Production Board

Introduction

When a nation goes to war, it must make the most of its resources. Manpower is mobilized. The people are persuaded to conserve precious raw materials for war production. The nation's sons and daughters are encouraged to volunteer for service — and even to make the "supreme sacrifice". In short, when a nation goes to war, a formerly diverse society must become a co-ordinated fighting machine.

When a nation goes to war, it fights not only on the side of God but also on the side of ballyhoo and bullshit, together with the darker divinities of bowdlerization and blue-pencil. The public must be informed and persuaded to do what is expected of it. The various publicity media must co-operate with the government, both in the negative sense of suppressing publication of material that might imperil the war effort and in the positive sense of expressing the government's war stance and enhancing public appreciation of its efforts.

The special place accorded to publicity and censorship in acquainting, mobilizing and maintaining the morale of the public during major national crises is no innovation of the twentieth century, nor for that matter is the practice of establishing publicity specialists to conduct this function.

As long ago as 1030, when St Olaf, King of Norway, drew up linesmen in battle order, he arranged for his bards to be present on the field within a shield force of the strongest and boldest warriors:

> Ye shall remain here and see the events which may take place and then ye will not have to follow the reports of others in what ye afterwards tell or sing about it.[1]

Wars, as the Canadian Royal Commission on Government Organization reported, have "a catalytic effect on the development of specialised information services in Government".[2]

But is it worth examining the development of these information services? On the one hand, there is the view that it is clearly a field that, at best, boils down to administrative trivia irrelevant to the war effort, let alone the context of politics.[3] On the other hand, there is the view that the very outcome of a war rests on the effectiveness of the propaganda organization and is central to political insight of developments.[4]

The Australian experience is worth telling, and is instructive. Very little has been written on the subject of government and media relations in World War II. There are very few sustained accounts of the government's censorship activities. There are a few myths still propounded and a few lessons yet to be learnt.

This book is a study of the Australian government's propaganda and censorship activities during World War II. Based on original research, it has extracted material from hitherto unopened government files and from private papers, and insight from personal interviews with leading figures of the period who were engaged in propaganda and censorship.

The little remembered Department of Information provides the focus of the study. As the principal agency responsible for publicity and censorshp, it excited controversy from the time it was created on 4 September 1939 to the time it was due for dissolution at the war's end six years later. At various times, Robert Menzies, John Curtin, Sir Keith Murdoch, Arthur Calwell, Chief Censor Edmund Bonney, Alf Conlon, Damien Parer, W. MacMahon Ball and Brian Penton, the editor of the Sydney *Daily Telegraph*, came to influence as well as be influenced by the Department's activities.

It began with a staff of less than a hundred and a budget of less than £45,000. By 1945, its staff had increased fourfold and its expenditure sevenfold. Five government Ministers were responsible for its activities during its war service. It continued to prosper for another five years. Although disbanded in 1950, it reappeared in various guises as the Australian News and Information Bureau, the Department of Media, the Australian Information Service of the Department of Administrative Services and now, Special Minister of State.

The Department's responsibilities included the censorship of all media, the management of shortwave broadcasting (later to become Radio Australia), the production and distribution of cinematographic films, the coordination and procurement of government advertising, the publication and distribution of pamphlets, posters and photos, the provision of editorial material to local and overseas media, and the maintenance of public morale.

This study chronicles the activities of the Department to highlight how changes in military and political circumstances influenced the Department's policy and practice. Although coverage is given to the range of the Department's activities, the operations and policies of its censorship arm receive particular attention. Of all the Department's functions, its censorship was at once the most controversial, least understood and most arcane. There are few public records of the Department's censorship policies — what they were, how legitimate they were, or how harshly or liberally they were enforced.

The accessible accounts of the Department's censorship activities are available mainly through the daily press reports. Brian Penton's *Censored!* encapsulates the received wisdom of the time. Nevertheless, his account, influential and vivid though it was, could hardly be expected to detail the fairness of censorship, since the press was the main object of censorship.

The only other account of censorship is to be found in Paul Hasluck's two-volume official history, *The Government and the People*. Even Hasluck's authoritative coverage seems to falter in this respect and appears influenced more by the popular judgements of the time than by any systematic analysis of censorship operations. For example, he concludes "from documents available" that censorship became more political under the Labor government and through ministerial intervention.[5] His evidence is based on selected incidents during Labor's time in office rather than a formal comparison of censorship activities under both administrations. It is possible to locate as many examples of political as opposed to military censorship under the Labor government's predecessor as well, even though the press did not seem as alert or as inclined to publicize them.

Although Hasluck rightly complains that many of the Department's files were incomplete, there are sufficient papers to permit the computation of broad statistical trends about the rate of censorship direction over most of the war period. A statistical examination of censorship instructions issued from 1940 to 1945 suggests that, if anything, there was more censorship carried out under non-Labor than Labor governments. This is particularly surprising, in view of the general low threat experienced by Australia under non-Labor governments.

Certainly political censorship flourished under both régimes. However, the political goals varied. Under Menzies, censorship delayed reports of embarrassing incidents in the guise of withholding information of value to the enemy. Under Curtin, censorship became obsessed with "prohibiting false impressions abroad" and "protecting the good name of Australia" in the guise of needing to project Australia as a worthy ally to overseas audiences, particularly the Americans.

The censors' concern with overall impressions can be

traced to one ironic feature in their background, which frequently has been overlooked. By 1944, most censors were themselves journalists. How these journalists accommodated their seemingly antithetical censorship functions remains central to the study. It seems that journalists were pleased to take jobs as censors because the experience of the Great War suggested that if censorship was needed, it was better for journalists, rather than quasi-military officers, to undertake this delicate task. Censorship bore some resemblance to the discipline of editing. Some censors began to subedit and correct grammar and spelling, to the chagrin of private journalists.

A fresh examination of Australia's most notorious censorship incident — the day the papers were suppressed in April 1944 — also discloses some insights. Today there remains a view that the government lost some of its censorship power through a High Court decision. However, there is little evidence for this in practice, although the press propaganda of the time might explain this mistaken impression. Indeed, a case can be made by the Censor winning on points. More significantly, the study places the censorship row into a new perspective, arguing that the incident was a direct result of the censorship concern with prohibiting false impressions abroad.

It is not surprising that the Department acquired a poor reputation. It was at one time or another berated by politicians, the press, the public, the government and the military services. Hasluck characterizes the Department as "singularly useless" in realizing the government's communication objectives.[6]

Thus one of the more intriguing riddles is how a Department created for purely wartime purposes continued to function when the war ended. It is especially perplexing that Arthur Calwell, the Minister who presided over the Department's transformation and survival in peacetime, as a backbencher had been one of the Department's most bitter critics: "if ever there was a Department that ought to be abolished, it is that Department", said Calwell about Information in 1942.

Yet why did the Department of Information survive beyond the war with increased resources? The issues with which the Department had to wrestle were by no means unique and had direct counterparts among its allies. The Department was modelled on the British Ministry of Information, whose Director-General conceded publicly that it was "the most unpopular department in the whole British Commonwealth of Nations".[7] Likewise, the United States Office of War Information, which performed similar expressive tasks, encountered difficulties in carrying out its mission.[8]

It also would be fair to describe Information as the department nobody wanted. Originally, it was proposed that a Propaganda and Censorship Bureau be established within the Armed Services. For various reasons, the government opted for a civilian agency modelled on the British Ministry of Information. However, the armed forces chose, to avoid where possible, the new Department's services and requirements.

To the Armed Services, the Department represented the chief government protagonist for full disclosure. It therefore was regarded as a major security problem. The Army and Navy were reluctant to furnish the Department with background on military conditions. In consequence, the private news-gathering organizations found the Department of marginal benefit. The Services felt the Department would not be tough enough to carry out censorship, therefore their censorship guidance to the Department proved capricious and inconsistent.

In 1942 and 1943, the Department lost its censorship, advertising and shortwave radio functions. A Cabinet sub-committee recommended its abolition. Yet it survived. There is a lesson here for advocates of small government. Can departments in themselves act in a political fashion to forestall their fate?

How the Department established itself as a dominant propaganda and censorship agency in the face of this lack of co-operation is carefully traced. The main finding is that the Department found itself with a new mission: the dissemination of information overseas. This freed it from competing with the local press and gave it much needed prestige. At the same time, it continued to influence the nature of censorship. To this day, the Australian Information Service has prospered precisely because it is dominantly concerned with providing information overseas.

People shaped and were shaped by the Department. Departments are worth studying on their own terms as mediators, guardians and significant institutionalizers of values. One commentator characterized it well when he said:

> The administrative system involves considerably more than ministerial mechanics or statics of the common view. It mirrors, reinforces, and sometimes helps realign the major interest groupings of society and by the same token mirrors deep ambivalences in all of us.[9]

This study aims to enrich understanding of the means by which those values are provided. Organizations can be treated as social systems. One can trace their special means of development, adaptations and resolution of internal and external conflicts. For example, organizations tend to seek staff with values similar to the established staff.[10]

The study looks at the way Ministers for Information managed their portfolio, how senior officers responded to and initiated policy, and how various sections within the Department developed their styles and values. In addition, the means by which the ministry influenced realignments in the structure of the press, commercial radio as well as the Australian Broadcasting Commission, are explored.

What happened then when the most powerful media magnate in Australia, Sir Keith Murdoch, accepted Menzies' invitation to head the Department? The media's enthusiasm for the appointment was brought to an end when Murdoch committed a major blunder. A new regulation gave Murdoch the power to dictate the wording of newspaper and radio news, if he so desired. The press and radio interests launched a savage attack, forcing Murdoch to withdraw. His promises to ease censorship and to move the spirit of the people were not kept.

A separate chapter assesses the Murdoch blunder and its implications for the Department's future progaganda and censorship activities. How two schools of thought developed about propaganda and censorship can be understood through the clashes between Chief Censor Edmund Garnett Bonney and the Head of the Shortwave Division, W. MacMahon Ball. Bonney and Ball proved the two strongest and most interesting personalities spawned by the Department. They fought over what was appropriate for overseas ears. While their struggle abounded in personalities, it was not fundamentally personal in nature. It rested on deeply held differences about what was desirable propaganda.

In the end, Bonney won. He brought the Shortwave Division under his direct control when he became the Department's new head in 1944. A study of the archives as well as private papers suggests that Bonney was not above the odd ploy to gain what he wanted. He seems to have justified the parody doggerel that circulated among his staff:

> My Bonney lies over the ocean,
> My Bonney lies over the sea,
> And sometimes I get the notion,
> Bonney also lies to me.

Finally, the study debunks the view of antagonistic relations between the Department and the media. While the more gladiatorial displays such as the censorship row of 1944 and the Murdoch blunder made headlines, the reality was that of a close and warm relationship.

Even at the height of the censorship row of 1944, the Victorian State Censor strolled off for drinks with the editors of the newspaper he had just officially banned. Care had been taken to ban the very last edition, so that advertising revenue would not be lost. The press came to the Department's aid when it confronted a Cabinet subcommittee recommending its abolition. The commercial radio stations tended to exert a far more severe censorship than was required by the Censor. The stations were most bitter when the Department ceased providing them with its local radio news service. While metropolitan papers found the Department's services of marginal benefit, the rural press used great amounts of its handouts with or without attribution. When the Department took responsibility for buying advertising for all government agencies, press criticisms of it all but died. One censor was appointed to the local AJA's ethics subcommittee during the war. Few of them found difficulty in re-establishing themselves in their journalist trade after the war. The media's hostility to the Department proved ultimately to be ritualistic. It had far more to gain with the Department than without it.

Notes

1. S. Sturlasson, *The Olaf Sagas*, trans. S. Lairrg; quoted in M. Ogilvy-Webb. *The Government Explains: A Study of the Information Services for the Royal Institute of Public Administration*. London: Allen & Unwin, 1965, p. 47.
2. The Royal Commission on Government Organisation, *Report 13 Public Information Services*. Ottawa: Queen's Printer, 1962, p. 61.
3. Neither of the British official histories of World War I and World War II accorded a place for the contribution of the Ministries of Information.
4. See, for example, L. Farago, "British Propaganda — The Inside Story". *United Nations World* 2, no. 9 (1948): 22-26.
5. P. Hasluck, *The Government and the People 1942-1945*. Canberra: Australian War Memorial, 1970, p. 403.
6. Ibid., p. 629.
7. The Hon. Harold Nicholson, MP, "Propaganda", *BBC Handbook 1941*. London: British Broadcasting Corporation, 1941, p. 27. See also Ian McLaine's *The Ministry of Morale: Home Front Morale and the Ministry of Information in World War II*. London: Allen & Unwin, 1979.
8. There are many accounts of the US Office of War Information. The more comprehensive ones appear in: US Bureau of the Budget, Committee on Records of War Administration, War Records Section, *The United States at War: Development and Administration of the War Program by the Federal Government*. New York: Da Capo Press, 1972, pp. 203-30; C.A.H. Thompson, *Overseas Information Services of the United States Government*. Washington, DC: Brookings Institution, 1948, pp. 17-92; and E. Davis and B. Price, *War Information and Censorship*. Washington, DC: American Council on Public Affairs, 1943, pp. 7-79.
9. M. Edelman, *The Symbolic Uses of Politics*. Urbana: Ill.: University of Illinois Press, 1964, p. 71.
10. W.A. Scott (with R. Scott), *Values and Organisations: A Study of Fraternities and Sororities*. Chicago: Rand McNally, 1965, p. 220.

1

Origins

"Caceothes scribendi, Suppressio veri"

During World War I, the Commonwealth government saw little need to create a special agency to promote the war effort. Public support for the coming conflict was evident even while the British were still agonizing over whether or not to declare war. An Australian government announcement that it would commit all its war ships and an expeditionary force of 20,000 men to be sent wherever the Home government desired was met with great enthusiasm. Crowds waited excitedly outside the newspaper offices to receive the latest cable news, singing "Rule Britannia", "Soldiers of the King" and "Sons of the Sea". "The war", as Manning Clark put it, "took hold of them like wave."[1]

There was spontaneous anti-German sentiment from the beginning. As early as November 1914, before Britain had created its special agency of war propaganda, headlines on Australian papers had screamed:

> Unrestrained German Savages!
> Frightful Barbarities!
> Men and Women torn open with Bayonets
> and Roasted to Death! . . .[2]

War news became good news for newspapers. A headline poster needed only to proclaim "A Great Battle" for paper sales to noticeably increase. Australia's burgeoning daily press was to approach its alltime peak in numbers and diversity.[3] This popularity went in hand with a heightened public regard for the nature of the reportage. One British writer, examining the effect on the relations between public and press, commented:

> The war lent newspapers in general . . . a new stature. A wider range of people were now accustomed to their morning paper. The biggest bloodiest war in history became a daily serial. There was no medium to compete with the Press.[4]

It was only when evidence of defeatist attitudes loomed in the latter war years, that an attempt to create a propaganda organization was made. A Directorate of War Propaganda was formed in 1918, to resolve inquiries about the state of the war, the intentions of Germany, the dangers of division within Australia, and false or biased statements. Based in Melbourne, with branches in other capitals, its function was to arrange speeches for meetings, provide lecturers, prepare articles for the press and arrange the distribution of leaflets. Established just before the Armistice, it was disbanded shortly after the war ended.[5]

In contrast to propaganda, the organization for censorship in Australia was well established and its effects felt throughout World War I. It was carried out by military rather than civilian officers. In harmony with the Imperial arrangements, the head of the organization bore the title Deputy Chief Censor (Australia). The Chief Censor was based in the British War Office. Censorship covered both personal mail, overseas telegrams and cables, as well as that of the press. Its authority was drawn from the War Precautions Act.[6]

The official historian provides evidence that during the operation of the organization, the press was strictly policed and occasionally totally suppressed. For example, an entire edition of a Perth newspaper was suppressed in December 1914. The Prime Minister, Andrew Fisher, despite his sympathy towards the press, continued to support the censors' decisions.[7]

The most notorious example of suppression occurred during the conscription referendum campaigns of 1917, when the then Prime Minister, W.M. Hughes, stopped the printing of the Queensland Parliament's *Hansard* containing the text of an anti-conscription speech by T.J. Ryan, the Premier of the state.[8]

One censor's report of the period supported allegations of undue suppression:

> I deem it my duty to say that many instructions issued to the press could not possibly be justified as an exercise of military censorship under the proclamation establishing a censorship of the press or under any War Precautions regulation which was *ultra vires* . . . there was no legal power to enforce them had they been challenged *qua* subject matter of the particular prohibition.[9]

A recent study has confirmed that the Australian censorship was perhaps the harshest of any country in the British Empire, with sometimes very little justification from the military standpoint.[10]

H.A. Rorke, a censor who served during both wars, testified to the lengths he was expected to go to fulfil his function during World War I:

> On one occasion I had to obliterate with a chisel and mallet matter which was typed in the forme in the office of a weekly publication . . . We were sort of secret service then . . .[11]

Although it is hazardous to generalize about the qualities of the censors of the period, some research is now coming to light. Censors were expected to undertake a good deal of intelligence-gathering in addition to their normal functions. The proportion of ex-members of the Australian Intelligence Corps (Military Intelligence) in senior positions within the organization was "highly significant".[12]

Fewster's authoritative analysis of military censorship during the Great War reveals a fairly consistent portrait of the first censors.[13] Most were too old or declared unfit for active service. The great majority were "business, professional and university men of high standing". Three were former Rhodes Scholars. Their prime reason for undertaking the work appeared to be King and Country. There was little personal prestige or profit to be gained. The censors' views, not surprisingly, were in line with the conservative ranks of Australian society. Some censors delivered speeches to recruiting rallies and most were antipathetic to those who questioned Australia's involvement in the war, such as the Labor Party, radical groups and even the press.

The press was critical of the competence of Australia's censors. Editorials admonished the censors for their general lack of knowledge and appreciation of newspaper operations. The Melbourne *Argus* of 29 December 1914 complained:

> The worst feature of the censorship . . . is that it has been placed in the hands of a staff of men whose only recommendation is that they are, or have been militia officers. For some unaccountable reason it seems considered necessary that work should be done by military or naval men, and the consequence is that gentlemen who in their own sphere, and doubtless not unworthy of respect, have been pitch-forked into positions for which they have had no training and possess no aptitude . . . They cannot pretend to have anything like the skill of a journalist of long training in detecting untrustworthy news when they see it.

Such public disparagements had their effect on the morale of the censors. One was moved to concede in December 1915:

> I suppose there has been no department of war service so unpopular — so despised — and so calumniated as the censorship . . . Almost everyone from the man in the street and in the office of the untutored scribbling journalist to those in high places, including even the very ministers under whose authority the service was carried on, have indulged in jeers and jibes . . . upon those who were endeavouring to protect the national interests.[14]

This lingering ambivalence, which was the lot of the censors, can be savoured from the menu designed for one of their reunion dinners. It features a coat-of-arms of three crossed pens above a newspaper, the "Daily War Truth", in which practically every word has been crossed out. In the background are a blue pencil and a pair of scissors. The motto comprises "Caceothes Scribendi" (an itch for scribbling and "Suppressio Veri" (suppression of the truth).[15]

For the censorship organization, the lesson of the Great War was that it could be effective in restricting the flow of military and even political information, but this was achieved at the cost of social disharmony and press antagonism.[16] The lesson for many newspaper proprietors was that no formal publicity organization would need to be established if the press itself fulfilled the censorship role. The censorship experience had disclosed the shortcomings of giving responsibility for censorship to a paramilitary organization. If censorship were necessary, better that it be conducted by sensitive and trained journalists or news-editors.

If these lessons were to be heeded in the defence planning after the war, they were not reflected in the *War Book*. This was a manual prepared in the Australian Department of Defence to provide, in a concise and convenient form, a record of all measures that would be required to go from peace to war. The manual aimed to ensure that once war was declared, all authorities affected would know the precise measures to be taken. Naturally, it had to be a tentative document and frequent amendments were required with knowledge gained of new types of warfare. The British government also circulated current editions of its own *War Book* to the Defence authorities in the Dominions.[17]

The Australian *War Book* provided for the setting up of a censorship organization under the control of the Army. The details were sufficiently elaborate for the Army, from 1938, to compile a list of World War I censors, as well as to maintain a censorship skeleton staff.[18] The *War Book* also proposed, if required, a "Publicity and Propaganda Bureau". Its main purpose was "consideration of matters connected with publicity and propaganda and in addition, the performance of advisory duties regarding press censorship." The Bureau was to be part of the Prime Minister's Department and representatives from the Department of

External Affairs and the Australian press were to be included as advisers.[19] In the event, the elaborate plans of the *War Book* did not materialize. Precisely why these separate organizations were set aside in favour of a Department of Information with a wider mission remains a mystery.

As late as 29 August 1939, the Armed Services understood the censorship responsibility to reside with the Chief of General Staff (Army).[20] On that day, the first confidential booklet of censorship rules for the guidance of Australian pressmen, broadcasters and motion picture companies appeared. It was issued under the authority of the Chief of General Staff.[21]

It is probable that Prime Minister Robert Menzies, in opting for a new Department of Information, was influenced by advice received from the British High Commission. In June 1939, the High Commission had informed him of preparations for the establishment of a Ministry of Information in Britain, in the event of war. A similar organization was suggested for Australia:

> In view of the fact special publicity machinery may be regarded as an essential part of defence arrangements under modern conditions of warfare, it is thought that the Commonwealth Government may wish to consider the desirability of making similar preparations in connection with their own defence plans.

The Commission outlined the proposed British ministry, including its publicity and censorship functions.[22] However, this plan was not incorporated in the Department of Defence's *War Book*.

This lack of co-ordination foreshadowed the organizational chaos that was to confront the Department of Information.

Notes

1. C.M.H. Clark, *A History of Australia V: The People Make the Laws 1888–1915*. Melbourne: Melbourne University Press, 1981, pp. 375, 377.

2. Quoted in M. Lake, *A Divided Society: Tasmania during World War I*. Melbourne: Melbourne University Press, 1975, p. 21.
3. H. Mayer, "Press Oligopoly" in *Australian Politics: A Third Reader*, ed. Henry Mayer and Helen Nelson. Melbourne: Cheshire, 1975, p. 642, table 1.

Number of dailies and owners 1903–1972

	1903	1923	1930	1950	1960	1972
Capital city dailies	21	26	20	15	14	16
Independent owners	17	21	12	10	7	4

4. P. Ferris, *The House of Northcliffe: The Harmsworths of Fleet Street*. London: Wiedenfeld & Nicholson, 1971, p. 196.
5. E. Scott, *Australia during the War: Official History of Australia in the War of 1914–18*. Sydney: Angus & Robertson, 1936, p. 467.
6. Ibid., pp. 60, 61.
7. Ibid., p. 58.
8. Ibid., p. 69.
9. Ibid., p. 76.
10. Kevin J. Fewster, "Expression and Suppression: Aspects of Military Censorship in Australia during the Great War". Ph.D. thesis, University of New South Wales, Duntroon, 1980.
11. *Sun* (Sydney), 28 February 1942.
12. C.D. Coulthard-Clark, *The Citizen General Staff: The Australian Intelligence Corps 1907–1914*. Canberra: Military Historical Society of Australia, 1976, p. 53.
13. Fewster, "Expression and Suppression", pp. 13-15.
14. Quoted from ibid., p. 320.
15. Ibid., loc. cit.
16. Ibid., p. 331.
17. P. Hasluck, *The Government and the People 1939–1941*. Canberra: Australian War Memorial, 1952, pp. 122-23.
18. Ibid., p. 181.
19. Ibid., p. 140.
20. Department of Defence, Defence Committee Minutes, 29 August 1939.
21. Hasluck, *Government and the People 1939–1941*, p. 179.
22. Office of High Commission, UK, to Menzies, 23 June 1939; A.A., SP 195/1, File 3/1/15.

2

The Beginnings

"The untidiest and administratively the most incompetent department"

The Department of Information came into being officially on 4 September 1939 by Executive Council Minute No. 123. Prime Minister Menzies announced its creation in Parliament during the afternoon of 8 September 1939. The new organization would be a wartime instrument, to be dissolved on the return of peace. He emphasized the Department's functions would be to "tell the truth about the cause", to keep the "minds of people enlightened and their spirit firm" and provide "soundly based truth". In practice, it would issue news about government wartime activities, supply information for publicity purposes, facilitate cinema and photographic work about the war effort and take over responsibility for the wartime censorship of publicity media from the Department of Defence.[1] Sir Henry Somer Gullett, Minister for External Affairs, was given responsibility for the new department.

The Minister seemed well suited to his responsibility. Gullett had been official war correspondent on the Western Front in 1917 and had written the history of the Australian Light Horse Brigade in Palestine. After the war he had worked for the Melbourne *Herald* as news-editor. In 1925, he was elected to the House of Representatives and became a Minister in 1928. During the thirties, Gullett resigned from the ministry because he regarded the then Prime Minister, Joseph Lyons, as lacking vigour and drive.[2] Parliamentarians from both sides of the House have described Gullett as an engaging, intelligent and articulate though not a particularly forceful speaker.[3] Sir Henry assured the House of Representatives that his department was not to become a mere instrument of propaganda or an organ to further partisan interests.[4]

Parliamentary reception to the announcement of the new department varied. Several recoiled from the concept. The leader of the Country Party, Archie Cameron, was particularly opposed. Distressed that censorship had been taken from military hands, he predicted that the Department would increase in size and cost — a common criticism. If censorship was to be a civilian function, the Department of External Affairs would have been more suitable. Irrespective of the organization, he wondered what the policy on the telling of the "truth" would be.

> Either we come out quite frankly and tell the whole truth . . . whether it pleases us or not; or — and I would adopt this alternative — we tell the public that certain information, for military and national reasons, cannot be divulged, and make no bones about it. We . . . should not . . . delude the people into believing that this new Department will do a lot of wonderful things which the Minister suggests that it will do.[5]

The most hostile Labor speakers were Mr G. Martens (Herbert) and Mr E. Ward (East Sydney). Neither saw any value in the new department. The Department of Information, at best, would serve up stale news, or ministerial statements, and the Department at worst, allow censorship to run rampant. Ward was suspicious that the Department was designed largely to popularize the war.[6] Mr M. Blackburn (Bourke) spoke at length on the potential danger to civil liberties.[7]

Senator J. Collings (ALP) asserted that the Department was under the influence of the press magnate, Sir Keith Murdoch. He claimed that recent appointees such as the Chief Censor, Percy Jenkin, C.P. Smith and Mr Hannan, a senior representative in the Department's Queensland office, were associated with, or former employees of, the Murdoch press: "The public is to be fed on news cooked in the Murdoch ovens and dressed with pro-Menzies sauce . . ."[8] While this was an understandable reaction, the bulk of the Department's senior officials, including W. MacMahon Ball (lecturer/broadcaster), J. Treloar (Australian War Memorial), L. Wigmore (Sydney *Sun*), C. Banfield, J. Legge, C. Burns (Melbourne *Argus*), J. Winkler (Sydney *Daily News*), Massey Stanley (Publicity Officer, Australian Country Party) and many of the censors were not associated with Murdoch press interests.[9]

This invective was not representative of the Australian Labor Party. The leader of the Labor Party, John Curtin, supported the creation of the Department. In his view it was one of the most important of the government's wartime activities and he devoted some forty minutes to elaboration. He welcomed particularly the shortwave radio service and approved of censorship being handled by civilians, trusting it would be conducted in a fair and responsible manner. The Department could perform a clearing-house role for government information.[10] Curtin had been sensitive about unfair press coverage of the Labor Party[11] and may have hoped that the Department might prove an effective alternative news outlet to the established press.

Most agreed such a department was needed. Most differed on the sort of structure desirable, its scope and its powers. Mr W.M. Nairn (Nationalist Party, Perth) agreed that the Department might be a "useful service in a limited sphere", but added that the Department should have been organized on less ambitious lines and a less costly basis.[12]

Mr A.S. Drakeford (ALP, Maribyrnong) favoured having civilian rather than military censors, but remained sceptical that he would receive more information than was available in the press. He warned that such censorship might attempt to suppress fair criticism of the government, or that it might follow slavishly censorship instructions from the British War Office. None the less, his final view remained that of guarded consent.[13]

The question that must have been asked of many critics of the Department was: what was the alternative? If the Department was unnecessary, would they agree also that providing special information arrangements during a national crisis was equally unnecessary? World War I and the experience of the military censors had not been forgotten. For many politicians, especially on the Labor side, the setting up of the Department was not the most sinister move the government could have made.

The press and radio responded to the new department in much the same way as Parliament:

> War conditions of course demand a certain reticence in news which might assist the enemy. For that reason we have willingly given our Government power, as the Governments of England and France have power, to impose certain limitations on expression. But it must not be allowed to degenerate into a bureaucratic censorship functioning as an end in itself.[14]

> This new Department can best justify its existence through the supply, rather than the needless suppression, of news.[15]

> The new Department should operate with restraint and objectivity, and with careful avoidance of Government propaganda. Its chief service must lie in informing the public of war activities and controversy, rumours and false statements from enemy sources.[16]

> If such a Department is to live up to its name, it should give a full service of official news concerning the war and its incidental activities, withholding only such "military" information that would be likely to be of help to the enemy. It should not withhold bad news, on the assumption that such news is calculated to have a dispiriting effect upon the people and thus lessen their will to see the war through. Psychology of this kind inspired the censorship during the Great War and the only effect it had was to weary and disgust the people.[17]

To all these editorials, Gullett and his department probably would have responded with an hearty "amen".

The provincial and suburban press were more enthusiastic in welcoming the Department. Always short of fresh news copy, they rejoiced at the prospect of a government agency dispensing at no cost such a significant news service. The Department's editorial section was to discover later that the greatest user of copy and photographs was the provincial press. Of 600 country and suburban papers offered the free news service, 60 per cent used the material in full, 30 per cent in part and only 10 per cent made no use of it at all. Thirty provincial dailies took a daily commentary on the war as well. However, many were not eager to indicate the source of the news, illustration and commentaries.[18]

Commercial radio stations were equally appreciative. In the past there had been little incentive for them to build up their news services. Their newspaper links had been sufficient, and in any case, commercial radio's principal output was family entertainment. The war demanded news coverage of more immediacy than the summaries of newspaper headlines or the occasional BBC rebroadcast that had sufficed in the past. The Department was well placed to provide the commercial stations with news of the war, and at no cost to the stations. The industry's journal, *Commercial Broadcasting* of 14 September 1939 set out its needs with disarming directness:

> Official news services by the Federal Government should be instituted immediately. It should not be left to a newspaper service or to some overseas news gallery service to tell Australia what is happening, particularly through the BBC. . . . The Commonwealth Government has control of both national and commercial broadcasting stations and should make available to all stations in both systems the news "free of charge" for the use of the public.

The commercial stations' interest in exploiting the Department's services was evident when the same journal protested that the Department was not distributing press releases to the commercial radio stations.[19] The Australian Federation of Commercial Broadcasting Stations co-operated in drafting regulations for the broadcasting of news commentaries, advertising and similar matter. These ultimately formed the basis of censorship instructions to commercial stations throughout the Commonwealth.[20] In later months, the Chief Publicity Censor was impressed with the control the commercial stations placed on themselves and reported that the rules for their own conduct probably were more rigid than required.[21]

The ABC's news resources also were limited. Before the war, the organization's attempt to broaden its news output was frowned upon by the Australian Newspaper Council. Headed by Sir Keith Murdoch, it disputed the ABC's right to rebroadcast BBC news (the licence for which was held by AAP) along with its own news. It was one thing or the other as far as the newspapers were concerned. Either the ABC collected its own news or it should continue to subscribe to the AAP service, including BBC broadcasts, and withdraw from the independent news field.[22]

Could the new Information Minister assist the ABC? The prospects were promising when Gullett convened a conference on the afternoon of 18 September 1939, bringing together the ABC, the Australian newspapers, represented by Sir Keith Murdoch, and commercial broadcasting representatives in the Federal Cabinet Room in Parliament House, Melbourne. Gullett pressed the newspapers to allow the ABC more flexibility in its news service:

> You must remember there's a war on, gentlemen, and the government could not possibly accept a situation in which the people of this country were not kept fully informed of what is happening. Your papers do not reach many people until hours after publication; and by then the situation may have materially changed. It isn't only people in distant parts of Australia who have to wait for their papers. Many living less than a hundred miles from the capital cities are poorly served by mails and paper deliveries and they must be kept fully informed of what is happening. Broadcasting alone can do that.[23]

Further discussion between the ABC and the newspaper representatives produced a new agreement. The ABC and the commercial stations would be allowed to use BBC rebroadcasts and commentaries, limited to ten minutes at a time.[24] Inevitably, the ten-minute rebroadcast of BBC material was extended later as the public demand for overseas war news increased.

The Department's view on the ABC's right to broadcast war news was subject to an overriding perception of the potential propaganda value. One senior officer recommended that the ABC should be subject to the Department's more direct guidance:

> Talks on the National Stations have on many occasions tended to play down the "war effort" and while it is desirable that freedom of speech should be allowed, it is not desirable that the general tenor of broadcasting in Australia should be to belittle Australia's part in the war . . . I have in mind something quite subtle, not propaganda, but rather giving a slight twist to talks which would, if properly handled, be unnoticed.[24]

As with the broadcasting stations, the film censors received full co-operation in both the distribution of films, as well as the suppression of portions of these films thought likely to prejudice the war effort.

In many respects, the effectiveness and prestige of the Department of Information rested on its relationships with the Armed Services. From the earliest months, that relationship was subject to considerable strain. To the Armed Services, the Department represented the chief government protagonist for full disclosure and therefore posed a major security problem. The Army and Navy were reluctant to furnish the Department with current background information on military conditions, however necessary, for propaganda. As a result, the newspapers were able to "scoop" the Department's releases with their own cable services, ridiculing the Department's objective of prompt information.[26]

Censorship was a particularly sore point between the Services and the Department. Publicity censorship had been removed from the para-military context. Nevertheless, many of the first censors were former military personnel, used to following Service orders and inclined to defer to the Services' advice about censorship. In consequence, in the first months of war, the military authorities were able to apply a strict censorship. In practice, they took over from the Minister, the issue and interpretation of censorship instructions. Furthermore, the Services proved capricious and inconsistent in their censorship "advice". Although censorship rules prescribed that illustration of ships, aircrafts, guns and armaments in general should not be published, such items were released by the arm of the Service concerned, without prior reference to the Department.[27] On 27 February 1940, protests from press and Parliament provoked Prime Minister Menzies to reaffirm publicly that all censorship powers were vested with the Minister for Information and the liaison officers from the Services were to advise and not direct censors.[28]

But was the Department's internal structure equipped to cope with the demands and tasks it was saddled with? During World War II, the Department's development and organization confronted more than the usual obstacles faced by a new agency. The principal staffing and organization agency of the Commonwealth government, the Public Service Board, which in normal circumstances would have been looked to for assistance, found itself concerned with many other pressing responsibilities.[29] The new-born Department would have to wean itself. The ministry as such came into being officially on 12 September 1939. Its first officers commenced work on 9 October 1939, with headquarters in Melbourne to maintain contact with the other defence-based departments.[30]

Gullett appointed his close friend, J.C. Treloar, formerly in charge of the Australian War Memorial, as the Department's first Director. Well versed in public service procedures, sincere and hardworking, Treloar emerged as the conventional administrator, as much concerned with means as with ends. With the high proportion of staff alien to the public service, Treloar may have chosen to emphasize this approach. In berating his staff for directly raising issues with the Minister, Treloar emphasized procedure above all:

> As a public servant I have been trained in a school where communications are sent to a Department and the distribution of the letters to the officers concerned is attended to in a central registry. Most of the senior members of our staff have come

to us from business offices where apparently personal correspondence is common. The method we are to follow can be quickly determined but I want my plan of organisation approved first . . .[31]

Treloar was less than successful, given the verdict of Hasluck, the official historian:

> It is difficult to be confident about the documents affecting the Department of Information. It was by far the untidiest and administratively the most incompetent department in the Public Service, if the state of its files can be taken as evidence. It fell far below the usual standard of both in recording what it did and in the custody of its records.[32]

In addition, Treloar proved ill-at-ease in dealing with journalists outside the Department as well, and responding to enquiries from the press and radio.[33]

His enduring influence was to be found in the planning and organization of the Department, which was approved by Cabinet on 18 October 1939.[34] The Department comprised the following elements: several Group Committees, together with the Editorial and Broadcasting Divisions, the Cinema, Photographic and Films Branch, and the Publicity Censorship Division. There were special arrangements within the Department for distribution, library and general administrative services.

The Group Committees were Gullett's special initiative. In October 1939, he wrote to some 500 organizations, such as trade unions, sporting clubs, friendly societies, local musical societies, etc., inviting representatives to meetings in each state capital, with the view to forming State Information Consultative Councils. These were to be composed of representatives from religious, educational, social, industrial, business and other activities, on the widest possible basis. The purposes of the Councils were twofold. Firstly, they were to act as the grass-roots public representatives to which the Department could distribute information on the war effort. Secondly, and more importantly, they were to act as sounding boards about the type of information required and the appropriateness of the publicity distributed.[35]

The need for the Group Committees was underlined by the public puzzlement about the Department and its role. A letter from a Tillie Gerson, published in the Melbourne *Argus* of 29 November 1939, is representative:

> Last week we were promised we would have some plain speaking in the House of Representatives on the subject of the new Department of Information, but no echo of it seems to have reached the public ear. For the successful presentation of war every right-minded Australian will willingly pay to the utmost of his or her ability . . . but . . . it is time the voice of the taxpayer was heard.

Through consultation, the Group Committees mainly were to serve as a means to allow the voice of the taxpayer to be heard.

Gullett appeared before enthusiastic meetings in Sydney and Melbourne in the first weeks of November. By acclamation, both meetings carried the following motion:

> That this meeting, representative of almost every public and private activity in the State . . ., religious, educational, social, industrial, commercial, recreational and other, in town and country, wholeheartedly welcomes and approves the action of the Commonwealth Government in establishing a Ministry of Information not only to supply facts and accurate details, and also, by all means within its power, to sustain and stimulate Australia's war effort and that those present assure the Government of their cordial support and assistance in this endeavour.[36]

Mr C.P. Smith of the *West Australian* was the man chosen to manage the committees. Smith had experience as a newspaperman going back to the Great War. He sustained Gullett's momentum and established the committees effectively and promptly.[37] By the end of March 1940, there were 93 Group Committees made up from 852 organizations. A further 30 groups, representing some 300 other organizations were in the process of forming. Each committee had a say in the State Council (the peak level of representation). Committees were to meet monthly to deal with questions placed before them by the Department of Information, views would be exchanged about the war effort and leaflets would be made available as requested. The demand for pamphlets and leaflets indicated the keen interest and effective organization established among the committees.[38] Even the official historian, who remained in doubt about the value of the Department, conceded that the Group Committee system influenced thousands of people to give more attention to the causes and nature of the war.[39]

The staff of the Editorial Division during the first six months comprised five men: one subeditor, one rewrite man, one man controlling pictures, and two men responsible for contacts with other departments and for general staff work. The responsibilities of this small group fell under the two headings of press releases and material for the Group Committees. The press releases produced included:
(a) daily war commentaries from External Affairs, Navy, Army and Air Force;
(b) Corporal's Diary and Soldier's Diary, contributed by members of the AIF;
(c) despatches from the Acting Official Correspondent;
(d) country bulletins consisting of items of various length, designed for the use of country newspapers;
(e) special articles and items for Victorian country press insert pages;
(f) weekly financial article;
(g) weekly review of neutral opinion;
(h) weekly clipsheet of Australian news for America and India;
(i) special articles, and preparation for Australian use of material from the British Ministry of Information;
(j) preparation of material used in the Broadcasting Division for press purposes;
(k) fulfilment of requests by newspapers for material;
(l) supply of pictorial matter (up to 750 prints and 130 ebonoid stereos were distributed each week).[40]

Group Committees were supplied regularly with weekly and monthly War Summaries, special articles for organizational journals, pamphlets, leaflets and illustrations, as well as a monthly survey of the Department's activities. By March 1940, the Department proclaimed that some 278,310 column inches of letterpress and 46,860 column inches of photographs had been distributed to 638 newspapers, 1000 organizations and specialist journals.[41] Little was revealed, however, of the extent to which the material was used.

The Cinema, Photographic and Films Branch was transferred from the Department of Commerce to Information,[42] to assist newsreel companies by way of supplying material or facilities. It developed beyond this support role and produced its own films in the latter part of 1940. Damien Parer already was gaining a reputation for his portrayals of Australians at war. *Anzacs March Again* was an early product from the Branch, co-produced with Fox-Movietone News and available free to all theatres. By the end of March 1940, some 1,200 photos by the Branch photographer had been taken covering all aspects of defence activity. Displays of enlargements were made available for exhibits around Australia.[43] In August 1940, a separate Films Division was established, giving the Department authority to spend money on its own film productions.[44]

The Broadcasting Division was planned as a purveyor of local radio programs. It began with fifteen-minute broadcasts on Sunday evenings, consisting of questions about the war sent in by the public and answers supplied by the Department. On Wednesdays, from 7.15 to 7.25 p.m., a special program went to air on the ABC to discredit the more serious misrepresentations and rumours received over the German shortwave bands.[45] Scripts were commissioned and distributed to commercial radio stations on such subjects as hints for women at home, saving resources and starting home farms, as well as morale boosters, which could be read by a local announcer at convenient times.

However, it was in the field of overseas broadcasting that the Division was to play its ultimate role. The first Australian experiments in overseas shortwave broadcasting were commenced in 1927 by Amalgamated Wireless

(Australasia).[46] These transmissions became well-known throughout Europe and Asia, especially the Kookaburra's laugh, which had been introduced for broadcasting to listeners in the remote northern parts of Australia, as well as adjoining territories. Broadcasts of cricket and football finals were beamed to those isolated from such events. Bi-weekly news sessions also were broadcast to New Caledonia and the New Hebrides.[47]

At the beginning of World War II, AWA estimated that there were some 8 million shortwave receivers in the world, and a potential audience of 27 million. The company's most powerful station at the time had a 10 kw transmitter. Due to changes in the ionosphere, this station was audible in the United States and Great Britain for no more than four hours a day. Yet "scores of thousands" of favourable letters had been received from listeners in America, Britain and over 200 other countries, including colonial settlements.[48]

In October 1939, John Curtin dubbed Australia the "Dumb Dora" or "Silent Susie" of the Pacific. In the face of unanswered German broadcasts, he argued that the Australian broadcasts should be available in Japanese, Russian, Dutch, Chinese and other languages. Gullett responded that he hoped to have a shortwave service operating within a month.[49] Sir Ernest Fisk, the managing director of AWA, was assured by Gullett that the company would be issued with a shortwave commercial broadcasting licence after the war, apparently in return for the government's use of his company's transmitter.[50]

On 5 December 1939, Cabinet authorized the newly established Department of Information to take responsibility for shortwave transmissions, in collaboration with the ABC. The Postmaster-General's Department hired the transmitters from AWA at £2.10.0 per hour and supplied them to the Department.[51] The Department's service was inaugurated on 20 December 1939 with a speech by Menzies, rebroadcast in Great Britain.

The decision to establish the station had been influenced by the Far Eastern Bureau of the British Ministry of Information and the Malayan Department of Information. Consequently, its service was saddled with a formidable task. It was to combat propaganda disseminated by enemy countries or countries with enemy sympathizers. Furthermore, it was to broadcast to areas where the Commonwealth "in the interests of the Empire, should have the greatest possible degree of influence".[52]

The Publicity Censorship was not established until 2 October 1939. Before the war, the government had applied censorship pressures to press and broadcasting stations. In October 1935, the Postmaster-General's Department disapproved of a script for radio 2SM and the commentary was not aired. D.G.M. Jackson, the Catholic publicist, recalled that Prime Minister Joseph Lyons forbade him to comment over the air about the Abyssinian crisis.[53] On other occasions, Lyons asked the press to play down or subdue their comments and reportage of the Anschluss, "in the national interests".[54] The most celebrated pre-war incident of censorship, however, involved radio station 2KY, which was cut off at a moment's notice on 21 October 1938 because the Postmaster-General, Archie Cameron, disapproved of the tone of the commentaries. Among the conditions by which 2KY had to abide was that "there shall be no radio comment which could be considered hostile to the Government's foreign policy".[55]

Why did the media, including the press, tolerate such interference before the war? One reason may have been that Australians still saw themselves as part of the Imperial family. Thus Australian foreign policy was British policy and not worthy of extended treatment for local news. The early censorship pressure was in tune with the media's consensus to maintain a simplified and pro-British foreign policy.

With the declaration of war, the censorship authority resided in the draft regulations for the Defence Act. It had been proposed that all censorship responsibility should rest with Army Headquarters, as specified in the *War Book*. A Chief Censor was to have been appointed under the Director of Military Operations and Intelligence and assisted by a Deputy Chief Censor for Communications and a Deputy Chief Censor for Publicity. ("Communications censorship" dealt with the censorship of letters, cablegrams, etc., and "publicity censorship" dealt with matter received via press, radio, cinema, booklets, posters, etc.) The proposed organization was to have broadened into various types of communications and publicity. On 25 August 1939, censorship was officially in readiness under the Defence (National Security, General) Regulations. These regulations prohibited the obtaining, recording, communication, publishing or possession of any naval or military information or any information on any other matter that could be directly or indirectly useful to the enemy; and the causing of disaffection or endeavouring to influence public opinion, whether in Australia or elsewhere, in a manner likely to be prejudicial to the defence of the Commonwealth or the efficient prosecution of the war.[56]

On 29 August 1939, the representatives of the press, radio and cinema received a confidential booklet of censorship rules published by the authority of the Chief of the General Staff, for their personal information and guidance. The day-to-day responsibility for censorship would be left in their hands. Provided the agencies assumed responsibility for not publishing, broadcasting or disseminating in any way matter that would infringe the Act or Regulations, they were not obliged to submit any item for censorship, unless the Chief Censor so directed. It was the media's responsibility to vet all copy prior to publication to avoid likely infringements.[57]

The Chief Censor, at any time, could compel any media agency to submit for censorship all matter proposed for publication or all matter related to a specified subject. This "order-to-submit" was intended not only as a warning but as a penalty in itself, which could hamstring the tight production schedule of most major dailies and assure chaos for a broadcasting station. This further encouraged media managers to submit doubtful items for appraisal and formal approval by Censorship. The "order-to-submit" was a relic of the Great War and novel to Australia. Britain never adopted the system, due to protests from the opposition in November 1917.[58]

The relationship between the Chief Censor and the organs of publicity clearly was to become a close and continuing one. The press organizations, the ABC, the Australian Federation of Commercial Broadcasting Stations and the film industry in Melbourne and Sydney appointed censorship liaison officers to consult with the censorship staff about problems that arose, as well as to communicate censorship policy to the media.[59]

Estimates of the Department's expenditure for its first nine months to 30 June 1940 were around £22,500. In fact, the total expenditure came to £43,787. This may reflect the fact that many sections of the Department came from existing parts of the Public Service and were not accounted for in the first public estimates. The staff to 30 June 1940 totalled 100, of whom 98 were appointed on a temporary basis, rather than permanent, since this was a wartime (temporary) organization.[60]

The Department was a "dog's breakfast" of an organization. Each area could, with little effort, be separated to operate on its own. The Broadcasting and Censorship Division disclosed this tendency from the beginning. If the Department's functions were as autonomous as this, the question arises, what was the common thread that would lend some co-ordination to those functions? Perhaps the government expected the Department to act as a general publicity organ. The grouping of like functions under one umbrella, the Department of Information, would sustain maximum efficiency and minimal overlap and duplication.

However, such an answer would have to be qualified by the fact that functions other than censorship and shortwave broadcasting were not exclusive to the Department. Government agencies such as the Service departments or even Supply and Commerce departments undertook similar publicity functions. The Department of External Affairs may have been an appropriate candidate for the publicity function, with its emphasis on overseas developments. However, the means by which the Department was to relate with these departments, let alone co-ordinate government publicity, simply was not given consideration.

Another question for the Department was how it should communicate with the media, beyond contributing hand-out material. Consultation would have to be undertaken when campaigns were being developed, or when a desired treatment was sought in response to a possible emergency. What machinery was available for this negotiation?

The answers at this stage are not easy to produce. What is clear is that the creation of the Department followed generally an unplanned and pragmatic course. However, the Australian disinterest in the lead-up to the war, partly encouraged by the press and government's previous attitudes, and the Department's tendency to recruit staff from among journalists and publicists, including censors, makes it difficult to depart from the impression that the Department was created to promote the war, as well as the war effort.

Notes

1. *CPD* (HR), 8 September 1939, p. 512.
2. C. Edwards, *The Editor Regrets*. Melbourne: Hill of Content, 1972, p. 25; and Dame E. Lyons, *Among the Carrion Crows*. Adelaide: Rigby, 1972, p. 61.
3. P. Spender, *Politics and a Man*. Sydney: Collins, 1972, p. 12.
4. *CPD* (HR), 15 September 1939, p. 643.
5. Ibid., p. 1599.
6. Ibid., pp. 1620-24, 1627-29.
7. *CPD* (HR), 28 November 1939, pp. 1604-08.
8. *CPD* (Senate), 23 November 1939, p. 1520.
9. Note on the Department's nucleus staff, December 1939; A.A. SP 195/1, File 3/1/15.
10. *CPD* (HR), 28 November 1939, pp. 1614-20.
11. See, for example, F. Dixon, *Inside the ABC: A Piece of Australian History*. Melbourne: Hawthorn Press, 1975, pp. 46-47.
12. *CPD* (HR), 23 November 1939, p. 1604.
13. Ibid., pp. 1631-34.
14. *Daily Telegraph* (Sydney), 6 September 1939.
15. *Adelaide Advertiser*, 11 September 1939.
16. *Sydney Morning Herald*, 9 September 1939.

17. Melbourne *Argus*, 13 September 1939.
18. *CPD* (HR), 23 November 1939, p. 1536.
19. *Commercial Broadcasting*, 18 January 1940, editorial. J.C.R. Proud, the Victorian State Publicity Censor, confirmed this in his note to the Director of 7 February 1940: "So far the Publicity Division of the Department of Information has centred its efforts almost entirely on the Press. This is having the effect of causing some heart burning among broadcasting authorities because they feel they had been left out of certain scoops" A.A., SP 195/1, File 3/1/15.
20. "Report on the Operation of Press, Broadcasting and Film Censorship from 2/9/1939 to 29/1/39" [sic]. This is clearly an error and should have read 'to 29/9/39'. State Publicity Censor NSW, Confidential Papers 1939-40; A.A., SP 106/11.
21. "Publicity Censorship Report on Activities", CPC 663, 2 January 1940: A.A., SP 109, Box 72.
22. This conflict was examined by the Joint Committee on Wireless Broadcasting, the "Gibson Committee", during 1940 to 1942. A personal account is given in Dixon, *Inside the ABC*; the conflict is studied afresh by Pam Mitchell in her History IV (Hons) thesis, "The Development of ABC News Gathering 1932-42", University of Sydney, 1974.
23. Dixon, *Inside the ABC*, p. 39.
24. Mitchell, "Development of ABC News Gathering", p. 46.
25. J.C.R. Proud to Director, 7 February 1940; A.A., SP 195/1, File 3/1/15.
26. L.G. Wigmore, enclosed draft article to Hugo Freeth of *The Press* (NZ), 17 October 1940; Wigmore Papers.
27. "Report on the Operation of Press, Broadcasting and Film Censorship", p. 2.
28. Full Cabinet Minute 16, in "War Cabinet Series", 26 February 1940 (also first agreed in War Cabinet Minute, No. 36 of 16 October 1939).
29. G.E. Caiden, *Career Service: An Introduction to the History of Personnel Administration in the Commonwealth Public Service 1901-1961*. Melbourne: Melbourne University Press, 1965, p. 271.
30. *CPD* (HR), 16 November 1939, p. 1233.
31. J.C. Treloar to L.G. Wigmore, 12 January 1940, A.A., SP 195/1.
32. P. Hasluck, *The Government and the People 1942-1945*. Canberra: Australian War Memorial, 1970, p. 403n.
33. Author's interviews with W. McM. Ball, L.G. Wigmore and C.E. Sayers, 17 and 18 February, 12 April 1976.
34. Hasluck, *Government and the People 1942-1945*, p. 201.
35. *CPD* (HR), 28 November 1939, p. 1612.
36. Sydney and Melbourne transcripts: A.A., SP 195/9, Item 13.
37. Author's interview with C.E. Sayers, 17 February 1976.
38. *Department of Information: Summary of Activities for the Period ended 31st March 1940*. Melbourne: Commonwealth Government Printer, 1940, p. 4.
39. Hasluck, *Government and the People 1939-41*, p. 202.
40. L.G. Wigmore, 11 June 1940, Wigmore Papers.
41. *Department of Information: Summary of Activities*, pp. 3-4.
42. *CPD* (HR), 23 November 1939, p. 1537.
43. *Department of Information: Summary of Activities*, p. 5.
44. "History of Films Division, Department of Information", (typed ms.), p. 1;

Publicity Censorship Division, Miscellaneous, Departmental History (1), Cinema and Photo Branch (2), Films Division; A.A., SP 195/10, Item 20.
45. *Department of Information: Summary of Activities*, p. 5.
46. *History of Overseas Shortwave Broadcasting in Australia*, Draft Report, ?1946 (unpublished ms., Hoey Papers, author unknown, ? Tom Hoey), p. 1.
47. I.K. Mackay, *Broadcasting in Australia*, Melbourne: Melbourne University Press, 1957, p. 104.
48. "History of Overseas Shortwave Broadcasting", draft report, pp. 1-2.
49. Melbourne Argus, 4 October 1939.
50. E. Fisk to H. Gullett, 23 November 1939; A.A., MP 272/2, (A/2).
51. "History of Overseas Shortwave Broadcasting", draft report, p. 2.
52. Cabinet Agendum No. 897, "World Wide Radio Broadcasting from Australia", 28 August 1945, Cabinet Secretarial I; A.A., CRS A2700 XM, Vol 17.
53. E.M. Andrews, *Isolationism and Appeasement in Australia: Reactions to the European Crisis 1935-1939*. Canberra: Australian National University Press, 1970, p. 24. See also Alan Thomas, "The Politicisation of the ABC in the 1930's: A Case-study of 'The Watchman'", *Politics* 13, no. 2 (November 1978): 286-95.
54. Andrews, *Isolationism and Appeasement*, p. 132.
55. Ibid., p. 160.
56. Hasluck, *Government and the People 1939-1941*, p. 179.
57. Ibid., pp. 179-80.
58. K.T. Fewster, "Expression and Suppression: Aspects of Military Censorship in Australia during the Great War". Ph.D. thesis, University of New South Wales, Duntroon, 1980, p. 316.
59. Hasluck, *Government and the People 1939-1941*, p. 180.
60. CPD (HR), 30 June-1 July 1949, p. 1903. There are a number of official discrepancies concerning staff numbers and budgets. Some of this may be accounted for by attributing the Department's costs to other departments. The above *Hansard* reference provides the following:

£ Expenditure, 1939-1945

1939-40	1940-41	1941-1942	1942-43	1943-44	1944-45
43,787	176,479	227,234	259,967	308,669	316,648

On the other hand, the Department's submission to the Pinner Committee of Inquiry in September 1945 showed:

£ General Expenses 1939-1945

Source	1939-40	1940-41	1941-42	1942-43	1943-44	1944-45
Hansard	21,758	112,657	140,065	168,362	206,281	175,714
Pinner	21,758	112,657	140,065	71,411	66,503	112,715

The reason for the disparity in the general expenses may be due to the cost-cutting mission of the Pinner Committee, encouraging the Department's accountants to present an austere picture. Another possibility may be due to the 1942 decision that required advertising campaigns of the Department of Information to be charged to the concerned agencies direct rather than form part of the Department's publicity expenditure vote. Whatever the reason, for the sake of consistency, the *Hansard* reference has been used because it includes definitive figures on staff as well.

3

The Early Development of the Broadcasting and Censorship Divisions

"We are fighting a war, and not arguing one"

The Broadcasting Division, based in Melbourne, began with a staff acting as editorial supervisors and commentary writers recruited for shortwave service. The ABC employed another group of newswriters, translators and announcers in Sydney. The Sydney staff of the ABC received talks and editorial guidance from the Melbourne staff of the Department.[1] The position was needlessly complicated and demanded someone to supervise and co-ordinate, someone conversant with overseas affairs, someone with the ability to recruit and train speakers who could broadcast in a variety of foreign languages, and someone with radio news and commentary experience. It was not until February 1940,[2] when W. MacMahon Ball was appointed as its head, that the Broadcasting Division began to operate effectively.

Ball, a senior lecturer in Political Philosophy at the University of Melbourne, was a regular contributor to the Melbourne *Herald*. From 1932 to 1939, he broadcast news commentaries for the ABC on a range of international issues.[3] Ball had intended to follow his father's vocation and enter the ministry. Much of this evangelical fervour remained in his university lectures, which he tended to pitch at young Christian idealists, and he gained satisfaction from provoking a lively audience response.

Ball became concerned that news about overseas affairs should come to Australia free from government influence. Past visits overseas had impressed on Ball the extent to which misleading and inadequate accounts of overseas affairs were received by Australians.[4] In part, this distortion had arisen from the conservative Customs policy of the Lyons government, which had prohibited the imports of many of the works of Marx, Lenin and Stalin. In 1934, this restriction proved intolerable to Ball and he formed the Victorian Book Censorship League, to "protect the rights of readers and booksellers".[5] He campaigned vigorously against the government's policy to supply information with its "blinker over the left eye".[6] Many publications that were available in Great Britain were prohibited in Australia. In September 1935, Ball met the Minister for Customs, T.W. White, but walked out of the discussions, criticizing the Minister as being "incapable of grasping the meaning of any viewpoint but his own". The Minister thought Ball "petulant".[7] Both were probably correct. Ball had more success with the then Attorney-General, R.G. Menzies. Menzies proved more receptive than White and lifted the ban on political books soon after.[8]

Ball realized that Customs policy alone was not entirely responsible for the inadequate coverage of overseas affairs. In 1938, after the ban was lifted, he singled out the press as having a case to answer:

> The interests represented by a non-Labor Government closely correspond on fundamental issues with the interests represented by the newspaper proprietors. There is no problem of censorship because there is no need for censorship.[9]

The principal overseas news source for Australia was AAP, which in turn was strongly influenced by British views in its coverage and interpretation of world events.

Ball remained concerned by the poor coverage of news from the United States and the Far East, arguing that this made it difficult for Australia to assume responsibility for its own foreign policy.[10]

For Ball, Australian understanding of foreign policies required four things that were not in existence in 1938. Firstly, an objective news service; secondly, an understanding of other countries' views; thirdly, frank, free and informed debates on foreign policy; and fourthly, training in critical interpretation of foreign news. He saw the ABC, despite its many shortcomings, as the most promising point from which to begin such reforms. The ABC should pick up and rebroadcast shortwave news from countries other than Great Britain. Expert reporters and commentators independent of the current AAP dominance should be employed. The intellectual standards both in reporting and commentary needed considerable upgrading. Finally, the ABC should cease its own policy of editing out news or views that were critical of government policy.[11]

Ball's commentaries for the ABC in the pre-war years, appeared to practise what he preached. In his chapter for the ABC *Annual* of 1939, entitled, "On Thin Ice", he argued that controversy was the corner-stone of truth:

> To be trained in the art of controversy is to be trained in the search for truth. To fear controversy is to fear truth. . . . It is unjust to condemn a public authority [the ABC] for not showing a degree of enlightened liberalism far in advance of the mental temper of the public which it serves. Yet the basic issue is clear. There can be no education without controversy, and there can be no controversy without freedom. To play for safety is the most dangerous way for democracy to try to live.[12]

Thus, in Ball's appointment, the Department not only acquired a manager for its Broadcasting Division but also a man with a vision of what the operation might achieve and why.

Although Ball was assigned to manage both local and overseas broadcasts, his energies were directed to the shortwave operation. His first steps were to increase the number of languages broadcast and to recruit skilled staff. By the end of March 1940, the Shortwave Division was transmitting eight hours a day to Northern Europe, Southern Europe, the United States, India, South America, the Netherlands East Indies, Japan, the Philippines and South Africa. It broadcast in five foreign languages: French, German, Dutch, Spanish and Afrikaans. News and talks formed the main part of the transmissions, explaining the "cause", reporting Australia's war effort and countering German falsehoods.[13]

An initiative of Ball's was the monitoring of overseas broadcasts, so that he would be briefed on what the enemy, neutrals and the allies were transmitting. This would aid prompt responses to enemy propaganda. The function accorded with his aim of gaining better access to the views of overseas countries, not only as they appeared in propaganda but as they appeared in other forms as well.

This "Listening Post", as it came to be called, was established by mid-1940. Its development was hastened by the close of the "phoney war" period. In some ways, it overlapped with the intelligence work of the Navy and Army, which had similar services.[14] The more general service of the Listening Post was encouraged and Ball continued to recruit his staff with enthusiasm and care. The PMG's Department provided his division with three landlines for receiving the broadcasts from sensitive receivers at Mont Park in Victoria. Each monitor was required to have a hundred per cent fluency in at least two languages other than English. Temporary monitors also were taken on, if they had fluency in one language. Monitors needed to be sensitive to the special political significance of overseas commentaries. The work proved demanding and sometimes monitors put in a 24-hour day. The information went to officials of the Navy, Army and Air Force. The Prime Minister received a telegraphic account twice a day. Daily summaries as well as weekly trend sheets were distributed to the press.[15]

The development of the Censorship Division also played

a major part in the government's policy on war news. A confidential booklet (the 1944 edition appears as Appendix A) prescribed the matters that were strictly forbidden for publication. Topics covered included the movement of troops, shipping and aircraft, defence installations, unofficial casualty lists and espionage. Matters that were not prohibited but required referral to the Chief Censor before publication included accounts of air-raids and bombardments, references to take-overs of factories and reports of the health or conduct of the troops. On matters of opinion as opposed to news, the policy was:

> Legitimate criticism will not be suppressed. Publication of statements likely to prejudice the recruiting, training, discipline or administration of any of His Majesty's Forces is prohibited. No attempt is made to define the limits of "legitimate criticism". Each case should be considered in its own circumstances and in doubtful cases the matter should be submitted to the Censor. As a matter of routine, complaints or criticism of administration are at once made the subject of inquiry, and this will be expedited if matter of this kind is submitted to the Censor or referred to the District Commandant or Department concerned. If necessary further reference can be made to the Minister.
> Statements of soldiers alleging bad treatment either in Australia or elsewhere should be submitted before publication. Such statements will then be forwarded to the proper authorities for investigation . . . It is not permitted to publish by statement, cartoon, illustration, photograph or cinematograph film any matter —
> 1. Evincing disloyalty, or likely to encourage disloyalty.
> 2. Likely to discourage enlistment in the forces or in an auxiliary service.
> 3. Likely to prejudice His Majesty's relations with foreign powers, or likely to offend such Powers. The imputation of hostile or unneutral acts to the subjects of a neutral power is prohibited.[16]

Therefore, from the very beginning, the provision for using censorship in a political context was established. The recurring and vague phrase "likely to" signalled, to the media, that it would be indeed a sensitive art to criticize or express an unfavourable opinion of the war effort.

Following the assent to the National Security Act and

the gazettal of the National Security (General) Regulations (Statutory Rules 1939, No. 87), the broad powers conferred by the dragnet clause of Section 5 and Section 16 of the General Regulations were drawn on for future censorship regulations. The sections placed in the hands of the Minister a censorship power as extensive as his own view of what was necessary or expedient in the interests of public safety, the defence of the Commonwealth or the efficient prosecution of war.[17]

In anticipation of the censorship task, both in communications (postal/cable) and publicity (media), the Army headquarters already had arranged skeleton staffs to man censorship posts in each capital city.[18] In New South Wales, the post began operating on Saturday, 2 September; its staff were summoned for duty the next day. The next few days were taken up with extensive briefings for the press, shipping companies and radio stations.[19] In the meantime, the Department of Information had been created on lines different to the paramilitary concept set out in the *War Book*. On 18 September, the Minister for Defence delegated to the Minister for Information the powers and functions conferred on him by Section 16 of the General Regulations dealing with publicity censorship. From then on, the two censorships were divided: publicity censorship being the responsibility of the Department of Information, whereas communications censorship was the responsibility of the Department of Defence, and later (after reorganization in December), of the Department of the Army.

Little censorship was in evidence during the first three weeks of war. The journal *Common Cause* submitted an article to the Department concerning a question asked in Parliament, which was deleted in part. Occasional lapses in respect of weather reports and shipping information were taken up with the relevant liaison officers, achieving the desired result without formal intervention being necessary.[20] It was not until 2 October 1939 that Publicity Censorship was established as a separate Division of the Department of Information.

Percy B. Jenkin, formerly of the Adelaide *News*, was the first Chief Publicity Censor appointed under the Defence Regulations of 25 August. On 3 November 1939, State Publicity censors were established for each state and took over the responsibility from the District Censors of the Army in each military district, following complaints of treatment of press items by Army censors.[21] On 1 March 1940, a Broadcasting Censorship Order was gazetted, transferring responsibility for broadcasting censorship from the Department of Defence to the Department of Information.[22]

Apart from the Melbourne-based Chief Publicity Censor, the NSW State Publicity Censor was in potentially the most sensitive position. On 14 December 1939, the names of people entitled to be censors under the Department of Information were gazetted and included the name of Harold Augustus Rorke as the first Censor for New South Wales.[23] Rorke was a veteran of World War I censorship operations.

Censorship staff who were not already part of the original staff maintained by the Department of the Army tended to be recruited from the ranks of journalists. Vacancies were not advertised: an examination of the archives files suggests the decision to join was generally spontaneous. Among the many who wished to serve but were not chosen was Wilfred Burchett.[24] In due course, Burchett joined the Department in the Broadcasting Division's Listening Post.[25] Not only were censors generally drawn from the ranks of journalists, they were to be male journalists. An annotation on a woman's application for a censorship position reads "it is contrary to policy to employ women censors here."[26] From 16 September 1939, Jenkin instructed each censor to maintain a diary of such non-routine events as important telephone conversations, important interviews, etc.[27]

The key to understanding and appreciating the behaviour of the Division of Publicity Censorship and the nature of its relationships with media, lies in the "censorship instruction". On 6 October 1939, a Press Censorship

Order (those for cinema and radio followed) was gazetted, giving the Minister power to appoint press censorship authorities. The authorities could set down those items that were to be censored by an order in writing *before* any matter intended for publication was printed and forbidding the printing of the whole or any portion of the matter submitted or direct that alteration be made in it.[28]

The effect of this was to shape censorship as an active as opposed to reactive relationship between censors and the press. Although censorship was still voluntary, it was only in the sense that the press voluntarily enforced the instructions of the censor. This allowed censors to foreshadow what should not be published. For example, if it were known in press circles that troops were about to depart, Censorship would provide guidance without request, to the effect that the colour of uniforms was not to be publicized, since this would indicate what ranks or types of troops were being dispatched. If a Minister were known to be travelling overseas, a censorship instruction would be circulated informing when information might be published and even in what terms. The instructions were meant to apply the guidelines to specific incidents. The instructions were usually quite brief and referred to one item only. In the first months, Censorship's notification of a prohibited reference frequently became the first advice that such an incident actually had occurred.[29]

It was the instructions rather than the actual censorship that were to form the point of issue between press and censors. The press felt that censors were anticipating legal precedents, especially in matters of censorship of opinion. The frequency of the instructions aggravated matters. These became an almost daily reminder of the dominance of publicity censorship.

In Parliament, Maurice Blackburn (ALP, Bourke) sought to make the legal distinction between restraint before publication and accepting the consequences of wrongful publication. He drew the analogy with the procedure in the case of a person charged under the Regulations with having endeavoured to influence public opinion in a manner prejudicial to the efficient prosecution of the war. Such a person would have an opportunity, *after* publication, to answer the charge before a magistrate and defend himself; whereas a censor prevented publication according to his own opinion of what was likely to be prejudicial. This distinction, noted the official historian, appeared to have been too subtle for general endorsement.[30] The censorship instruction was to become more formidable than the formal excision of copy. To round out Censorship's special position, the Censorship Order of 6 October 1939 made it an automatic condition of all censorship that the act of censorship on any copy published was not to be indicated or publicized.[31]

Though it hinted of some difficulties, the Censor's official report at the end of March 1940 gave an optimistic picture of censorship administration. Censors were working to a set of broad general principles, it reported. It was inevitable that on occasions the interpretation of these principles would differ, but every submission was considered carefully and decisions were made without "fear or favour". They would be wrong sometimes, the report conceded, but censors were never vindictive or unreasonable. It argued that censors frequently were caught between two demands. On the one hand, they had been accused of too severe treatment of copy; on the other hand, protests had been made against their leniency in dealing with the same copy. It concluded that, apart from some socialist journals, press and broadcasting stations had complied with regulations and instructions.[32]

Although Censorship had a vast array of legal provisions and statutes to support its work, it was subject both to institutional and to technology constraints on its discretion and powers in Parliament and shortwave broadcasting.

In recognition of its status, parliamentary debates recorded in *Hansard* could be censored only by agreement between the Speaker and the member concerned. However, the press or radio reports of the debates remained subject to censorship. Public information about the war effort from enemy, allied and neutral countries received on radios with shortwave bands also presented problems. These stations occasionally gave the names and movements of merchant ships, notice of their conversion to armed cruisers, and the like. Sometimes the BBC mentioned that Australian troops had not only arrived at a general location, such as the Middle East, as then allowed by Australian censorship rules, but went further and announced the actual point of disembarkation.[33] In these circumstances Censorship passed copy that had originated from this source, since it was anomalous to suppress information that had been published to the world.[34] In April 1940, for example, the BBC broadcast of a departure of a British liner effectively cancelled censorship instructions withholding reference to it.[35]

While Parliament and shortwave broadcasts restrained censorship treatment of war facts, they did little to restrain a discernible tendency to suppress critical opinion. In bringing in the all-embracing National Security Act, Menzies sought to assure civil libertarians that the powers were necessary and would be used responsibly:

> the greatest tragedy that could overcome a country would be for it to fight a successful war in defence of liberty, and lose its own liberty in the process. There is no intention on the part of the Government to use these powers when they are granted, as I am sure they will be, in any way other than to provide the security of Australia . . .[36]

These sentiments became subject to changing war conditions. As the "phoney war" period drew to a close, the government adopted a harsher view of those sections of the press that seemed less than sympathetic with Australia's war effort, or who, in particular, publicized the life and ideas of Soviet Russia.

While the Australia First's *Publicist* appears to have received the first order to submit, on 9 January 1940, the socialist journals received the most attention.[37] The Melbourne communist-oriented *Guardian* received its order to submit on 7 February 1940. In response to representations from the Council for Civil Liberties, Gullett made it clear that the journal would not be allowed to interfere with the war effort and that "special action" was threatened.[38] By 9 April, Gullett was convinced that the communists were adversaries and that their journals should be treated more harshly than non-communist publications. He wrote to Jenkin:

> The attitude adopted by Censorship towards this [communist] copy should be stiffer than that adopted to other newspapers. It must be borne in mind that Australian Communists are now clearly hostile to constitutional government in Australia. They are to be regarded as the declared and active enemies of the Australian and Empire war effort, and as a force engaged in sabotaging of the Australian industrial effort associated with the proper conduct of war . . .[39]

On 19 April, Gullett named eight papers that were to be subjected to censorship conditions so severe, he expected them to cease publication. The papers had their copy called up and were instructed not to publish material concerned with the war, Russia or its government, strikes within the British Empire or any allied country, or industrial unrest. One of these, *Soviets Today*, ceased publication almost immediately. Publication of the whole of its copy, including its title, was prohibited by the NSW Censor under the special rules. On 23 April, further regulations were gazetted to provide for "permits". J.V. Barry, a distinguished lawyer and member of the Council for Civil Liberties, protested that this system of licensing of the press had been abandoned in England in 1695.[40]

Gullett offered to ease censorship conditions if the union journals purged themselves of their communist editors.[41] In fact, Gullett admitted in Parliament that matter that was prohibited in communist journals might be permissible in other newspapers. Communist journals were deemed enemies and ripe for special censorship.[42] There was very little reaction or concern among other press interests to this suppression. The public, in turn, was not informed of the issues. One exception included the teaching staff of the University of Melbourne. In the Melbourne *Argus* of 14 May 1940, thirty-two members of the staff protested over this suppressive trend:

We do not question the Government's right in war time to prevent publication of information likely to assist the enemy. But it does not appear to us to follow from this that the Communist press and trade union journals should be totally prohibited from discussing the war . . .

Other correspondents were less sympathetic. "Vigilo", in the *Argus* of 15 May, wrote:

Cannot the teaching staff of the University realise that the British nation and Australia are at war? Their attack on censorship is ill-timed. These critics are concerned about freedom of speech yet they defend flooding the country with senseless talk which loyal citizens, concerned about the conduct of war, are not anxious to hear.

The teaching staff responded in the *Argus* of 27 May that their point was not understood and that they were loyal citizens who had no wish to detract from the war effort.

A further step was taken on 24 May, when Archie Cameron, then Deputy Prime Minister, signed an order prohibiting nine communist and trade union publications:

We are fighting a war, and not arguing one . . . I do not care what was said when the National Security Act was passed. Conditions have changed entirely since that time, whatever they may have been. Today, any act directed against the internal peace, security and good government of this country is aimed at this country and has to be dealt with . . . If other newspapers wish to meet the same fate, they have only to act in a similar way.[43]

The publications concerned had delayed the loading of ships and output from coal mines, according to Gullett. They whispered "poison". The only hope for the publications, and similar ones, lay in the unions' freeing them of communist control.[44]

Maurice Blackburn protested that the National Security Act had become far harsher than the British one, on which it was supposedly based.[45] Australian censorship did not slavishly follow the advice of Imperial authorities, according to Menzies. Wartime censorship followed similar principles, but methods could be varied "to meet local demands".[46] Blackburn criticized the Minister's policy as locking up people in case they committed crime.⁴⁷ On 15 June 1940, Blackburn's simile was to become literal truth. The Australian Communist Party was declared an illegal organization and its members went underground until the Labor government lifted the ban in December 1942.⁴⁸

In the process, the Department had demonstrated its value for government in ways beyond its "clearing house/public rally" model. The Censorship Division had shown itself amenable to the whims of its Minister. The discrimination against communist publications would have been more understandable had the party been prohibited *prior* to the banning of the journals. Irrespective of whether the communists as a group were enemies, Gullett imposed on the Department's censorship the beginnings of a double-think on censorship interpretation. It was not *what* was said, but *who* said it. Identical copy in publication A could be passed, where it was prohibited in publication B.

However, the government was saddled with other problems that were not so readily amenable to censorship action. The close of the "phoney war" may have served to legitimate the banning of the communist publications, yet lack of genuine military action from November 1939 to March 1940 had had other less desirable effects on public attitudes. It was no easy task to awaken the public from its delusions of safety or to impress it with anything approaching a sense of sacrifice. Many had come to accept that everything would come out right in the end, irrespective of whether they were personally involved. Many union leaders saw it as an imperialist war. There seemed no burning sense of purpose. The public was actually enjoying boom conditions: prices were kept down, there was full employment and interest rates were down. There was also a general view that the tottering government, due for re-election in late 1940, was unlikely to tamper with taxes for fear of losing crucial seats.⁴⁹

The government had been considerably weakened in early 1940 with the by-election loss in the seat of Corio (R.G. Casey's former seat) and when its Trade and Customs Minister was forced to resign. Menzies recast his

Cabinet and a new coalition was formed on 14 March. Archie Cameron had become the Minister for Commerce and Navy, as well as Deputy Prime Minister. Gullett was appointed as the Vice-President of the Executive Council, Minister in Charge of Scientific and Industrial Research and now only Assistant Minister for Information. His former portfolios of External Affairs and Information went to John McEwen and Menzies.[50]

Government administration lacked direction or real commitment in this period. William Dunk, at the centre of much of the Public Service activity, conceded the administrative war machine was developing, "one could say with truth, slowly". This languor affected Public Service accountability: "It was a piece of cake in avoiding the checks and balances, divided authority and fear of consequences that rule procedures in democratic government in peace time."[51]

For many Australians, casualty lists remained the main touch with reality when Germany resumed its offensive in April. Denmark, Norway, Holland, Belgium, Luxembourg and France all fell. The resignation of Chamberlain, the British Prime Minister and Dunkirk evacuation made dramatic news, but Australians seemed more complacent than ever. According to the official historian, the government seemed incapable of communicating the war position and its relevance for Australians with any effectiveness.

Precisely why Menzies took personal responsibility for the Information portfolio in March 1940 is not clear. He may have sought to reduce the frequency of "sniping" attacks on him appearing in the daily press:

> I, as Prime Minister, have to devote at least one third of my time (and I work fifteen hours a day, seven days a week) to warding off blows aimed at me, not from the front, but from those who are supposed to be my supporters — "snipers", people who shoot from behind, people who think a fine round of mouthfilling destructive criticism is a contribution to make to the war.[52]

If nothing else, the development of the Broadcasting and

Censorship Divisions suggested the Department had a potential that needed more cultivation.

Notes

1. "History of Overseas Shortwave Broadcasting in Australia", Draft Report ?1946 (unpublished ms., in Hoey Papers, author unknown, ?Tom Hoey), p. 2.
2. Melbourne *Argus*, 16 February 1940. His appointment officially took place on 2 February 1940.
3. Author's interview with W.M. Ball, 18 February 1976.
4. Author's interview with Stephen Alomes, ANU student examining Ball's career, 10 May 1977.
5. P. Coleman, *Obscenity, Blasphemy, Sedition: Censorship in Australia*. Brisbane: Jacaranda Press, 1962, p. 115.
6. W.M. Ball, "The Australian Censorship", *Australian Quarterly*, no. 26 (June 1935), p. 10.
7. Coleman, *Obscenity, Blasphemy, Sedition*, p. 116.
8. Ball correspondence with author, 20 August 1977.
9. W.M. Ball (ed.), *Press, Radio and World Affairs: Australia's Outlook*. Melbourne: Melbourne University Press, in association with Oxford University Press, 1938, p. 25.
10. Ibid., pp. 9-33.
11. Ibid., pp. 129-32.
12. W.M. Ball, "On Thin Ice", *ABC Annual*. Sydney: Australian Broadcasting Commission, 1939, pp. 155-57.
13. *Department of Information: Summary of Activities for the period ended 31st March 1940*. Melbourne: Commonwealth Government Printer, 1940, p. 4.
14. W.M. Ball, evidence to Gibson Committee, 22 July 1941; *Report of the Joint Committee on Wireless Broadcasting*. Canberra: Commonwealth Government Printer, 25 March 1942, p. 20.
15. Author's interview with H. Ferber, 16 February 1976.
16. P. Hasluck, *The Government and the People 1939-1941*. Canberra: Australian War Memorial, 1952, p. 180.
17. Ibid.
18. Ibid., pp. 180-81.
19. "Report on the Operation of Press, Broadcasting and Film Censorship from 2/9/1939 to 29/1/39 [sic], State Publicity Censor NSW, Confidential Papers 1939-40; A.A., SP 106/11.
20. Ibid.
21. *War Cabinet Minute*, No. 36 of 16 October 1939.
22. *Commonwealth of Australia Gazette*, No. 44 of 1940, 6 March 1940, pp. 541-43.
23. Ibid., No. 170 of 1939, 19 December 1939.
24. Burchett application, 21 September 1939; A.A., SP 109, Box 72.
25. W. Burchett, *Passport: An Autobiography*. Melbourne: Nelson, 1969, pp. 143-44.
26. 16 June 1941, annotation between CPC 2852 and 2853; A.A., SP 109, Box

73. However, I suspect that this meant women censors could be employed in the *communications* censorship operation.
27. Jenkin to Censors, CC 9, 16 September 1941; A.A., SP 109, Box 72. The censorship diary could be regarded as analogous to a war diary of a military unit and was a chronological account of events. Like a war diary, it did not present the complete picture, but was potentially valuable as an insight into the censorship operations. Apart from one belonging to Tom Hoey, the Victorian Publicity Censor, 1942-45, located among his personal papers, no other diaries were found during the course of research. Most probably were destroyed after the war.
28. *Commonwealth of Australia Gazette*, No. 99 of 1939, 6 October 1939, pp. 2105-06.
29. J.C. Proud to Chief Censor, 21 February 1940; A.A., SP 109/3, Box 53.
30. Hasluck, *Government and the People 1939-1941*; p. 181.
31. In the *Publicity Censorship Directions* issued on 31 October 1944 (para 11(1)):
"A person shall not print or publish in Australia —
. . . (e) any matter in such a way as to show that any alteration, addition or omission has been made by, or under the direction of, a Publicity censor; or
(f) any statement to the effect that publication of any matter has been forbidden by Publicity Censor.
32. *Department of Information: Summary of Activities*, pp. 5-6.
33. Melbourne *Argus*, 27 February 1940.
34. "Report on the Operation of Press, Broadcasting and Film Censorship", p. 2.
35. Melbourne *Argus*, 10 April 1940.
36. *CPD* (HR), 7 September 1939, p. 164.
37. Mansell to Bonney, 27 May 1943, gave a list of the newspapers in New South Wales (with dates) that at some time or other were served by Censorship with total or partial orders to submit: *Century* (9/1/40), *Ironworker (30/5/40), Publicist* (9/1/40), *Forward* (24/5/40), *Smith's Weekly* (7/6/41), *Common Cause* (8/4/40), *Voice of the Jobless* (27/5/40), Forward Press P/L (3/5/40), Daily News Printery (3/6/40); as well as papers that were banned from publication through gazettal action: *Tribune* (12/4/40), *Soviets Today* (18/4/40), *Militant* (18/5/40), *World Peace* (21/5/40); A.A.; SP 109, Box 55, File 338.32.
38. *Civil Liberty*, 3, no. 4 (July 1940): 3.
39. Gullett to Jenkin, 9 April 1940; A.A., SP 195/1, File 72/1/5.
40. *Civil Liberty* 3, no. 4 (July 1940): 3-4.
41. *CPD* (HR), 23 April 1940, p. 375.
42. Ibid., 22 April 1940, p. 291.
43. Ibid., 24 May 1940, p. 1294. The nine publications were: The *Tribune* (Sydney), *Soviets Today* (Sydney), *Communist Review* (Sydney), *The Wharfie* (Sydney), *The Militant* (Sydney), *World Peace* (Sydney), *The Guardian* (Melbourne), *The Workers Star* (Perth) and *North Queensland Guardian* (Townsville).
44. Ibid., pp. 1273-74.
45. Ibid., 3 May 1940, pp. 559-60. In Great Britain, the provisions were liberalized in November 1939, after protests from the Council of Civil Liberties Union.
46. Ibid., 17 May 1940, p. 1037.

47. Ibid., 24 May 1940, p. 1036.
48. Hasluck, *Government and the People 1939-1941*, pp. 589-91.
49. P. Spender, *Politics and a Man*. Sydney: Collins, 1972, pp. 52-53.
50. G. Sawer, *Australian Federal Politics and Law 1929-1949*. Melbourne: Melbourne University Press, 1963, p. 104. Gullett, with other government Ministers, died in a plane crash at Canberra, 13 August 1940.
51. W. Dunk, *They Also Serve*. Canberra: privately published, 1974, pp. 41-43.
52. Hasluck, *Government and the People 1939-1941*, p. 237.

4

Murdoch's "Department of Expression"

"Touching the spirit"

While Menzies was considering how he might stir the populace to appreciation of the deepening crisis in Europe, the press was becoming jaded and increasingly cynical in reporting the war. The official historian felt the government needed to demand more of the people, if Australia were to respond properly to the reverses suffered overseas. For this to occur, "it would be necessary first to prepare the minds of the people".[1]

On 21 May 1940, at the meeting of his War Cabinet, a special inner cabinet of Ministers concerned with the war effort, Menzies urged that the morale of the public would have to be raised. Nothing less than the best publicist and journalist in Australia could counter the impending public trauma and re-energize public involvement with the war effort. Sir Keith Murdoch was that man.[2]

Before accepting the position, Murdoch consulted with his fellow newspaper proprietors. The prospect of Murdoch in charge of the Department of Information was welcomed unanimously. R.A. Henderson, general manager of the *Sydney Morning Herald*, wrote to Murdoch:

> Referring to our conversation today, the proposed appointment is acceptable to us and you can depend on our trust and

co-operation . . . wish you every success in your task. There can be no doubt of the seriousness of the [war] position and [the] necessity for us to do what we can . . .[3]

Murdoch was given a new kind of position: Director-General of Information. Although below ministerial status, it ranked above that of Department Secretary, with access to the War Cabinet and the Prime Minister. Treloar remained. Menzies also arranged similar positions for his other troubled areas of Munitions and Economic Co-ordination, appointing Essington Lewis, of BHP, and Sir Ernest Fisk, of AWA, respectively.

In appointing Murdoch, Menzies gained one of the most enterprising and influential press proprietors in Australia. Although fairly humourless, a poor public speaker and with a tendency to hire employees with attitudes in harmony with his own, Murdoch had established the largest media empire ever seen in Australia. He had had a substantial impact on the creation and success of the Lyons United Australia Party government, and was liked and respected by the leading political figures of his time.[4]

His father, Patrick John Murdoch, a minister of the Free Presbyterian Church, ensured that the young Murdoch was brought up a righteous and thrifty man. Equally influential for Murdoch was Lord Northcliffe, the British press magnate, who took him under his wing when Murdoch came to London. In a note to Northcliffe in March 1920, Murdoch disclosed:

> I will not say more than that you have been the biggest force over me here, largely on account of the kindness you have shown me, but even more largely from the example I have steadily seen in you, and the standard you have set me . . . If I never meet you again I would retain this influence to the end of my life.[5]

Later admirers and detractors alike dubbed Murdoch "Lord Southcliffe".[6] One of the more savage accounts depicted him as "The Man in the Paper Mask":

> no more than a paper mask, life-like and ingenious, but still a mask, hiding a calculating, undertaking, insatiable seeker after worldly riches and temporal power.

It seems clear that Murdoch was attracted by the power and prestige the government position would give him. Menzies provided Murdoch with the draft news release that described the nature of the task. It read in part:

> The Director-General will be concerned with the informative and psychological side of the war effort. In particular it will be his function, subject to Government policy and direction
>
> a) To present the progress of the war and its true colours without minimising reverses, while at the same time giving due weight to those factors which will enable a balanced public judgement to be formed;
> b) To keep the Australian people informed of the progress of Australia's war effort and of the work done in relation to manpower, industrial organisation and finance;
> c) To keep all sections of the community adequately informed as to what their duties are at the time of crisis, so that as far as possible, every citizen will know what his own task is and will be encouraged and directed in its performance;
> d) To organise in all parts of Australia committees and groups to play their part in the creation and expression of sound public psychology and the furtherance of our efforts in relation to manpower and supply;
> e) To arrange for *and control* the utilisation of every avenue of publicity, including broadcasting and cinematograph films, for the achievement of the purposes previously indicated.
>
> The Director-General, whose functions will thus be an integral and important element in the organisation of effective national service, will be adequately provided with funds and financial authority for the doing of his work, and in relation to all media of contact with the public, will be given all the powers necessary to see that private interests and normal routine are made subject to the national needs.[8]

Murdoch suggested eliminating the words "and control". The Prime Minister agreed and in that form the statement duly appeared in the papers on 8 June 1940.[9] In a later note to Murdoch on 24 June, Menzies set out the "substance of the discussions between us and reached by Cabinet". The words "and control" reappeared in the text. This time, Murdoch did not suggest amendment.[10]

Despite the provocative final sentence, the announcement was greeted with considerable acclamation. The *Daily Telegraph* of 11 June warmly commented: "The appointment means that Menzies has a man in this key post whom not only he, but all of Australia can trust." Many newspaper proprietors may have hesitated to be critical at a time when a positive national effort was being summoned. Murdoch's new position and ability to renegotiate the ABC's news-gathering arrangements on the basis of more favourable conditions towards the press may have assisted the widespread acceptance of his appointment.

In his first statements, Murdoch confined himself to well-meaning platitudes, hinting at an evangelical conception of the Department:

> The Department of Information will exist to serve the people and for no other reason. There will be no conceivable bias or selfish interest . . .[11]

In a radio talk, he described the Department as being "an instrument informing, rallying, and leading great and immediate tasks."[12] His parting speech to his staff at the Melbourne *Herald* shed light on the roles he desired for the press:

> The world of newspapers is of paramount importance in a democracy in war-time, and if it were not that I was going to serve newspapers outside, I certainly would not be leaving you now . . . In the past there have been places in our newspaper lives when speculative journalism has been sound journalism. I believe that time is past. I believe that during the next few months nothing but the most complete truth telling will be your duty.[13]

He talked of the Department's task as being something of a crusade, in that he was to "stir the inner thoughts of men, or go deeper and try to touch the spirit. It is very difficult and of course carries its own considerable share of danger."[14]

Murdoch's first move made significant inroads into the ABC and commercial radio stations' news sessions. He appointed three senior journalists, C.E. Sayers

(Melbourne *Age*), T. Holt (Sydney *Daily Telegraph*) and A.M. McLaughlin (*Sydney Morning Herald*), to prepare scripts to supplement news sessions. MacMahon Ball was as bemused as others in the Department:

> Sir Keith Murdoch had some very vague kind of picture that he would collect together, in Melbourne, the brightest and the best journalists who were in Australia, so that they could present the war effort in a way that was accurate within the limits of security possible . . . He always seemed to have a spiritual picture of his role: that there would flow from him, his energy and from his conviction of the righteousness of the struggle in which we were involved . . . and this was somehow energised to the people of Australia through the highly skilled work of the wonderful journalists and writers that he would enrol.[15]

However valuable such appointments proved, Murdoch was yet to formulate a detailed plan to realize his aims. On 19 June 1940, Murdoch submitted two related proposals for War Cabinet approval. Firstly, he wanted to increase the Department's role in radio. Regular nationwide broadcasts emanating from the Department about the international situation would be mandatory for all ABC and commercial stations. The schedule consisted of a 7-7.23 p.m. broadcast, Monday to Saturday. Sunday evenings, a 9-9.30 p.m. musical session was to be broadcast. It would include a ten-minute inspirational talk on the war.[16]

The second proposal involved an increase in his censorship powers. Murdoch sought a regulation that allowed him the right to insist that a journal or broadcasting station publish the facts in an "appropriate" form.[17]

Both proposals reflected Murdoch's desire for a more positive way of disseminating important information on the war. He informed the War Cabinet that he wanted his organization to be a "department of expression" and to avoid becoming a "department of suppression".[18] Murdoch already had discussed the proposals with Menzies and was assured of his support which resulted in both proposals being approved.[19]

Murdoch's first proposal concerning radio was implemented on 26 June 1940. For the first time, radio stations carried the same national news session. The broadcast began with ten minutes of overseas news (BBC and Australian), followed by five minutes of interviews with prominent persons or workers connected with war industry, such as munitions, and concluded with commentaries and local news.[20] Neither commercial stations nor the ABC were overjoyed by the proposal. The commercial stations, though pleased to have their long sought-after war news sessions, were nonplussed that the most popular evening broadcasting period had been given up to the program. This meant foregoing the best time for advertisers, moving other advertisers to less favourable times and "upsetting listeners so that one of the dullest sessions ever broadcast could take the place of the most popular sessions."[21]

The ABC also had reservations about the program, but decided against pursuing them, lest they stir Murdoch into assuming control over the whole of its activities.[22] However, ABC audiences began to complain. According to Frank Dixon, cries of stale news were heard. ABC listeners regarded the sessions as falling below the standard of the earlier bulletins. Murdoch put this down to teething problems. If necessary, he would engage another three journalists to make it successful. ABC staff doubted whether even twenty journalists would make a stale news bulletin sound interesting to listeners. The chairman of the ABC referred all complaints to Murdoch. Murdoch remained unconvinced and persisted with the view that it was a "good show".[23]

There were some criticisms in the press, but they were fairly mild. The press was in an ambivalent position. Murdoch had solved the problem of the ABC's news competing with its efforts. Stale news on the radio meant that press news was more desirable than ever. Nevertheless, it is unlikely that Murdoch was trying to undermine the ABC. Perhaps a more reasonable interpretation is that he was trying to show the ABC how "professionals" would go about producing a news program. However, Murdoch and his journalists seemed insensitive to the scheduling requirements of radio. He misjudged the effect of substituting such news sessions for the entertainment usually heard at that time. Murdoch expected people would grow accustomed to the news sessions as long as the stations continued the program.

The second stage of Murdoch's proposals, the regulation of "misleading impressions" in the media, also was developed in June. The War Cabinet had reasons other than Menzies' personal endorsement for viewing the regulations with favour. Up to March 1940, the Australian government had found it difficult to maintain the public's interest in the war. The most substantial war development had been the departure of the first convoy of the 2nd AIF (6th Division) for the Middle East some three months before. The public's enthusiasm for the cause had slackened. The following month, the Germans invaded Denmark and Norway. By the end of May, Holland, Belgium, Luxembourg and France were doomed. By June, the mood of the Australian public finally had responded. The gross AIF monthly recruiting figures from September 1939 to September 1940 chart the change clearly:[24]

Month	No. Recruited
1939	
September	—
October	7,853
November	9,991
December	1,810
January	811
February	217
March	1,316
April	5,441
May	8,000
June	48,496
July	21,022
August	32,524
September	1,049

In June 1940, the government found itself unable to cope with so many willing recruits. There were not enough uniforms to clothe all the recruits, arms and ammunition were not available to equip them and few camps existed in which to train them. The main reason for the decline in

July was the Cabinet's decision on the 11 July to temporarily limit enlistments.[25] The press was bound to return to its favourite theme of bottlenecks. Its commentaries would be likely to suggest that the government had been unable to organize the war. Censorship, which had been used to cover such stories in the past (on the basis that they revealed vital industrial intelligence to the enemy), was no longer enough. The recruits themselves soon would become aware that they were being discouraged. They need not read about it in the newspapers: they were part of it.

Murdoch's proposals to regulate dissemination of such impressions allowed the government to answer the inevitable outcry without appearing unduly suppressive. Instead of the odium of censorship, the government could oblige the press and radio to publish its account for the edification of the public.[26]

Murdoch realized that this would require considerable finesse. Unlike the radio stations, the press was not normally subject to licensing or ministerial overview. On 1 July 1940, Murdoch convened a conference with news editors and controllers, to seek their views about the Department's role. The editors accepted his invitation and seized on the shortcomings of Censorship. Murdoch said he was concerned about "wilfully biased" and "deliberately incorrect" news. Would not this be better subject to government correction than censorship? In certain circumstances, he argued, the government should have the right to say that a published statement had been harmful; to say, here is the truth, print it, and print it where we tell you. The media representatives were unconvinced. It was a denial of freedom of the press. Censorship, odious as it was, was more than sufficient. These proposals smacked of dictatorship.[27]

Murdoch regarded such objections as reflections on his own bona fides. Sir Lloyd Dumas has suggested that the Attorney-General's Department had made the regulations broader than Murdoch intended.[28] Murdoch had been cautioned about the provocative aspects of his proposals. Sir George Knowles, Secretary of the Attorney-General's Department, wrote to Treloar as early as 19 June 1940:

> The alteration which Sir Keith Murdoch has made . . . is going a long way, in that it would be possible under that alteration, if the Director-General so desired, to require an editor to make available space to the amount of, perhaps, a whole page of publication of the matter as a statement, i.e. without payment.

At the same time, Knowles had no doubt that the regulation would not operate in this way, providing its conditions were more circumscribed.[29] Murdoch annotated this memorandum with "should stand".

On 17 July, Murdoch's regulations were duly gazetted. Newspapers, broadcasting stations and cinemas that were disseminating "misleading information" could be compelled to publish with equal prominence the "correct" version which would be supplied by the Director-General of Information.[30] The outcry by the press was swift and vigorous:

> The Director-General, if he should become sufficiently intoxicated by his excess of authority, or sufficiently piqued by criticism of himself or the Government, could order the whole issue of a newspaper to be occupied by "material supplied" by his Department. It is no answer to say that the powers will probably be used little, if at all. The powers are there, and experience has shown all too clearly that excessive authority placed in political and bureaucratic hands is very liable sooner or later to be abused . . . It is precisely the system adopted by the Dictator countries, whose propaganda Ministries achieved their ascendancy over the newspapers and the public by enforcing the publication only of matter suited to the purposes of their masters.[31]

> The Commonwealth Government can force you to read statements or opinions which your papers passionately disagree with or believe to be incorrect.[32]

> The regulation is a crime against the very ideals of freedom for which Australia entered the war . . .[33]

> The regulation is objectionable and a dangerous and unnecessary attack on the liberty of the Press and the public.[34]

Members of the public appeared no less disturbed. Excerpts from the letters published in the press disclose the widespread bewilderment:

> Some Ministers invite criticism every time they speak, and so we may soon find ourselves reading "corrections" intended to gild bedraggled lilies, but exciting further criticism which will have no vent; closed vents lead to trouble . . .
>
> The Director-General "does not intend to abuse his powers" but the present Government may not weather the next election. We may then have a Prime Minister without Mr Menzies' extraordinary capacity for doing many diverse jobs . . .
>
> Even an imbecile who has watched the trend of the present Government towards dictatorship can interpret the last move which is aimed at preventing any expression of opinion that might jeopardize its chances at the forthcoming elections . . .[35]

John Curtin congratulated Murdoch for appointing himself editor-in-chief of every newspaper in Australia.[36]

The row over the regulation had repercussions within Cabinet as well. After the full Cabinet meeting of 18 July 1940, the Postmaster-General, Mr H. Thorby, protested he had not been consulted about the regulations, even though they concerned his broadcasting portfolio responsibility and he threatened to resign over the matter.[37]

Murdoch was upset by the row. There had not been a similar occurrence when he implemented his broadcasting plans. His attempts to placate his critics were based on the worthy intentions underlying the regulations, and on his reputation. If Murdoch could not be trusted, no one could:

> If I had sought to be suppressive . . . I would not have asked for the power to correct persistently damaging misstatements. I would have been satisfied to use the ample powers that exist of suppressing publications by censorship . . . suppression by censorship should be avoided where possible, and that the best answer to the persistent misstatement is the power to correct adequately. That is all the new regulation is intended to mean . . .[38]

Ironically, the regulation resembled a proposal submitted by the civil libertarian, Maurice Blackburn, in November 1939:

A newspaper which prints its own opinions about the war should be compellable [sic] to print the department's answer to such views and arguments. I believe that would only be fair. I regard newspapers as public utilities discharging public functions, and I believe that they, as well as radio stations, should be compellable [sic] to publish replies . . . The only way to deal with opinions is to answer them not to repress them. Once the people believe that the Government has no answer to such opinions . . . Only the person who has no answer will take refuge in repression and suppression . . .[39]

His biographer argues that the regulation was Murdoch's first major error, and it was to prove the greatest of his professional life.[40] Murdoch might have salvaged his regulation had he taken up the matter with Blackburn and the Council of Civil Liberties. (Blackburn made no attempt to resurrect his proposal in the debates about the regulation that ensued in Parliament.) Murdoch also might have bolstered his case if he had provided convincing examples of what he proposed. He might have had his department provide a dossier of "persistently damaging" statements that appeared in the press, to suggest how the censorship powers were inappropriate or ineffectual, and that something in the nature of his regulation was needed.

Such precautionary measures were not considered by Murdoch. He had been accustomed to making judgements about what was right, and appears to have come to believe that he only would desire what was right. His success in business and political circles attested to this view. His religious upbringing may have inspired him to take this course. The press, for its own good, should be shown the right path. As Australia's top publicist, Murdoch could not accept that he was remote from public opinion. He had become stale through his lack of contact with the public.[41] It is probably not entirely coincidental that Murdoch sponsored the first Australian public opinion (Gallup) polls some months later.

On 19 July 1940, Menzies and Murdoch realized the hopelessness of their position. Menzies agreed to review the regulations. A considerably weaker version of the regulations was gazetted on 31 August. This provided that instead of the Director-General having the power to require publication of his own matter when he believed it necessary in the interests of defence or the prosecution of war, he should have the power only in case of misstatements or misrepresentation of facts concerning the prosecution of war; and then, in the first instance, he should furnish a statement to the newspaper concerned and request that it be published. If this request were not complied with, he might, with the approval of the Minister, require that the statement be published in such a form as he specified. He could not direct what space it should occupy, only that it should have a corresponding position and prominence and display equal to that of the original statement it sought to correct. It was specifically provided that space usually occupied by the leading articles or editorials was excluded and that newspapers could not be required to publish comments as distinct from statement of fact.

The regulation was never applied.[42] The more the official historian, a former journalist himself, compared the two regulations, the more convinced he became that nothing fundamental was at stake. The point at issue, in his view, was one of property rights.[43] The press was concerned that the regulations would preempt valuable advertising space. But there was more to it than this. As far as the press was concerned, Murdoch had demonstrated he could not be trusted.

Murdoch's set-back over his regulation stimulated other changes to his policies. The ABC saw to it that the Department no longer imposed the broadcasting of 7-7.23 p.m. news sessions.[44] The commercial stations also wanted the arrangement changed, to which Menzies agreed. The 23-minute program was replaced by a news commentary inserted between the regular news broadcasts. The commentaries were no longer mandatory and in August they were well on the way to being dropped by the Department.[45]

Murdoch conferred with the Federation of Australian

Commercial Broadcasters in Melbourne on 14 and 15 August 1940, on how they might assist the war effort. Apart from gaining agreement to the treatment to be given to the forthcoming election, Murdoch found those who attended the meeting more and more intransigent. His proposal for an experimental production of one or two serials dramatizing the war effort was declined. The industry journal, *Commercial Broadcasting*, reported "that it was considered that the Government should allow radio production of this nature to remain in the hands of private enterprise."[46]

The result of the 1940 federal election proved indecisive. Menzies lost seats, but Curtin failed to gain enough to form a government. Two independents held the balance of power.[47] Menzies, now desperate to negotiate a National government similar to the Churchill-Atlee arrangement, cultivated a more conciliatory attitude to the opposition. He asked Curtin to name the conditions that might form the basis of an agreement. Curtin responded with a long list that implied a total review of the war effort. Included on the list was the request for "a complete overhaul of the Department of Information and its activities". Menzies, in his reply to Curtin of 22 October 1940, declined to respond to such points in detail, but expressed confidence that a basis of agreement could be found.[48] In the event, an Advisory War Council was established on 28 October, to develop a consultative and advisory link between the government and the opposition. The government, which appointed Murdoch in June, was no longer matched in either enthusiasm or effectiveness.

To understand the censorship practices under Murdoch it is necessary to appreciate his obsession with turning the Department's interests from suppression to expression. He hoped that censorship would be lessened if his policy could be implemented. Censorship policy as such attracted little of Murdoch's attention or interest. When he first took office, Murdoch spoke of liberalizing censorship:

> we should be able to help by clearing channels when they need clearing, by adding a note of authority sometimes, by con-

siderably increasing the behind-the-news matter in the editors' rooms, and even by explaining the workings of the censorship, so that the public will know how extremely little censorship is actually done in this country . . .[49]

Murdoch's neglect of censorship did not mean that it would not be given direction. It meant it would be subject to many directions.

With the end of the "phoney war", Archie Cameron, the newly installed Minister for the Navy, authorized the "New Rules for Naval Censorship". In March 1940, he introduced three classifications for naval news. The first was the news that was prohibited under all circumstances: mainly troop and shipping movements, and the like. This was not a departure from the previous rules. The second was information that could be published "only after announcement has been made by a member of the Naval Board". This covered such matters as the appointment of officers, the fitting of vessels, transport, munitions, damage sustained, etc. This effectively reintroduced the senior service to the jurisdiction of censorship. The third category reinforces this interpretation. This was information that was to be "referred to the local Navy Authority for permission to publish", and concerned such matters as the construction of buildings, and photographs or articles referring "even indirectly to technical matters of concern to the Navy".[50] In effect, naval matters could not be reported without first referring them to the Navy. The new rules did not cover ministerial statements. The ground had been laid for papers to publish freely only what the Naval Minister wanted published. Even before Murdoch's appointment, then, it was a difficult matter to press on with independent news or views, especially after the government's suppression of the communist journals.

After Murdoch's appointment, the censors continued to receive and act on directions, capricious or otherwise, from all quarters of government. The following examples are illustrative:

On 2 July 1940, editors and broadcasting managers were guided on the promotion of the War Loan campaign:

A warning is issued to Editors and Broadcasting Managers against allowing articles or talks which attack the present system of raising war funds by additional taxation and by public subscription to War Loans, urging instead the issue of interest-free state credit money. Such arguments are calculated to dissuade the public from subscribing to War Loan and to patriotic funds and are therefore liable to weaken the war effort. Their publication is therefore directly opposed to the Censorship rules under the National Security Act.[51]

The relevance to military security is difficult to see. In July, editors and broadcasters were instructed that: "No photograph of General Blamey and staff, arriving in Palestine in civilian clothes, is to be published."[52]

Such instructions, while suggestive, fail to capture and reflect their political intentions. Extracts from the censors' diaries do this much better. These suggest that, in 1940, Ministers other than the Minister for Information came to direct the Censorship Division; that some of these instructions were relayed by means as informal as a telephone call to censors; that some of these Ministers assumed the right to control the release of news; and that some of these influences amounted to overt political censorship.

On 26 June 1940, an entry[53] in the diary of the State Publicity Censor for Victoria, C. Burns, suggests that Murdoch was prepared to suppress publication of an article without evidence of the existence of the copy:

Approx 1540 hrs. 26 June 1940
Deputy CPC (Chief Publicity Censor) called SPC (State Publicity Censor), Mr Burns urgently into a conference . . . It was urgently reported by the Secretary to the Prime Minister . . . that he had been informed that *Truth* newspaper proposed to publish a false and scandalous article personally attacking the private life of the Prime Minister. (The Deputy CPC consulted the Director-General and reported that the Director-General *had* instructed that publication of the article would be inimical to the public interest at this critical juncture of the war. If necessary an order to submit to Censorship must be served on the *Truth*.) SPC therefore called personally on Mr F.V. McGuiness, Melbourne editor of the *Truth*. Mr McGuiness gave an assurance that he had absolutely no knowledge of the existence of any such article. He had never

even heard the rumour; he had not made any enquiries of any kind concerning the personal life of Mr Menzies; and no member of his staff had been asked to do so. If any such story was astir in Sydney he felt sure he would have been consulted but he had heard nothing of the kind. If he received anything of the sort from Sydney, he undertook to submit it voluntarily for Censorship. The result of this interview was conveyed to (the secretary of the Prime Minister) with certain advice. As a result (the secretary) requested that no further action be taken unless requested.

The precedent for secretaries of Ministers conveying instructions to censors was not confined to that of Menzies' secretary. The secretaries of other Ministers also were active:

2335 hrs. 3 September 1940
Mr. Moroney, sec Minister for External Affairs, phoned instructions from Minister placing stop on reference to a man named Vois alleged to be aboard the steamer *Notou* being associated with the Commonwealth Government in the purchase of Nickel in Noumea.

The ministerial intervention with regard to censorship was characterized less by outright suppression than by delay. Ministers chose this strategy so that they could be in a position to prepare their view of the incident — a view that would suggest that they were on top of the situation. Archie Cameron, Minister for the Navy, used this tactic frequently:

24 August 1940
Mr. Neil reports —
At 1045 on Saturday . . . I received a telephone message at my home from Mr A. Cameron, Minister for the Navy. Mr Cameron's message was substantially as follows. "Further to my telephonic communication with you this afternoon, from now on please understand that I will make all statements pertaining to Naval matters for publicity releases in the future."

This entry followed Cameron's release of an account of the activities of an enemy raider in the Tasman Sea. The first news of the incident had been released by the Prime Minister of New Zealand.

2150 hours 29 August 1940
Melbourne *Argus* telephones CLO (Censorship Liaison Officer)/Navy, pointing out that *Sydney Morning Herald* reported that "shipping circles" in Sydney were concerned that a ship was overdue at Noumea. CLO/Navy advised that Navy had no statement for publication and asked that previous arrangements concerning news affecting the Tasman raider should prevail, i.e. only statements *to be passed* are those made officially by the Minister for the Navy.

Although film censorship generally was carried out without problems of the kind that daily confronted press and broadcasting, odd decisions still were made. The Metro-Goldwyn-Mayer blockbuster *Gone With The Wind* was shorn by some fifteen minutes for Australian cinema goers because it was thought that some sequences and dialogue would prejudice recruiting. Among the cuts was a statement by Captain Rhett Butler: "most of the miseries of the world are caused by wars and when wars are over, no one ever knows what they were about."

The censor insisted on cuts of only about seven minutes. The distributor voluntarily disposed of the additional eight minutes, to demonstrate good faith and to ensure unimpeded presentation of the film in Australia.[54] Ironically, these cuts coincided with the one period when the government was embarrassed by the numbers volunteering for war services.

Murdoch found himself saddled with such petty matters as having to apologise for the censorship imposed by the Services. In October 1940, a ship carrying child evacuees from Britain came via Melbourne. Anyone at the waterfront could have witnessed its passing. However, Murdoch defended a Navy instruction to suppress the news:

> It might seem foolish that newspapers and broadcasting stations should be asked not to mention travels of a large ship containing many hundreds of children evacuees before it reached its last port, but all reasonable people agree that the Admiralty's policy was wise . . . It was true the children were near the end of the journey when they passed through Melbourne, but had Melbourne any right to ask that a wise Admiralty policy should be changed simply to give little earlier publicity than Admiralty thought right?[55]

The more probable reason for the delay was Archie Cameron's instruction that statements on naval matters were to be issued only as he so authorized. Either way, Murdoch's duties had strayed from his lofty mission. He was now supporting the red-tape and opaque censorship principles that he had vowed to do away with.

The influence of the Services on censorship infuriated the press. Errol G. Knox, president of the Australian Newspaper Council, chose to highlight the matter in his address to members in November 1940. Knox conceded the need for security censorship, but argued that "the tardy and inadequate release of news when the enemy already has full information is to my mind evidence only of the futility of officialdom."[56]

The press was not alone in its annoyance with the system:

> It seems to me censorship defeats itself. That the Navy Minister considered it necessary to say "Any rumours regarding the loss of any other vessel off the Australian coast were unfounded" clearly proves this . . . It should not have been necessary for people to await the BBC broadcast from London to know the locality in which the disaster occurred . . .[57]

The editor of the Melbourne *Herald* wrote in his diary:

> (June 1940) Now we are making virtues of our vices. Now, we newspapermen are told, we must prepare people for the worst; we must *not* emphasize hopeful notes in communiques and speeches about fighting in France. What might have been censored a few weeks ago becomes the highest form of patriotism . . .
>
> (July 1940) A dumb captain marches his men in the rain all day then refuses to let them change before dinner. Some gross 16 lb hammers are ordered in mistake for 4 lb hammers. Middle aged executive is permitted to enlist and does nothing in particular that would not have been done by adult 14 year old or not too bright pensioner — The offence is not to permit these things, but to mention them.[58]

Cognizant of the growing resentment, Menzies promised a "revision" of the censorship principles on 2 December 1940. His principal concession was:

Where news is received by the Press or by broadcasting stations before a public announcement is made, the Chief Censor should afford the department concerned the opportunity of stating whether security considerations are involved . . .[59]

This was hardly a revision. If anything, it formalized the process that had developed already through Murdoch's neglect. The new system continued the arrangement of warning Ministers and their departments of "incidents" about to be reported. If a security reason could not be offered to restrain the reporting, the arrangement served to delay publication and to alert the agency to prepare its gloss on the incident.

Under Murdoch, an anti-Labor bias continued to feature in censorship procedure.[60] An article by J.T. Lang, in the publication *Century* concerning the shortage of defence equipment, was prohibited. The paper's editor, N. McCauley, wrote a leading article on the subject, but this also was banned. Finally, in exasperation, McCauley retyped an article that had already appeared in the Sydney *Sun* on the same topic. This too was rejected. McCauley then discussed the article with the Censor on a line-by-line basis, but was informed none of the material was publishable. McCauley then showed the original *Sun* clipping to the Censor, who was alleged to have responded, "You have trapped me!" The following day, the ban on the *Century* article was eased substantially.[61]

In Parliament, Eddie Ward (ALP, East Sydney) castigated the work of the censors. Until the end of 1940, *Hansard* records disclosed few censorship advocates among government members. Even the Deputy Prime Minister, Arthur Fadden, conceded that the censorship staff may have been poorly selected.[62] It is typical of that time that reports of the parliamentary debate on censorship referred to Ward's criticisms in only general terms. The illuminating and provocative illustrations recounted by Ward, and recorded in *Hansard* were not published.

The set-back to Murdoch's expressive regulations affected other divisions of the Department, including the

Department's publicity area. At the end of October 1940, the Department announced that it was allowing a cameraman from the American *March of Time* series freedom to see and film whatever he pleased. No specially conducted tours would be arranged. It was trying to avoid "expressive" tactics. It was just a resource, and would not interfere:

> The Department's job was to make facilities available for him. Conducted tours on lines similar in some European countries gave most visitors the impression of being sidetracked — and that was to be avoided.[63]

However, the Murdoch ledger was not all gloom and despair. In July, Murdoch had reported that Australia's war effort already was becoming better known in other parts of the world as a result of the efforts of the Department. A cable service of Australian news to the United States had been commenced, and a separate bulletin was to be beamed twice a day. A similar service was planned for the United Kingdom.[64]

The American Division of the Department of Information was established by Murdoch in August 1940, as a small unit headed by R.J.F. Boyer, a commissioner of the ABC, in an honorary capacity. It was designed to operate like the American Division of the British Ministry of Information, in keeping Americans informed of the work carried out by Australia. This modest beginning was to spawn the first Australian News and Information Bureau, based in New York. In more dire times, when the war entered the South West Pacific, the Division's interest shifted to that of maintaining and improving relations between Australian and American servicemen.[65] Murdoch also supported Ball's Shortwave Division; its budget was increased and the staff became more effective and versatile as a result.

All these developments, however, were largely unsung and of little consequence to the crestfallen Murdoch. More importantly, his prestige and position had been tarnished. On 14 November, Menzies announced Murdoch's departure. He was to continue in an advisory capacity, particularly in regard to the emerging and promising area of overseas publicity.[66] The sourness left by this episode may be inferred from his company's (the Herald & Weekly Times) eulogy on Murdoch's death in 1952. This otherwise comprehensive account of Murdoch's career omits reference to his period as Director-General of the Department of Information.[67]

The Department survived his departure. Menzies indicated that he would soon appoint a new Minister for Information. The Advisory War Council discussed the Department's future on 25 November 1940. Members from both sides of politics agreed that its results had been lacklustre and its censorship operations in need of reform. Labour members felt that more "definiteness of purpose and imagination should be infused into the administration", if the Department was to justify its existence.[68]

In December, the Department's estimates for the 1940-41 period drew considerable criticism. An increase in its vote to the order of £60,000, bringing its total annual estimate to £193,000, attracted widespread comment and criticism in Parliament. Archie Cameron, no longer a Minister, was particularly hostile. He said it was one of the worst conceived of departments — a mismanaged department of bits and pieces. It had no history and should have no future, and he pressed the government to bow to the inevitable and allow the Department to pass into oblivion.[69] The Treasurer, Arthur Fadden, replied that a review by the Advisory War Council indicated the Department should not only continue but extend its activities, particularly its overseas publicity role. He foreshadowed changes that would satisfy even Mr Cameron.[70]

Notes

1. P. Hasluck, *The Government and the People 1939-1941*. Canberra: Australian War Memorial, 1952, p. 238.
2. Ibid.
3. C.E. Sayers "Keith Murdoch, Journalist", ANL, MSS 2823, Folder 84, p. 553.

4. Ibid., p. 20. See also *Keith Murdoch — Journalist*. Melbourne: Herald & Weekly Times, 1952, p. 21.
5. Sayers, "Keith Murdoch", p. 300.
6. A.A. Calwell, *CPD* (HR), 25 March 1941, p. 176.
7. J. Hetherington, *Australians: Nine Profiles*. Melbourne: Cheshire, 1960, p. 82.
8. On 6 June 1940, Menzies submitted this draft for Murdoch's agreement; Sayers, "Keith Murdoch", pp. 556-58; emphasis added.
9. The official historian erred slightly in this regard, and appears to have relied on the original draft rather than the amended one, which was published, when citing the duties of the Director-General. See Hasluck *Government and the People 1939-1941*, pp. 238-39.
10. Sayers, "Keith Murdoch", p. 558.
11. Melbourne *Argus*, 8 June 1940.
12. Sayers, "Keith Murdoch", p. 561.
13. Ibid., p. 553.
14. Ibid., p. 554.
15. Author's interview with W. MacMahon Ball, 18 February 1976.
16. Melbourne *Argus*, 9 July 1940. The session began on 26 June.
17. Hasluck, *Government and the People 1939—1941*, p. 239.
18. Ibid. This was not the first occasion that the "expression/suppression" concept was raised in the context of government information policies. George Creel, who headed the US World War I propaganda agency, recalled in March 1917, (see *Rebel at Large — Recollections of Fifty Crowded Years*. New York: Putnam, 1947, p. 157) that when the Navy and Army were pressing for firm censorship, he argued that "expression, not suppression, was the real need".
19. Hasluck, *Government and the People 1939-1941*, p. 239.
20. K. Murdoch, evidence before the Gibson Committee, 20 October 1941; *Report of the Joint Committee on Wireless Broadcasting*. Canberra: Commonwealth Government Printer, 25 March 1942, pp. 300-01.
21. Editorial, "Dictators-not required", *Commercial Broadcasting*, 1 August, 1940.
22. F. Dixon, *Inside the ABC: A Piece of Australian History*. Melbourne: Hawthorn Press, 1975, p. 44.
23. Ibid., p. 46.
24. Hasluck, *Government and the People 1939-1941*, p. 613.
25. Ibid., p. 220.
26. The American and British governments flirted with regulations of a similar nature, although they were dropped before being made public. Bruce Catton recalls the Director of Information of the War Production Board receiving and discarding the following suggestion: "What we ought to do . . . is to get out a simple press release whenever WPB does anything and require all of the papers just to print that press release exactly the way we write it, without adding anything of their own or leaving any of it out. Then we wouldn't have all this confusion and people's minds wouldn't get so upset."
See *The War Lords of Washington*. New York: Harcourt, Brace, 1948, p. 63.
27. Sayers, "Keith Murdoch", p. 564; Melbourne *Argus*, 19 July 1940, p. 2.
28. Sir Lloyd Dumas, *The Story of a Full Life*. Melbourne: Sun Books, 1969, pp. 67-68.

29. Knowles to Treloar, 19 June 1940; A.A., SP 195/1, File 3/1/1A.
30. National Security (Information) Regulations, Statutory Rules 1940, no. 137.
31. *Sydney Morning Herald*, 18 July 1940.
32. Sydney *Daily Telegraph*, 18 July 1940.
33. Sydney *Sun*, 18 July 1940.
34. Melbourne *Age*, 18 July 1940.
35. Letters to the Editor, Melbourne *Argus*, 19 July 1940.
36. Ibid.
37. Ibid.
38. Ibid.
39. *CPD* (HR), 28 November 1939, p. 1608.
40. Author's interview with C.E. Sayers, 17 February 1976.
41. C. Edwards, *The Editor Regrets*. Melbourne: Hill of Content, 1972, p. 84.
42. There is no record of the revised regulation actually being applied. In 1943, the Chief Publicity Censor, E.G. Bonney, invited the Department of Air's Public Relations Directorate to resort to the regulation instead of censoring a Sydney paper alleged to have persistently published damaging articles. The invitation was apparently declined. See E.G. Bonney to Wing-Commander F. McDonnell, Director of Public Relations, Department of Air, 29 September 1943, Hoey Papers.
43. Hasluck, *Government and the People 1939-1941*, pp. 240-41.
44. Melbourne *Argus*, 25 July 1940.
45. K. Murdoch, evidence before the Gibson Committee, 20 October 1941, p. 301.
46. *Commercial Broadcasting*, 29 August 1940, p. 6.
47. G. Sawer, *Australian Federal Politics and Law 1929-1949*. Melbourne: Melbourne University Press, 1963, p. 125.
48. P. Weller and Beverley Woyd (eds), *Caucus Minutes 1901-1949: Minutes of the Federal Parliamentary Labor Party, Vol. 3, 1932-1949*. Melbourne: Melbourne University Press, 1976, pp. 243-44.
49. Melbourne *Argus*, 8 June 1940.
50. Censorship Instruction C, March 1940; T.C. Bray Papers, ANL, MSS 2519.
51. Bray Papers.
52. Ibid.
53. All the diary entries following were compiled by Tom Hoey in 1944 for a confidential paper entitled "Extracts from Diary of 1940.41", in Hoey Papers.
54. C. Burns, 5 July 1940, "Censorship of Films Likely to Affect the Recruiting Campaign"; A.A., SP 109, Box 48, File 320.08.
55. Melbourne *Argus*, 18 October 1940.
56. Ibid., 13 November 1940.
57. Ibid., 12 November 1940.
58. Edwards, *Editor Regrets*, pp. 81, 83.
59. Melbourne *Argus*, 3 December 1940.
60. *CPD* (HR), 12-13 December 1940, pp. 1064-70.
61. Ibid., p. 1067.
62. Ibid., p. 1069.
63. Melbourne *Argus*, 31 October 1940.
64. Ibid., 9 July 1940.
65. R.J.F. Boyer to E.G. Bonney, 10 December 1943; A.A., SP 195/9, Item 17.

66. Melbourne *Argus*, 16 November 1940.
67. *Keith Murdoch — Journalist*.
68. Melbourne *Argus*, 26 November 1940.
69. *CPD* (HR), 12-13 December 1940, p. 1068.
70. Ibid., pp. 1068, 1075.

5

Foll's Consolidation

"Certainly there has been a bungle today"

Senator Hatill Spencer Foll, the Minister of the Interior, became the third Minister for Information on Friday, 13 December, 1940. Former employees of the Department have remained singularly unimpressed by Foll's ability and contribution to the Department.[1] Menzies, too, thought little of Foll, and was said to have quipped to one of the staff, "I understand you don't suffer Folls gladly."[2] Nevertheless, Foll was underrated. His administration proved effective and his influence was enduring.

Like Murdoch, Foll had a positive conception of what the Department was supposed to achieve, matched with a personal enthusiasm for the portfolio:

> I was very interested in the Department of Information. I always had a desire to be associated with the Press and Publicity. I was a part-time journalist for a period in Qld . . . and composed my own election material.[3]

Foll saw the Department as one that should promote Australia's interests abroad rather than at home. This was an elaboration of Murdoch's "department of expression" theme, in that it met a need for a co-ordinated promotion initiative. But unlike Murdoch, Foll demonstrated a capacity to attend to the administrative implications of his policies. This capacity, perhaps more than any other, spared him from the set-backs that bedevilled Murdoch. Foll represented the Service Ministers in the Senate and thus was in a position to require that the Service departments kept him briefed on military developments. He also had sat on the Advisory War Council in War Cabinet sessions from October 1940. Tactically, he was well placed to handle the Information portfolio.

On the day of his appointment, Foll expressed his desire for the Department to be given a further opportunity to prove itself: "I ask that the past shall be forgotten and that the Department shall be allowed to begin again with a clean slate . . ."[4] Foll intended taking more direct control of the Department and the Director-General's position lapsed on Murdoch's departure. The control of the Department was formally handed over to Foll by Murdoch on 18 December 1940 at the Melbourne headquarters, where they conferred for some hours. Anxious to learn as much as possible before commenting on new policies, Foll informed reporters: "I am coming to an entirely new Department . . . it is not on all fours by any means with the ordinary Government Department. That is why I am moving carefully."[5] However, later that day he announced changes in the original conception of the Department. When peace returned, the Department would not necessarily end: "The Department is now regarded as a wartime activity but I am satisfied that its work will endure after the war . . . Australia must become better known abroad and Australians must realise that their years of fancied isolation are ending."[6]

Among his most enduring contributions was Foll's decision to establish an Australian News and Information Bureau, based in New York. This branch of the Department was created to foster stronger links with the United States, by keeping it informed of Australia's war effort.

Although the Bureau was conceived by Murdoch, and had already been provided for in the budget, it was Foll who brought it to life. The Bureau had a staff of nine, including an editorial assistant, a shortwave recordings/transcriber, a photographer librarian and associated administrative staff.[7] In January 1941, Foll appointed David W. Bailey to take charge of the Bureau. Bailey, a Tasmanian, was a journalist with wide experience. He had been on the editorial staff of the Melbourne *Herald* and *Sun*, and had worked in London with AAP as second-in-command. At the time of his appointment, he was in charge of the New York office of AAP.[8] Bailey's achievements were to be recalled by later Ministers for Information. His example paved the way for other overseas branches.

In a matter of weeks, the Department had been reoriented. Foll's objective of gaining overseas publicity for Australia was evident in the phasing out of the local information policies. The Group Committees network and organization were discontinued, since they were becoming costly to service and were of declining benefit. Contact with community groups would be continued by the Editorial Division's provision of news to the 1,200 journals published by those groups throughout the Commonwealth.[9] Five "unnecessary" state branches of the Department were closed later in the year, which saved £34,000 on the budget estimates. The Department had "branched out in other directions", said Foll.[10]

The background of Charles Holmes, who in September 1941 became the new Director of Information, reflected the policy direction pursued by Foll. Holmes was not a journalist, but was experienced in tourist promotion. He had been general manager of the Australian National Travel Association, had published a handbook on Australia for circulation overseas and had founded the journal *Walkabout*.[11]

Other staff and organization moves included the appointment of Charles Bateson, the publicity officer, from his Interior portfolio to a new position of Principal Information Officer, to control the Department of Information's editorial, broadcasting, photographic and film activities.[12] C.E. Sayers was appointed the Department's editor and the poet Kenneth Slessor, then based in England as the official war correspondent, was sent to cover the increasing military involvement of Australians in the Middle East.[13] Foll wanted to transfer the Department's headquarters to Canberra, but a shortage of office space prevented this. Instead, the Film Division was transferred from Melbourne to Sydney, to be closer to the centre of the commercial film industry.[14]

Local radio programs dealing with the war and supplied by the Department were cut back to fifteen minutes. These were broadcast nationally each Sunday evening. This created difficulties for many broadcasting stations that wanted an authoritative service but did not want to expend resources. As an alternative, they offered £180,000 worth of "free time", for quarter-hour sessions of authoritative and topical war news, morning and evening. But Foll declined their offer.[15]

The Secretary of the Australian Federation of Commercial Broadcasters commented bitterly: "Senator Foll believed it was not the function of the Department to supply news services. In this, of course, he differed from Sir Keith Murdoch."[16]

Foll was concerned with the cost (£30,000) of providing landlines to broadcasting stations. Where would the money come from? Eventually, Foll agreed that the twenty-one commercial country stations whose service area was not covered by the ABC news service could receive landlines to take the ABC news. However, it was not only landline costs that perturbed Foll. The special difficulties in maintaining a local news unit to serve these radio stations meant a considerable expense.

As part of his overseas policy, Foll's aim was to develop the shortwave service. From discussions he had with the Advisory Council, Foll knew that Curtin would support him in reallocating resources from local to overseas radio. He planned to increase the power of the shortwave transmitters and was considering additional transmitters.[17] Eventually, local news offered by the Department under Foll for use by commercial radio was confined to fifteen-minute sessions each Sunday.[18]

Foll's interest in pursuing an overseas information policy

did not prevent him from undertaking local information activities. He later recalled the creation of the Advertising Division, to co-ordinate all government advertising, as his greatest achievement.[19] Its genesis lay in the rivalry of the Armed Services. By the time Foll became Information Minister, the recruiting figures had fallen considerably. In response, each of the Services engaged in their own recruiting drives, which resulted in their out-bidding each other for premium advertising space. Foll drew this to the attention of Menzies and the Advisory War Council, proposing that his department establish a division to co-ordinate government advertising budgets, particularly those for the Services, so that resources would not be wasted. Other major campaigns, such as the forthcoming second War Loan campaign, which might interfere with the space needed for the recruiting drive required special co-ordination arrangements. Foll's proposal for an Advertising Division was approved and established in February 1941.[20]

The Advertising Division took over all advertising negotiations other than the placement of small, routine vacancies notices. The functions of preparing copy and the production of layout or recordings remained the responsibilities of the individual advertising agencies. The allocation of advertising space and time was to be the responsibility of the Advertising Division. In March 1941, I.B. Hutcheson, sales director of Lever Bros. Pty Ltd, was appointed Controller of Commonwealth Government Advertising. A Deputy Controller was appointed a few weeks later.

Hutcheson's first move was to negotiate "master contracts" for all newspaper advertising. Instead of, say, five different government ads being purchased each at the, say, 1,000 column-inch rate, the space could be negotiated and purchased at the cheaper 5,000 column-inch rate. Similar arrangements were developed for radio time, poster positions and theatre slides.

This effective centralization of publicity could have been viewed at yet another attempt to apply by stealth the "expressive" function. By centralizing advertising contracts, Foll put the Department in a powerful position. The media could be rewarded or punished by gaining or losing the lucrative master contracts. The provincial papers were among those who openly protested that the Department was not giving them adequate consideration in the master contracts. Foll forestalled such claims of improper patronage with the establishment of an Advertising Agency Advisory Board, made up of representatives from the leading advertising agencies, that was to advise the Division on purchasing policies.

While there was some resistance to the new Division from other government agencies, such as the Military Board,[21] the advantages of central oversight and purchase of all government advertising became apparent. Campaigns were better co-ordinated and advertising rates more favourable. In Australia, the advertising for the War Loan campaign cost 0.5 per cent of the public funds raised, whereas in Canada, where no central purchasing policy existed, it was 5 per cent.[22]

The Advertising Division gave the Department two advantages it had sought from the beginning. Firstly, it established an agreed and useful departmental role in relation to publicity for other agencies of government. Secondly, the media had to accustom itself to the new role of the Department as one of its chief paymasters. Not only was it the provider of government publicity on the war effort, it was now the chief agency presiding over the placement of government advertising to the media. A semi-commercial relationship was being established: for if editors and leader-writers were to ridicule the Department's publicity efforts, this would be tantamount to heaping ridicule on a treasured client. Ultimately, it is difficult to be more than speculative. Nevertheless, whereas the year in which the Advertising Division was established was a year that the government itself took a hammering, the Department itself enjoyed its least hostile press.

The new direction in which Foll steered the Department

proved a substantial stimulus for the Shortwave Division. Its controller, MacMahon Ball, had come to regard the Division's work as special, set apart from the mainstream objectives of the Department. ". . . it was so different", he remarked. "We were not trying to do anything *to* the people of Australia".[23] The qualities Ball sought in his staff added to this separateness. The Listening Post required special abilities, not only of a multilingual nature, but also in physical resources (to tolerate the incessant aural pounding received through wearing headphones during the long hours), and a background in European education (to be familiar with local dialects, idioms, geography, emotions, opinions and minority disputes).[24] By no means atypical was staff member Helen Ferber. She had been recommended to Ball by a university associate and had worked in a voluntary capacity from the beginning of 1940, when the Listening Post was established. She was fluent in German, French and Italian. "We were basically academics doing this thing for the war. We were doing things that 'they' [journalists] couldn't do."[25]

The Listening Post was not the only section in which Ball sought special qualities in his staff. Although Ball liked and respected journalists (who did much of the news editing), he believed many of the news commentaries and talks were better given by academics with special interests in international affairs.[26] Ball drew on the talents of such learned figures as Professor K.H. Bailey, L.F. Crisp and A.G.L. Shaw to prepare and present such talks as "This Week of War".[27] Geoffrey Sawer, then a lecturer in law at the University of Melbourne, joined the Division to look after the political warfare and news presentations.[28] R.I. Horne, a former schoolmaster, was invited to prepare talks on Australia, but remained to take charge of the news commentaries from 1941 onwards. Horne was transformed from an academic to a radio-talks man.[29]

Concurrent with the Division's growing specialization, Ball proceeded to rationalize the overseas transmissions. In July 1941, he disbanded the remainder of the Sydney shortwave staff of the ABC, concentrating the operation at the Melbourne Headquarters. The ABC continued to supply studio space and make available its music library, while the Postmaster-General's Department and AWA continued to supply the transmitters.[30] The Division's work was well received and, by October 1941, it was transmitting some 13,500 words — the equivalent of 13½ newspaper columns — each day.[31] The output consisted of ten minutes of news, four to five minutes of commentary and a ten-minute talk on the war effort. By late 1941, the Division was transmitting nine thirty-minute sessions each day.[32]

Encouraging responses were received from American listeners, whose letters between March to July 1941 totalled about two thousand. American broadcasting network executives were pleased with the news sessions.[33] The propaganda talks were regarded by one network as "the spiciest in the world, better than Hitler when he really goes to town".[34]

By this time Ball was running the most productive and respected of the Department's divisions. Foll was delighted with his work, as was Curtin. By July 1941, the shortwave service was costing some £17,000 annually, the Listening Post, £3,000. Ball had 33 full-time staff and 6 part-timers. The government proposed to substantially upgrade the transmissions with three additional transmitters, estimated to cost £250,000.[35]

Ball held to his conviction that the Division's work, though increasing, was specialized and self-contained, and did not require supervision from either Principal Information Officer Bateson, or his Minister.[36] Foll recalls:

> Ball was a very capable man, but he made it perfectly clear that he would only continue the work he was doing provided he wasn't interfered with, but he wouldn't have taken instructions from any other executive member above him in the Department. He wanted to rule it, and he did rule his section . . .[37]

Listening Post transcripts went straight to the Prime Minister; Foll was to receive only courtesy "drop" copies later. In the absence of government guidelines, Ball began to develop his own overseas propaganda policy. Foll, for his part, was pleased that the Shortwave Division was one of the few of his troubled Department's divisions that could be left to its own devices.

Less pleased with this development were the censors in the Department. Tom Hoey, the censor for Victoria, recalled Ball's style of operation with less enthusiasm and possibly a degree of envy: "Ball was a law unto himself with Shortwave. It was an academic station run by academics rather than trained broadcasters and journalists, who take a rather tougher approach."[38] Ball probably was aware of such views. He certainly would not regard the description "academic" as pejorative in the least. Hoey took it as a sign of weakness that Ball presented opposing viewpoints occasionally, even those of the enemy, on the war effort. Ball would have taken this as a sign of strength. Truth came via controversy.

Although Foll's main concern, like that of his predecessor, lay with the Department's "expressive" rather than "suppressive" functions, he was aware that reforms of the censorship function were needed. On the very day of Foll's appointment, the censorship instructions reflected the tendency for Censorship to discourage accounts of the war effort from other than official sources:

> Mr Curtin's reference to anxiety concerning the Australian Medical Services may not be published.
>
> A statement by the Minister of the Navy will release a story of an incident at Nauru. Press reports are to be limited to the Ministerial statement. No conjectures or theories are to be advanced nor may the subject be expanded except within the limits of any further Ministerial statements.[39]

W.M. Hughes, the new Naval Minister, proved no less active than his predecessor, Cameron, in using censorship instructions to harmonize press treatment of his ministerial releases.

In the beginning there was little that Foll, a Minister junior in rank to the Service Ministers, could do to change this situation. He promised that the press would be given the opportunity to take a more direct interest in the workings of Censorship, and to examine copies of all censorship instructions as they were issued.[40] His first move was cosmetic, though thoughtful. On 3 January 1941, he decided that if the substance of the censorship instructions could not be changed, perhaps their tone could. Where possible, censorship instructions would explain the reasons behind the prohibitions. The aim was to soften criticism from the press by making the censorship instructions appear to be a reasonable request rather than a prohibition.[41] For example, on 20 February 1941, the censorship instruction read as follows:

> Army headquarters has issued two statements for publication today by both Press and Broadcasting. One deals with the intensification of Australia's war preparations, but its use is permissible only on the condition that the full text is published. The second article deals with Australia's defence measures. Further speculation on this second subject is forbidden and an urgent request is made for publication of the statement by both mediums.

This policy allowed censorship instructions, on occasions, to become bearers of corrigenda. In March 1941, advice was received of an amendment to a speech by the Acting Prime Minister, Fadden, in a statement issued the same day. It concerned a story that a contingent of the AIF and the New Zealand Expeditionary Force had taken up duty in the Middle East. The original of the official statement read: "and so have contributed in a small measure to the final victory." The statement should have read, according to the instruction of 12 March 1941, "and so have contributed in *no* small measure to the final victory."

However, just as the growing interservice rivalry for publicity provided Foll with the opportunity to establish his Advertising Division, so interservice rivalry allowed Foll to insist on the primacy of his censors as the final arbiters and co-ordinators of censorship policy. A statement about the discovery and rescue of German raider victims from Emirau Island provided Foll with his opportunity. The statement had been drafted and was to be released after the victims' ship arrived in Australia, but it was released by the Minister for the Navy, Billy Hughes, *before* the ship reached port. This breached the standing regulation prohibiting the publicity of shipping movements outside of ports, a policy Murdoch had earnestly though thanklessly defended a few months earlier. Naval authorities in Melbourne said nothing, but insisted that the statement publicizing the Air Force role in the rescue be prohibited. Newspapers were allowed to publish the names of officers brought to Australia by plane, only to have them censored, then released again. Bitter recriminations between the Service Departments were reported. Air Force representatives claimed the Navy sought full credit, while the Navy argued that the information released by the Air Force should not have been disclosed. Both were probably right. With some relish, Foll announced:

> Certainly there has been a bungle today . . . My Department was in no way responsible for it, but I am concerned to try to devise a scheme which will make it impossible for such a thing to happen again. Effective consultation between the two Service Departments concerned and the Department of Information, which has all the machinery for the handling and issuing of statements, would have saved all the trouble.[42]

On 7 January 1941, Foll proposed to Cabinet that the release of such statements, as well as censorship within the Services, should be co-ordinated by the Department of Information. Service Ministers were reported to be upset, but his proposal was accepted. The absence overseas of Percy Spender, the Minister for the Army, would have helped Foll's proposals.[43]

It was an important victory, but a limited one. Ministers continued to use censorship to discourage unofficial accounts of incidents (usually embarrassing to the government). There was still a long way to go before censors could truly co-ordinate the release of sensitive information. Sometimes censors only became aware of an official release when press and broadcasting station representatives protested that a Minister had made a statement that hitherto had been prohibited.[44] The publication of opposition statements, one of the principal sources of "unofficial accounts", continued to be discouraged. On 5 February 1941, the press was instructed that "Any references by Mr Curtin to the Australian Navy are to be withheld until further instructed."[45]

Menzies' desire for National government appear to have had the effect of restraining censors from excising copy that discussed positive aspects of Russia or socialism. For example, in February 1941, in a note from Captain Laughlin of the Army, R.H. Croll (Acting Chief Publicity Censor) was asked his advice on some journals dealing with socialism and suspected of being subversive. Croll's remarks seem mild compared with previous censorship policy concerning socialist literature:

> *Philosophy of Anarchism* — it is subversive in that it is full-circle anarchistic . . . but I cannot imagine that with the world as it is, enough people would buy it and read it to make it dangerous. I would not interfere . . . *Women's International League Monthly News Sheets* — The organisation is just ultra-idealistic and is run by women who are idealists . . . The news sheet is critical of Great Britain in relation to China, and particularly in relation to the Burma Road; but on the whole I do not think that there is such a subversive tendency in the paper that immediate action should be taken. I would "wait and see".[46]

When Russia sided with the allies later that year, the censorship of such material ceased. In fact, anti-Soviet propaganda had to be reduced. The anti-Soviet film *Comrade X* was among material ordered withdrawn by Menzies.[47]

Word spread among the press of the more reasonable attitude of the censors. There was the celebrated account of the military authorities wanting to prohibit the comic strip "Wally and the Major", on the grounds that it was subversive to address a Major in the terms Wally used. The Censor refused to act unless officially requested. Even the military authorities came to recognize some of their foolishness.[48] In May 1941, Foll announced that cable and wireless messages to Australian newspapers from Britain no longer would be subject to censorship in Australia, if they had been cleared at the British dispatch station.[49] This was a major concession, preparing the way for Australian censorship to be brought into line with the more liberal British policies, which had been sought by both the press and the opposition. In July, Menzies apologized for the "grievous blunder" by which a censor had interpreted an instruction to suppress some aspects of a parliamentary debate to mean a general prohibition of the debate.[50] The incident was regarded as a genuine error by the press and opposition rather than as any sinister design on the part of Censorship.

But just when the censorship organization and procedures seemed to be operating smoothly, its senior staffing was in flux. In June 1941, Percy Jenkin, the first Chief Censor, replaced Treloar, who joined Lieut-General Sir Thomas Blamey's staff.[51] However, pressures of previous censorship administration had taken their toll. Jenkin's health suffered and he died some months later. The position of Chief Publicity Censor then fell to R.H. Croll, formerly the Deputy. Croll, a veteran of censorship in the first war and a well-known writer and humanist, introduced a more liberal style of administration. But Croll had retired from the Department of Education in 1933, and had foreshadowed his resignation from Censorship in May 1941.[52]

After consulting with Murdoch and Errol Knox, Foll decided to appoint Edmund Garnett Bonney, of the Melbourne *Argus*, as the new Chief Publicity Censor.[53] Bonney was well respected and admired by the press. He had been editor of the *Argus* since 1938 and had worked for the *Sydney Morning Herald* and the *Argus* as a lead writer. For two years, he had been news editor of the Melbourne *Sun*; for six years, chief of staff of the Melbourne *Herald*; editor-in-chief of the Adelaide *News* for six years; and general president of the Australian Journalists Association.[54]

Bonney was appointed on 4 April 1941 and soon acquainted himself with the policy desired by the War Cabinet. The Cabinet was becoming increasingly concerned about statements that, though in themselves were fair comment and did not disclose or compromise security arrangements, could be used by the enemy as propaganda material. On 28 and 29 April, Bonney introduced new censorship guidelines that were to divide censors and the press for the remainder of the war. As Fadden later announced:

> Every responsible person in Australia must feel concerned at the reaction which had followed publication overseas of comments on the war which had been made in certain quarters in this country . . . Government advices [sic] showed that these comments, *which did not in any way reflect Australian public opinion*, had a damaging effect on the Empire's war effort.[55]

In accord with government policy, a *Daily Telegraph* cable to London was suppressed by Bonney and the action publicly endorsed by Fadden (the Acting Prime Minister) because:

> it gave an untrue version of opinion here and might have *added to the propaganda resources of our enemies*. Consequently the censorship authorities acted correctly in rejecting it.[56]

It was Bonney's special mark to consolidate this policy into a working style for censors. News statements and opinions became sensitive not so much because they directly affected the war effort, but because the information they contained might be of use as enemy propaganda. Bonney had broadened the task of censorship to one that asked not only does this article compromise military security, but would this article, if used selectively by the enemy, damage the morale of Australians or our allies? Thus in August 1941, thirty-eight copies of the *Radio Times* were seized and stereoplates of two pages were destroyed under the direction of the State Publicity Censor. The inflammatory article in question expressed a view that the United States might not be in a position to fight in the Pacific, if the situation called for it. Accounts of the suppression were also suppressed.[57]

In addition to these changes, Foll saw a need for the headquarters of Censorship to be relocated in Canberra. In July 1941, Foll explained that if problems occurred when Parliament was meeting, it was useful to have the Chief Censor to give on-the-spot rulings and to iron out problems with the Press Gallery.[58] Uniformity of censorship then would be guaranteed.[59] The effect was to place Bonney at the source of the more newsworthy statements about the war effort that could be of value to enemy propaganda — parliamentary debates.

By late 1941, Foll had achieved, unheralded, and with little obvious encouragement, a Department of Information with a positive role to play. The Advertising Division's activities gave it a reputation for efficiency that it had sorely needed, in the face of continued parliamentary scrutiny of its expenses. The press and commercial radio also appear to have given it a more tolerant, even respectful coverage. The Shortwave Division was fulfilling the hopes of all parties as an independent Australian voice. The Australian News and Information Bureau had performed effectively. The Films Division was establishing a strong reputation for producing quality work, especially through the efforts of Damien Parer. The Editorial Division had reconciled itself to the fact that its main clientele would be provincial, suburban and specialist journals. Under Bonney, even Publicity Censorship appeared to attract less criticism.

Not everybody agreed with this assessment. By late 1941, Hitler's troops had been stalled at the Russian front. As the war entered this less dramatic phase, public disenchantment with the Menzies government was again apparent. The trade unions remained unenthused by Menzies' policies and there seemed a general lack of public confidence.[60] The official historian singled out the Department of Information for particular criticism: "It was almost impossible to find evidence that the Department knew clearly what it was trying to do, except to serve a general purpose of handing out information about the war."[61] He felt the Department should have devoted a greater effort to reviving public morale and less to its overseas initiatives. This is not entirely fair, because domestically the Department had become a conduit for other government agencies. Hasluck gave backhanded praise to its overseas direction by emphasizing the Department's lack of local initiative: "The department was directing propaganda to countries overseas . . . but its domestic activities were unenterprising . . ."[62] Hasluck was on firmer ground when he berated the Department for its lack of initiative in conducting surveys of public opinion, following its dissolution of the Group Committee system. However, when such surveys were carried out by the British Ministry of Information, the public and press jeered at "Cooper's Snoopers" (after its Minister, Duff Cooper), fearing the survey was to be used to spy on them.[63] Hasluck's criticism of the Department's abandonment of local propaganda campaigns might have had more force had he shown that the local media, particularly the metropolitan press, wanted or even needed it.

No local propaganda effort could have stemmed the tide against Menzies. On 29 August 1941, the Menzies ministry was no more. The Country Party, together with Foll, Spender, Spooner and Hughes, joined to form the Fadden government. Public opinion had moved towards the formation of a National government. The Australian Public Opinion Poll of October 1941 asked: "Should all parties in the Commonwealth Parliament join together in a wartime government?" The response was 78 per cent in favour, 14 per cent against and 8 per cent undecided.[64] However, public opinion was not to determine such issues. Two independents retained the balance of power, and joined to reject the Fadden budget. The government fell on 7 October 1941.

The Department, which seemed close to achieving a workable role with the public, Parliament and press, even an uncanny stability, was to find itself thrust into the maelstrom of a new environment, together with an inexperienced but ambitious Labor government.

Notes

1. Ball, Sayers, Wigmore, Hoey, Sawer, Hamilton, Ferber and Horne in their interviews all recall Foll as lack-lustre and were hard-pressed to explain why he might have been chosen as Minister.
2. Author's interview with I. Hamilton, 3 May 1976.
3. Author's interview with H.S. Foll, 10 February 1976.
4. Melbourne *Argus*, 14 December 1940.
5. Ibid., 18 December 1940.
6. Ibid., 19 December 1940.
7. *CPD* (Senate), 17 September 1941, p. 331.
8. Melbourne *Argus*, 10 January 1941.
9. "Statement of Activities", Department of Information, 23 April 1941, (Departmental History Files); A.A., SP 195/9, Item 18.
10. Melbourne *Argus*, 16 July 1941.
11. The ANTA organization was established in 1929. The Commonwealth government had encouraged its work before the war with regular grants amounting to £20,000 annually in 1937 and 1938. Its function was to direct overseas publicity for the encouragement of travel to Australia and to cooperate with transport, hotel and business interests in Australia, on all matters concerning the reception and accommodation of tourists. A.A., M 301/1/2. Holmes' appointment is officially set at 4 November 1941, but he took up duties in September. *CPD* (Senate), 20 November 1941, pp. 629-30.
12. *CPD* (Senate), 2 July 1941, p. 652.
13. Melbourne *Argus*, 30 December 1940.
14. Ibid., 26 February 1941.
15. R. Dooley, Secretary, AFCB, evidence to the Gibson Committee 23 July 1941; *Report of the Joint Committee on Wireless Broadcasting*, Canberra: Commonwealth Government Printer, 25 March 1942, pp. 99-100.
16. Ibid., p. 100.
17. Minutes of Advisory War Council, 7 February 1941, A.A., CP 815/4, Item 87.
18. R. Dooley, evidence to the Gibson Committee, 29 January 1942, pp. 620-21.
19. Author's interview with H.S. Foll, 10 February 1976.
20. Detailed accounts of the Advertising Division are to be found in: K. Unstead, "Commonwealth Government Advertising" *Institute of Public Administration (Australia) Journal* 6 (new series), no. 8 (December 1947); R.D. Ansell, "Advertising in Relation to the Public Service", ibid., and *CPD*, (HR), 30 May 1941, p. 83.
21. The Army claimed that there still remained some "free" advertising space for recruiting and that "the intervention of the Advertising Division of the Department of Information will not be advantageous to the Army . . . the Army recruiting staff includes serving officers with experience of journalism and other forms of publicity." See F.J. Alderson, Publicity Officer of Military Board, to the Secretary of Military Board, 13 March 1941; *Australian War Memorial*, File SP 1029.
22. Unstead, "Commonwealth Government Advertising".
23. Author's interview with W.M. Ball, 18 February 1976.
24. An account of the almost sphinx-like qualities sought of Listening Post

staff is found in "The NBC Listening Post", *RCA Review*, 3 October, pp. 143-44.
25. Author's interview with H. Ferber, 16 February 1976.
26. W.M. Ball, correspondence with author, 20 August 1977.
27. W.M. Ball, General Files; A.A., MP 272, Bundle 3, Item 24/2.
28. Author's interview with G. Sawer, 20 April 1976.
29. Author's interview with R.I. Horne, 18 February 1976.
30. "History of ShortWave Broadcasting in Australia", Draft Report, 1946 (unpublished ms., in Hoey Papers, author unknown, ?Tom Hoey), p. 3.
31. 7,500 words were new and the balance was made up of repeated extracts. Evidence of C.H. Holmes to Gibson Committee, 27 October 1941; *Report of the Joint Committee on Wireless Broadcasting*, p. 401.
32. Subjects for talks included the Australian Territories, Australian Prime Ministers since Federation, the Army Medical Services, and D. Copland on price-fixing; ibid., p. 402.
33. W.M. Ball, evidence to Gibson Committee, 27 October 1941; ibid., p. 404.
34. Ibid., 22 July 1941, pp. 88-89.
35. Ibid., 22 July 1941, pp. 89-90. The estimate rose to £290,000, but was approved by Cabinet on 15 September 1941, (Cabinet Agendum 602).
36. Author's interview with G. Sawer, 20 April 1976.
37. Author's interview with H.S. Foll, 10 February 1976.
38. Author's interview with T. Hoey, 16 February 1976.
39. T.C. Bray Papers, ANL, MSS 2519.
40. File note, 21 December 1940; A.A., SP 109, Box 53, File 337.03.
41. Sayers first discussed the idea with Bateson, who submitted it to Foll for his endorsement on 31 December 1940. Foll annotated the proposal with "Agree" on 3 January 1941. On 18 February, a formal circular to censor from P.B. Jenkin, then Director of the Department, advised that: "While censorship instructions ordinarily must be brief, we should explain why the prohibition is necessary . . ." From Paper on File 337.03, A.A., SP 109, Box 53.
42. Melbourne *Argus*, 3 January 1941.
43. Ibid., 8 and 10 January 1941.
44. Burns, State Publicity Censor, to Chief Publicity Censor, 17 May 1941; A.A., SP 195/5, Item 11. Burns expressed the position thus:
Censorship is frequently requested, on behalf of a Commonwealth Minister, to prohibit publication of certain specific items of news. The purpose of these temporary prohibitions is apparently to prevent any unofficial disclosure of the news until the Minister concerned can make a formal statement.
45. T.C. Bray Papers, ANL, MSS 2519.
46. A.A., SP 109/10, Item DCPC 600-770.
47. However, Foll, who was aware of the value of resisting ministerial requests for censorship, replied: "need not take any steps at present to withdraw this film. It is merely entertainment." Cable Bruce to Menzies, 1 July 1941, AA., CP 815/4, Item 46.
48. C. Edwards, *The Editor Regrets*. Melbourne: Hill of Content, 1972, p. 93.
49. Melbourne *Argus*, 9 May 1941.
50. *CPD* (HR), 3 July 1941, pp. 827-28.
51. Melbourne *Argus*, 26 June 1941. In June 1942, the Army Public Relations Directorate was created. Treloar played no part in its creation or formation, but returned to take charge of the Military History Section.

52. Melbourne *Argus*, 9 May 1941.
53. Foll to Murdoch, March 1941, Murdoch Papers, *ANL* MSS 2823, Folder 55; and author's interview with Foll, 10 February 1976.
54. Melbourne *Argus*, 5 April 1941.
55. Ibid., 29 April 1941, emphasis added.
56. Ibid., emphasis added.
57. Hoey to Bonney, 5 May 1944, A.A., SP 109/5, Box 66.
58. Melbourne *Argus*, 7 July 1941.
59. *CPD* (Senate), 25 November 1941, pp. 772-73.
60. Don Whitington, *The House Will Divide: A Review of Australian Federal Politics*. Melbourne: Lansdowne Press, rev. edn, 1969 pp. 88-89. See also Professor A.P. Elkin's 1941 survey of public opinion, *Our Opinions and the National Effort*, cited in P. Hasluck, *The Government and the People 1939-41*. Canberra: Australian War Memorial, 1952, pp. 381-83.
61. Hasluck, *Government and the People 1939-1941*, p. 383.
62. Ibid., p. 384.
63. Marjorie Ogilvy-Webb, *The Government Explains: A Study of the Information Services for the Royal Institute of Public Administration*. London: Allen & Unwin, 1965, p. 61.
    Keith Murdoch did toy with the idea of the Department undertaking surveys of the public when he was Director-General. The notes of Sylvia Ashby, founder of the first independent market research company in Australia, record that Murdoch contacted her to discuss the first public opinion poll representative of all Australia. Murdoch hoped to canvass the views of the Australian public to the war effort, its attitudes to Ministers, including the Prime Minister, and whether or not the broadcasting efforts of the Department were appreciated. A questionnaire was developed and agreed upon. However, one day before the interviewing was to be conducted, the row about "Cooper's Snoopers" broke in Britain. Murdoch withdrew the Department as sponsor and substituted his *Courier-Mail*. Cited in David Jones, "Advertising Research: Myths, Legends and Realities", *Broadcasting and Television* 28, no. 1172 (16 March 1978): 39, 78.
64. Hadley Cantrill (ed.), *Public Opinion 1935-1946*. Princeton: Princeton University Press, 1951, p. 29.

6

The Department under Ashley

"I honestly don't see how it can be rehabilitated"

Senator William Patrick Ashley was appointed Postmaster-General and Minister for Information in the first Curtin Labor government on 7 October 1941. The Department had slipped in the Cabinet pecking order. Ashley was the twelfth of nineteen Ministers.[1] Furthermore, the new Minister hitherto had not expressed interest in the portfolio, nor had he contributed to debate on the subject to Parliament.

Born in 1886, Ashley had enlisted for the Boer War at the age of fourteen. He was elected to the Senate largely on the strength of the "donkey vote". At that time, names on the Senate ballot papers were placed in alphabetical order, and Ashley came to be derisively labelled as one of the "Four A's". Ashley's parliamentary performance was poor. He possessed, according to Whitington,[2] a harsh voice and an "almost grotesque Australian accent", complete with an inability to sound "h's" as consonants. Ashley was no visionary, but a backroom politician, a numbers man, wily, cautious, though at times "devastatingly blunt". Dubbed "Bill the Fixer" for his ability to deal with all members of the Labor Party, Ashley's political strength derived from his astuteness in picking the way Cabinet numbers would go and positioning himself accordingly. He was an unusual figure, even for a Labor Minister. He lived in a small flat at a Sydney seaside suburb, wore shabby, double-breasted blue suits with tan shoes, and followed horse-racing as his main spare-time interest. In later times, he was able to translate his enterprise with political matters into a tobacco retail business and become one of the few Labor parliamentarians to retire on a fairly comfortable income.

Ashley's earliest statements about his Information portfolio followed a similar path of opening statements on the Department. He wanted to relax censorship and asked the press for suggestions about how improved relations might be attained:

> My intention is to see that censorship is relaxed to the greatest extent possible consistent with national security and effective prosecution of war. I want to brush aside all obstacles to a smooth working system.[3]

In practice, Ashley cared little for the Department and was more interested in finding ways to cut its budget. On becoming Prime Minister, Curtin's task was to carry out his promise to relieve the lower-income earners of the onerous tax proposed by the defeated government. This meant identifying government programs that had fat that could be trimmed. The Department of Information seemed an attractive proposition. Few would bemoan a cut in its budget.

The first Labor budget in October 1941 made cuts to the Department's advertising campaigns for promoting surplus primary produce. Its overall 1941–42 estimate was to be cut from £238,000 to £158,000 and the advertising campaign from £50,000 to £15,000.[4] How the Department was supposed to cut back was not clear until much later. Ashley informed the Senate that the £80,000 cut would be made in two areas, the major one being the advertising campaign on behalf of the Department of Labour and National Service, with the balance spread as evenly as possible over the other services. He was unsure whether staff reductions would be necessary.[5] Ashley probably was not sure himself as to where the axe would fall.

Indecisiveness was to become the hallmark of Ashley's leadership. Former employees of the Department recall him as a neglectful Minister. Bob Horne, Tom Hoey, MacMahon Ball, Lionel Wigmore and Geoffrey Sawer all thought little of his contribution.[6] Sawer recalled Ashley's lack-lustre style: "he made no impression on me as a man capable of personally intervening in matters and himself contributing to what we were doing and how we should do it, the way that Calwell and Evatt certainly did."[7] On the other hand, Ian Hamilton thought him underrated as a Minister. Although clearly no intellectual, Ashley had a simple, direct view of matters. None the less, even Hamilton was hardpressed to pin down the nature of Ashley's contribution to Information.[8]

Ashley's administration was sorely tested after 8 December 1941 with the dramatic entry of the Japanese into the Pacific War. Devastating reverses were suffered by the British at Singapore and the Americans at Hawaii. In the guise of German raiders, the war had pressed close to Australia before, but this was the first time there was a sustained series of dramatic reverses for the allies.

A startled government ordered many important changes. The size of newspapers was to be reduced to conserve resources. There would be fewer photographs. Private motoring would almost cease. Taxes were to soar. Industry and military conscription, shunned so long by the Labor Party, would be introduced. There would be no holidays that Christmas.[9]

The progress of the war continued to deteriorate. In January 1942, the Japanese forces had taken Rabaul. In February, Port Moresby and Darwin were bombed. In March, Japanese troops entered Rangoon and occupied Lae and Salamaua. AIF troops were withdrawn from the Middle East to defend the Australian continent. General Douglas MacArthur fled the Philippines and arrived in Australia. In April, the American forces surrendered in Bataan, and the General Headquarters of the South-West Pacific Area was established in Melbourne. In May, the Battle of the Coral Sea was fought, allied forces had to withdraw from Burma, the Germans began their offensive in the Western Desert, and Sydney Harbour was visited by Japanese midget submarines.

Australians needed little stirring from the government about these reverses. There was sufficient from enemy action. On 16 January 1942, Radio Tokyo began to broadcast news of those Australians taken as prisoners of war. Listeners were encouraged not to miss further radio transmissions. "We will make every effort to give you details of your loved ones," it announced. Later sessions were arranged so that POW information was interspersed among the news and propaganda.[10] A poll taken during July 1942 disclosed that 49 per cent of the population now were listening more frequently to radio than a year ago.[11] On 7 February 1942, *Smith's Weekly* pressed that some central body such as the PMG's Department should take over control of all broadcasting and arrange groups of "synchronized stations" to reduce the potential enemy bombers using the local broadcasts as a beam to direct targets in capital cities. The public was receptive to strong central government intervention. In May 1942, a public opinion poll revealed that 41 per cent were in favour of the government taking over more industries, 41 per cent were against and 18 per cent were not sure.[12] In June 1942, 60 per cent were willing to agree that state governments should be abolished.[13]

Curtin had made a desperate appeal to the Americans at the bitter close of 1941: "Without any inhibition of any kind, I make it clear that Australia looks to America free of any pangs as to our traditional links and kinship with the United Kingdom."[14]

The American Commander, General Douglas MacArthur was someone for whom Australians were totally unprepared. He appeared in turn to be a mystic, an egotist and a master dramatist.[15] In World War I, MacArthur had worked in the US War Department's Bureau of Information from 30 June 1917. His duties included censorship and liaison with the press. So successful was MacArthur that, after only nine months, he received a warm note from twenty-nine correspondents praising his "unfailing kindness, patience and wise counsel".[16]

MacArthur's effective command of public relations in Australia was recorded by one of Blamey's advisers in the following terms:

> General MacArthur, on his arrival, made an instant impact with his personality and style. It was obvious from the outset that his personal public relations policy had been carefully planned. He went to great pains to gain the good-will of the waiting pressmen the moment he stepped off the train at Spencer Street. In a carefully prepared statement, he made it clear — on his very first day — that with the help of Almighty God, he planned to return to Manila, as soon as possible. From that day onward General MacArthur was perceived to the world as a man with a mission; a veritable Lancelot following the quest of the Grail. He eschewed all social arrangements; it was claimed he worked long hours, he prayed for divine guidance daily. On Independence Day, 1942, while most of the American world was celebrating, the Melbourne press announced that General MacArthur had commenced work an hour earlier and finished only at midnight. His press photographs show him only in profile, looking over the horizon — Manila-wards.[17]

It was not entirely co-incidental that this was also MacArthur's best camera angle.

MacArthur became the Supreme Military Commander of the South-West Pacific from April 1942 onwards. In commenting on the appointment, one official historian described it as "a notable surrender of sovereignty" on the part of the Australian Government.[18]

Against these fast-moving military and strategic developments, it remains one of the ironies that the Department of Information, designed to take a major role in such circumstances, was to contract its activities through yet another 'reorganization'. Cabinet Ministers, particularly the Rt Hon. Herbert Vere Evatt, K.C. (Attorney-General and Minister for External Affairs) and the Hon. John Albert Beasley (Minister for Supply and Development) regarded the ABC and the Department of Information as agencies with senior officials unresponsive to their demands.

On 7 January 1942, Ashley summoned senior officers from both the ABC and the Department to a meeting in Canberra, to discuss what the government required of them. Evatt and Beasley were in attendance as well. The ABC had failed to broadcast a statement of Beasley's that week. Consequently, its acting general manager, T.W. Bearup, almost was forced to resign, and would have had not the ABC Chairman, W. Cleary, personally intervened on his behalf.[19] The attacks on representatives of the Department, on Holmes (Director), Robert E. Hawes (Deputy-Director NSW) and Ball (Shortwave Division), were equally severe. In the view of Evatt and Beasley, the Department had neglected to respond to the new war position promptly enough and had, in some way, not "maintained a united front".[20]

The savagery of the abuse remains vividly in Ball's memory.[21] Members of the Department were told that anyone not prepared to work in the new environment and under the Labor government should get out. Two days later, Holmes made his resignation public. Ashley responded as promptly with a telegram accepting his resignation, adding that the Department had needed overhauling. Infuriated, Holmes accused Ashley of gross neglect as a Minister for Information, and rejected his comments as "contemptible and false". He berated Ashley for never indicating what he required of the Department and for visiting his headquarters only once in the previous three months.[22] With three other senior officers, Holmes departed. Hawes was appointed in Holmes' place, pending a review of the organization.[23]

A reorganization, if not a purge, had been on the cards since 8 December 1941. The Censorship Division, which had yet to relocate its headquarters from Melbourne to Canberra, lost little time in seeking a breakaway role. Bonney wrote to Curtin on 15 December:

> Our association with the actual Department of Information should, I submit, be merely one of location. For example, Censorship may soon have to make a few appointments to give extra supervision which changed conditions call for . . .[24]

It was not until 22 December that Bonney finally moved to Canberra, informing Holmes: "I feel half-dead, but hope that in a few days we will evolve order out of chaos, and begin to function in a business-like way."[25]

On 12 January 1942, three days after Holmes' resignation, Bonney boldly advised Ashley that the Department was no longer relevant to Censorship, and that all censorship matters should be sent to the Chief Publicity Censor (Bonney) direct:

> To avoid any possible misunderstandings in the future may I suggest that you inform Mr Hawes that so far as Censorship is concerned, he has no responsibility and no authority. I like him personally, and I believe that if this point were made absolutely clear at the outset, he and I could co-operate happily. I have had some unhappy experience in the past, and to ensure efficiency — and it would damage your reputation as well as mine if Censorship did not function efficiently — it is imperative that the Chief Censor should have to consult nobody but his own Minister, and that the Services must be compelled, if they will not do so voluntarily, to address all Censorship communications to me, and route none through the Director [of Information] . . . The Department of Information has fallen by the wayside. If Mr Hawes can remould it so that it will become an effective instrument for war propaganda he will have a full time job, and will get many a headache. Certainly he will have no time to tinker with Censorship. I feel sure that you will realise this, and reaffirm your recently expressed determination to cut the painter between the two Departments [sic] giving the head of each equal status. This will not mean any lack of co-operation on my part, and as I have said I feel sure that when once Mr Hawes fully understands the position he also will be 100% co-operative with me . . .[26]

The fact that Bonney was not among those called before the Cabinet with other Department officials at the earlier meeting, may have assured him of his stronger position. Nevertheless, it remains an audacious letter for a public servant to communicate to his Minister and indicative of the growing confidence and power that Bonney had acquired.

Likewise, the Shortwave division was subject to conflicting loyalties. After 8 December 1941, Holmes recommended to Ashley that the Department's responsibility for the Shortwave Division be clarified in the current crisis to cover *all* aspects of its operations, including broadcasts locally (the ABC's responsibility) as well as overseas. On 29 December, the ABC, not wishing to relinquish its shortwave involvement, pressed Ashley to increase its responsibility to embrace the entire shortwave service.[27]

On Sunday, 18 January 1942, a ministerial conference finally determined the shape of the Department under Ashley. Censorship went to Curtin, as Minister for Defence Co-ordination. The ABC took charge of the Shortwave Division and Advertising went to Treasury. The new headquarters of the Department would be located in Canberra. The Office of the Director would be replaced by the more conventional one of Secretary. Norman McCauley, the Industrial Liaison Officer for the Department (and a Labor Party appointee)[28] was appointed the Assistant Secretary in charge of a Canberra "Secretariat". Hawes was appointed Secretary. Ashley announced that "the changes would add to the status and efficiency of the Department, and improve the services to the Australian public and the fighting services abroad".[29]

In September 1942, Ashley explained the reasoning behind the carve-up to the Senate. Censorship went to Defence Co-ordination because, as Postmaster-General, Ashley had a conflict of interests with his function of overseeing broadcasting, which was also subject to censorship. Shortwave Broadcasting went to the ABC because it was the "appropriate" organization for conducting this work, and because the Gibson Committee's (on Wireless Broadcasting) report supported this transfer as well. The Advertising Division had been transferred to Treasury because it was the proper department to handle financial matters. The Department's officers could be called upon to act for each department in the handling of their campaigns.[30]

The only new function given to the Department was the modestly staffed, Inter-Allied Relations Division. Earlier known as the American Division, and formed in 1940 to promote good relations with America, it would concentrate its activities on relations among Australian and American and other allied Service personnel.[31] R.J.F. Boyer would continue as its honorary director.[32] The only promise of a future or potential in the new department lay with the activities of the Canberra Secretariat, the new headquarters. Small branch offices in each capital city formed part of the plan. Some of the branch offices closed by Foll in 1941 were reopened and developed.[33]

The official description of the Department in its decidedly slimmer role remained hopeful:

> The Department of Information is the clearing house and co-ordination point of all broadcasts and motion picture film publicity, and is becoming more and more a clearing house for all publicity in relation to the war activities.[34]

The new arrangements had the virtue of freeing the Department from its thorny censorship functions, but the transfer of its Shortwave Division cast doubt on its ability to pursue overseas information policies. It seems hard to imagine Ashley agreeing to this had he also not had the responsibility for the ABC.

With this reorganization, Ashley's department had a new look:

```
                         Minister
                         Secretary
                    (based in Melbourne)
┌────────────────────────┬────────────────────────┐
Melbourne                Canberra                 Sydney
Administration           (Assistant Secretary)    Films Division
Illustration Section     Publicity Co-ordination  Inter-Allied Relations
Cinema Branch            Censorship Liaison       Advertising
Services Liaison         Editorial                Co-ordination
                         (Aust/Overseas Publicity)
                         ┌──────────┴──────────┐
                         London              New York

Hobart      Newcastle    Brisbane    Adelaide    Perth       Townsville
Press       Press        Press       Press       Press       Liaison
Officer     Officer      Officer     Officer     Officer     Officer
                         GHQ                                 Film Depot
                         Liaison                             Aust.
                                                             Territories
```

The strongest impression to be gained is that of a dispersal of functions among the three capital cities, probably because it was difficult to transfer all functions to Canberra, where there was a shortage of office space.

One unintended effect of the reorganization was that it became easier to defend the Department's budget because of the transfer of its censorship, advertising and shortwave services to other departments. The cost of Publicity Censorship before its transfer was £17,000; of the Advertising Division £19,208; and of the Shortwave Division, £28,540. This totalled some £64,748 for the financial year 1941-42. Ashley later conceded in the Senate that he had achieved his budget cuts by transferring the expenditure to other departments.[35] Still, there were many who expressed their appreciation that the Department had reduced its expenditure from £213,000 to £117,000 during the year.[36] The fact that expenditure on particular fuctions, in some cases, had actually increased seemed barely to have been grasped. Some note was made of the fact that under Defence, Censorship's expenditure appeared to increase, but the implications of this were not pursued.

While the Department's reorganization may have served the government's need to purge it of its less-than-responsive officials, pressing demands for dealing with local news remained. The fact that important war news for Australians was now to come from the Pacific rather than Atlantic and Mediterranean areas had worrying implications for commercial broadcasters in particular. In the past, they had managed to get by with edited or direct rebroadcasts of BBC news. However, BBC news now was more concerned with, and for that matter better equipped to cover, the European theatre of the war. There was need for a service to concentrate specifically on Pacific developments.

The stations had been aware of their weakness in supplying war news generally. In the wake of Foll's phasing out of local news sessions from the Department, one major broadcasting network raised the possibility of an independent news service. In November 1941, the Macquarie Broadcasting proprietors discussed an idea put by 4BH Brisbane, which "thought it necessary for the Macquarie network to supply a news service which could combat that of the national stations". While the idea was welcomed by the meeting, it was felt that the estimated cost of £15,000 would be inadequate and that the newspaper affiliates probably would want to handle the news on an individual station-by-station basis. Thus little further action was pursued, though the problem remained.[37]

The ABC confronted problems in this vexed area as well. The near disastrous meeting for its officials in Canberra on 7 January 1942 impressed the ABC Chairman of the government's concern to see that the ABC reviewed its war news policies. It was vital that it be more responsive to developments in the Pacific. On 8 January, Cleary informed Evatt how such a policy could be implemented. It only could be carried out if the ABC provided a nationwide news service at least once a day to all stations, national and commercial. To ensure uniform news control, and to ensure the co-operation of the commercial broadcasters, Cleary recommended that the service be offered free and the landline costs underwritten by the government.[38]

On the same day, Cleary counselled ABC staff on the primacy of Pacific war news and the need to avoid references to local political disputes:

> From this afternoon there should be no reference in State News to Federal Politics and policies. There should be no reference to statements by Federal Ministers. There should be no comment on the war situation . . . The next part is highly confidential. This is an outline of the high policy of the Federal Government. Broadly, the emphasis should be on our maintaining the territorial integrity of Australia. The Australian interest is paramount at the moment and involves a successful handling of the aggressor in the Pacific. It is also desirable to play up the American angle in regard to assistance to Australia. This outline of high policy involves all sections of the programmes.[39]

For all intents and purposes, Cleary had the ABC take on the function of the Department of Information, in the sense that it was to serve the public information needs of the Australian government. On 16 January 1942, Cleary informed Evatt of the new policy, commencing with the phasing out of ABC commentaries. The ABC's reply to enquiries from the public about this change declared that this procedure had resulted from adjustments due to daylight-saving and that events of the past few weeks required more emphasis to be given to the Pacific war. Regular listeners seemed more concerned that "Advance Australia Fair" had replaced the "British Grenadiers" as the theme that heralded the news.[40]

Cleary's proposal that the ABC offer a news service to all stations required a renegotiation of news-gathering arrangements with the Australian Newspaper Proprietors Association. Ashley convened a meeting on 10 February, with Curtin attending, to canvass this as well as other matters. Knox, then president of the Association, pressed Curtin to adjudicate in the long running dispute between the press and the ABC about news-gathering arrangements. Curtin declined, but suggested instead that the "gentlemen's agreement" continue until the release of the report of the Gibson Committee.[41] The meeting proved a stand-off, but Cleary appeared to come out of it with an enhanced reputation. He had remained calm and courteous throughout, and the points he raised, though not accepted or rejected by Curtin, seemed sound and convincing.[42]

The next day, the ABC fared even better. A meeting of representatives from commercial and ABC broadcasters, presided over by Ashley, discussed the problems of a radio news service. The commercial representatives wanted all radio stations in the Commonwealth to broadcast three five-minute bulletins each day, prepared by the Department of Information. Speaking on behalf of the commercial broadcasters, A.C. Paddison suggested that the sessions consist of "essential news" and bear the "imprimatur of the Government". "That does not mean", he added, "that the service must bear a particular label. So long as the Government accepts responsibility for giving the news, we shall be satisfied."[43] This was a warmed-over version of earlier proposals that Foll had rejected, when the Department reduced its bulletins.

Cleary countered with his plan that the ABC make its news available to all commercial stations at least three times each day, free of cost, provided the broadcasting of the service was made compulsory to all stations. The commercial stations also could broadcast any or all of the overseas bulletins they wished. The generosity of the offer was unexpected, and the commercial broadcasters readily agreed. Ashley informed Curtin of the excellent results from the second meeting. There remained the headache of paying for the landlines, estimated at £75 per day. Curtin agreed that amount should be underwritten by the government, and as Dixon notes, another chapter in the history of news broadcasting in Australia was thus written.[44]

The government also did well out of the decision. In some respects, it was confronting the problem that had perplexed Menzies: how to encourage dissemination of responsible news to the community without being accused of manipulation. The ABC Chairman's skill in making a virtue of necessity seems to have made all the difference.

Anti-government backlash, on what must have been a fairly open secret, was slight. In March 1942, the dropping of commentaries by the ABC was raised in Parliament. To one enquiry, Bearup, the ABC's Acting General manager, had replied to a question on the change in news policy in the following terms:

> It is evident you assume that the Commission in entirely responsible for all broadcasts that are made from its stations. That is not so. The Act under which the Commission works gives overriding authority to the Government through the Minister. In these circumstances I am sure you will understand that it would be improper for me to indicate whether, and if so, to what extent such authority is exercised or to express an opinion on the merits of the broadcasts to which you take exception.[45]

Curtin, pressed by the opposition for an explanation, tabled two items of advice received by Cleary, which claimed that in February 1942, "No instruction has been given by the present government that criticism of domestic and political policy or actions should be suppressed." The second advice received by Cleary was an instruction from the Postmaster-General in 1939, to the effect that: "Commentaries must be free of criticism of government action or policy . . . Commentators were to make no reference over the air to the fact that restrictions were being imposed upon their freedom."[46]

The revelation that the Menzies government had issued suppressive instructions to the ABC in 1939 may have tempered this backlash. However, the basic implication of the Bearup note remained. The fact that no instructions had been given about domestic policy or actions had little to do with the possibility that the government was concerned about *overseas* rather than domestic news. In the best 'pre-emptive buckle' traditions, Cleary himself had given the instructions, with the informal and obvious approval of Evatt and Curtin. Had it not been a time of crisis, the explanations and evidence might well not have sufficed, and there may have been longer-term political implications for a government dependent on the support of two independents.

A more visible consequence of the reorganized Department of Information lay in the growth of public relations sections in other government agencies. The major ones were the Army Directorate of Public Relations, with 54 staff,[47] RAAF with 8,[48] Munitions with 11, Allied Works Council with 7, Labour and National Service with 7, War Organization of Industry with 5, and the Rationing Commission also with 5,[49] Press releases formed a large portion of these departments' publicity output. Dissatisfaction with the Department of Information's service was widespread. None used the Department exclusively, even for the distribution of their own releases. The Department mainly was used for distribution of educational or general information articles of little topical interest, or when interstate distribution was required to cover the provincial press. The press was the overwhelming preference in the media choice, compared with radio, cinema or poster publicity.[50]

By 1942, the most controversial government public

relations agency was the Army Directorate of Public Relations. Its origins can be traced back to the end of the "phoney war", in May 1940, when the Army considered a serious need for such an agency had arisen. At the time, the expansionist policies of Murdoch, Director-General of Information, may have overtaken further development of such an agency. In May 1941, the Military Board of the Department of the Army revived the idea and informed the *War Book* Officer that it was reconsidering the agency's establishment.[51] On 7 April 1942, the Army Minister, and Deputy Prime Minister F.M. Forde announced the appointment of Errol G. Knox as Director-General of the Directorate of Public Relations. Knox, at the time, was managing director of the *Argus* newspaper and president of the Australian Newspaper Proprietors Association. He had served in World War I, rising to the rank of Major, Air Staff, RAF and was awarded the MBE, as well as being mentioned twice in dispatches. The appointment was said to correspond to a similar one in the British War Office, "to promote better understanding between the Army and the public".[52]

The Directorate's organization had some novel features, none the less. It included the subsection of Military Intelligence concerning publicity, propaganda and the facilitation of press work. Other duties included accreditation of correspondents in war areas and field and press censorship on behalf of field commanders. Its new activities were vague: co-operation with the public relations section of MacArthur's headquarters, liaison and co-ordination with Military Intelligence, liaison and co-ordination with publicity censorship, and co-ordination of military publicity with other government agencies.[53] With the exception of Knox, its staff of fifty-four were servicemen.[54] Although many of the staff came from already established Service positions, the Directorate attracted criticism over the size of its establishment. The press was irritated by its Service style, and Knox was to find it awkward operating as a civilian in charge of servicemen. His lack of military rank made it difficult to exchange information with British and American Army officials, who held similar posts at the level of major-general.[55] Eventually, he was accorded the honorary rank of brigadier.

Early in its operation, the Directorate became the centre of a minor, though significant, row with the press. It was reported to have authorized an investigation by two detectives to pinpoint the source of a news story about how Ashley, as Information Minister, failed to receive an invitation to an important conference between press representatives and Blamey on national discipline and morale. The snubbing was first reported in the Sydney *Sun* on 14 June 1942.[56] The Sun's reporter, William Bissell, was interviewed, but gave little assistance to the detectives. He later reported the interview in his paper. Knox "unequivocally repudiated" responsibility for interrogating the reporter. However, Knox was involved. His reasons for the investigation were given "off the record".[58] The press soon learnt of them. The *Truth* accused Knox of Gestapo tactics and hypocrisy. Knox was judged to have broken the press code when he sent police to question a reporter on the source of information, and in directing that the privacy of telegraphic transmission be interfered with. Knox was branded a liar associated with a "morass of mendacity which has never been equalled in Australian public life". The incident was seen as typical of the Directorate's "army of pannikin soldiers". It was costly and overlapped with the work of other agencies. The article concluded: "When the ghost of Knox, the Director-General of Army Public Relations, is laid low, let there be inscribed upon the tablet that marks its last resting place — 'Here lies one who sought to save Democracy by Tramping on it'."[59] It seems not entirely insignificant that the incident arose over the snubbing of Ashley. After the *Sun*'s story, Ashley was reported in the following terms:

> There can be no doubt as to the authenticity of the story in question, added Senator Ashley, who said both he and his Department were totally ignored regarding the Melbourne conference, and he could not understand the Gestapo

methods that had been adopted since the conference was held.[60]

In Parliament, the Army Directorate had to become accustomed to criticism that usually was reserved for blunders by the Department of Information. Its large staff and its role aroused concern.[61]

Relations between the Department of Information and the Directorate usually were formal and cool. On 14 July 1942, McCauley of the Canberra Secretariat informed Ashley of the difficulties he had experienced in getting material for a series of "Salute the Army" broadcasts. Wigmore, the Department's Press Officer in Melbourne, contacted Army Public Relations for information, but was informed "approval could not be given for such broadcasts unless the scripts were first submitted for Army scrutiny". The point was that approval was not sought, assistance was. State Publicity Censorship could vet scripts. On another occasion, Wigmore had contacted his former Director, Treloar, then in charge of the Military History Section, for material on the AIF's Middle East campaigns. He was referred back to the Public Relations Directorate.[62]

For its correspondent accreditation and publicity functions, the Directorate tended to regard the whole of Australia as its operational area. It overlapped with the Department of Information's own press accreditation system. However, the Department managed to persuade government that the Directorate's press control system be confined to Australia's northern operational areas.[63]

The frosty relations between the two agencies were reflected in a Cabinet request that they rationalize their photographic resources. The question before Cabinet was: "If one or the other organization is sufficient, can Australia, in view of its manpower and financial position, afford two organizations of this type?" The official reply was "Agreement not reached."[64]

The blossoming public relations section became a political issue. Fadden, the Leader of the Opposition, pressed for an official review of government publicity services, to improve co-ordination and efficiency. He singled out for criticism the work of the Army Directorate. The *Daily Telegraph* supported Fadden's assertions, adding that it had received three identical statements about tea being supplied to shearers. One had come from the Head Office of the Rationing Commission, another from the Deputy Director of Rationing in Sydney, and a third from the Department of Information in telegraphic form.[65]

The following propaganda radio broadcast prepared by RAAF Public Relations, in which Group Captain McCauley is interviewed in connection with the exploits of his men in Malaya, is typical of the time:

> Thousands of men in the R.A.A.F., fighting in all theatres of war, are building up for Australia a model of offensive spirit unsurpassed throughout the world. Nowhere did the R.A.A.F. give a finer example of this than during its widespread operations in Malaya. There our fighter and bomber squadrons did magnificent work. Against incredible odds they destroyed many enemy warships and transports, bombed and machinegunned troops concentrations, and demoralised the Japanese whenever and wherever they encountered them.
>
> During the Malayan fighting, men of the R.A.A.F. in Malaya did not return. But we remember them. Their courage lives in the memories of their comrades who had returned to Australia to carry on the fight — who wait grimly for a chance to avenge their deaths.
>
> Tonight Group Captain McCauley, of the R.A.A.F., is in the studio. He's going to tell you how the R.A.A.F. acquitted itself in Malaya; how it upheld the finest Anzac traditions. You'll be proud of the R.A.A.F. when you hear Group Captain McCauley — and proud to be of the breed that produced these gallant sky-men.
>
> HERE IS GROUP CAPTAIN McCAULEY:
> GROUP CAPTAIN MCCAULEY: R.A.A.F. units operated in Malaya, Singapore, Sumatra and Java. In Malaya, the Australian wing flew Bristol Buffalo fighters and Lockheed Hudson bombers and reconnaissance aircraft. The Buffalos alone destroyed 51 enemy planes in the air.
>
> The Hudson did coastal and sea reconnaissance and bombed land and sea targets. Largely to them goes the credit

for the arrival in Singapore of six large convoys of reinforcements and equipment.

Not only did they give us warning of the approach of the enemy convoys towards Khota Dahru, Endau and Palembang, but they afterwards bombed Jap. troopships, landing craft, and troops on the beach. Each time they sank transports, ships and barges and killed large numbers of the enemy.

At Khota Dahru the R.A.A.F.'s aim was so sure that the first Jap attempt at landing failed, and the Japs were forced to withdraw. At Palembang Japanese losses were so heavy that their penetration down the Palembang River was delayed 12 hours.

In day attacks on enemy aerodromes and at night when parachute flares were used a great many enemy aircraft on the ground were destroyed.

ANNOUNCER: Our boys seem to have been right on the job, Captain.

GROUP CAPTAIN MCCAULEY: Yes they were first-rate. Throughout the campaign they showed great initiative, and there were many acts of gallantry.

ANNOUNCER: Will you tell us about some of them?

GROUP CAPTAIN MCCAULEY: During the retreat down the West Coast of Malaya, near Butterworth, Sergeant Cormie of one of the fighter squadrons, provided air force crews for two armoured cars which would otherwise have had to be abandoned. Sergeant Cormie kept one car in action against the enemy all the way to Kuala Lumpur and the army took over the second one.

Flight Lieutenant Max White, Flight Commander of the Buffalo squadrons lost both his followers who were shot down over Penang. He re-fuelled and re-armed and set out alone to attack Japanese troops moving south. Max White did not return.

Flight Lieutenant Widmer found that his aerodrome had been strafed by enemy fighters. He shot down one and drove the others off.

Flying Officers Plenty and Hewitt while on coastal patrol were shot down into the sea by Jap. fighters. Plenty kept his crew in the air-craft for 15 minutes and held their dinghy under water to give Japanese planes coasting about them the impression that the crew of the Hudson had been killed. When the Japanese left, Plenty and his men rowed the dinghy to a nearby Island and later sailed a sampan 300 miles down the coast where they were rescued. On returning to their station they resumed full duty immediately.

The ground-staff too was responsible for exceptional acts of resolution. Often they had to re-arm and re-fuel air-craft while enemy bombers flew overhead, and, sometimes, while bombs were falling near the aerodromes.

Flight Sergeant Wheatley, at Palembang, rescued the crew of a Blenheim bomber which crashed and caught fire while taking off. He carried them to a ditch and after the air-craft's bombs had exploded arranged for the men to be medically treated.

The morale of all ranks was high. At Palembang, squadrons operated at maximum strength for two days against large numbers of the enemy although the only defending ground forces were two Dutch Battalions of native troops. During evacuation the aerodrome defences were manned by airmen 200 of whom were armed with Dutch rifles, and they then acted as a rear-guard to cover the operation. The conduct and bearing of all ranks were exemplary.

The majority of the personnel who were engaged in the campaign have now returned to Australia and are being dispersed throughout operational units here. The infusion of these experienced personnel will disseminate uptodate knowledge of Japanese equipment and methods. This will undoubtedly add to the fighting strength of our air force.

ANNOUNCER: And that is the story of the R.A.A.F.'s brilliant part in the Malayan campaign. We are much obliged to you, sir, for giving up part of your leave to tell us how the "Australia will be there" spirit persists in this war as it did in the last. Thank-you and Cheerio.

GROUP CAPTAIN MCCAULEY: Cheerio.[66]

It was inevitable with the expansion of public relations sections in other agencies and the reduction in the Department of Information's functions that the continued existence of the Department would be called into question. Certainly, the Department needed only to make one wrong move for its role to be challenged. Such an occasion came with its "The Jap as he really is" or the "hate" campaign.

In March 1942, the Department, in reaction to the continual news of allied defeats in the South-West Pacific, prepared a campaign to increase the public's awareness of the "nature" of its inscrutable foe. The propaganda was unashamedly racist. Advertisements appeared in newspapers showing the Japanese as he was regarded before the war: bespectacled, studious, polite, a lover of goldfish and cherry blossom. Below this illustration stretch bomb-wreckage, above which a grinning Japanese airman was about to release his load of "daisy-cutter" bombs filled with bits of bicycle-chain, bottle-tops and razor-blades. The general theme was: Did you fall for the idea that the Jap was a pleasant little fellow, a polite little yellow man? Did you admire the beauty of the cherry-blossom festivities in quaint villages? And even if you did, did you not feel always there was something sinister about him, that beneath the mask of obsequious politeness there lurked a devil? For make no mistake, in his heart he always hated you, has looked forward to the day when, sustained by his illusion of Japanese divinity, he would torture, murder and enslave. Each press advertisement concluded: WE'VE ALWAYS DESPISED THEM — NOW WE MUST SMASH THEM![67]

A series of 7½-minute radio sessions also were prepared and lodged with all stations throughout Australia. They were to go to air every evening. The sessions began with thirty seconds of bells chiming "Waltzing Matilda". One script ran:

> This is a message to those of the Japanese near enough to our shores to hear it — close enough to feel the hot anger rising in a race slow to hate but fierce and relentless in their hating when there's a need for it. We haven't bothered to hate you before just as we haven't feared you any more than we do now. We've simply regarded you as a bespectacled ape-like race that lent colour to the theory of evolution. Not only are you physically short-sighted — you're mentally myopic. Some of us listen to your amusing broadcasts. We know that you don't think they're funny because you haven't a sense of humour. If you had, you wouldn't waste your time addressing Australians not to fight. You've apparently never heard of Gallipoli, where the spirit of Anzac was born. You've never heard of Menin Gate, Passaendale, Hill 60. Or of Villers Brettoneux where the Australians broke the great Hindenburg Line and paved the way to Germany's defeat in the last war. Yet you suggest that Australians shouldn't fight! Its like your dirty hides to talk such impertinence. You know, as we know, that the people of this great Commonwealth hide beneath their complacency a fighting spirit that you little runts with all your hordes never could and never will curb. All that you

have succeeded in doing is to weld our people into one fierce fighting whole — fighters on sea, land and air, fighters in factory and workshop, fighters in the home and in the field, fighters who are prepared to give all — all their strength, all their possessions to put you back where you belong. You know this you would-be lord of Asia, and your bombast and insolence are only to mask your feelings. You are aware of your inferiority but dare not own up to it, — but we know it and we know that you can be beaten by people with the will to win just as surely as the Russians are proving it to the Germans. You have succeeded in starting a surge of Australian Nationalism that is grown and growing into a torrent of blood and sweat that you will find unquenchable.[68]

The broadcasts began on 24 March 1942. The reaction was immediate. The public saw it as crude, repulsive and offensive.

Such hysterical mouthings are not merely unworthy but serve to disgust the nation.[69]

What irritates is the vindictive hate expressed in these too frequent utterances. It is one of the same impotent types of propaganda that the Germans used for a few months in 1915, until it was laughed out both by their own people and the enemy . . . What does stand out clearly is that the Japanese make remarkable soldiers.[70]

All sectors of the public appeared offended by the campaign. A.M. Lillicrapp, honorary secretary of the Mangrove Mountain Fruitgrowers Association, wrote:

I am directed by the members of the Mangrove Mountain Fruitgrowers Association to make known to you our disgust at the purple blurbs of hate, put over by you, at the instance of the Minister for Information. If the sentiments expressed are supposed to represent the views of the average Australian then we must disassociate ourselves, even at the expense of being thought unpatriotic.[71]

Some support for the campaign came from Clive Ogilvy, country vice-president of the Australian Federation of Commercial Broadcasters. He wrote to Ashley:

It does appear that . . . [the] radio presentation is misunderstood by the critics of the anti-Japanese propaganda. This might be so, but, at the same time, I am sure that your story "sells" in the majority of Australian homes . . .

> Surely, these armchair critics do not suggest that your Department of Information should advise Australians to love this enemy. At least one of your critics suggests we take a Christian view. This might be accepted if we were not fighting a cunning, unsavoury heathen . . .
>
> I unhesitatingly support your campaign and your officers responsible for planning this propaganda.[72]

The majority were not "sold". Three weeks after the broadcasts began a Gallup Poll disclosed that, of those who had heard any of the sessions, 44 per cent thought them a good idea, 54 per cent thought they were not and 2 per cent were undecided.[73] On 7 April 1942, two weeks after the initial broadcast, the campaign ceased. It had cost £4,468 for press advertisements alone,[74] but the cost to the Department's reputation was undoubtedly greater. Any pretension the Department had to expertise or finesse in local publicity had been dispelled.

Curtin decided on a review of the Department. Originally, a Cabinet Committee was planned, consisting of Chifley, Ashley (on whose order the campaign had ceased) and Curtin himself. However, pressure of work forced Curtin and Chifley to step aside, and Scullin and Lazzarini, the Minister for Home Security and Minister Assisting the Treasurer, replaced them.[75] The Committee was appointed by Curtin on 28 April 1942, to "report on the work and cost of the Department of Information". On 22 May, it presented its report to Curtin. It contained four recommendations:

> That the Department of Information be abolished.
>
> That the work of the Press section be drastically reduced and carried out by the Prime Minister's Department.
>
> That the Photographic section be taken over by the Department of the Army.
>
> That the ABC, under the Postmaster-General's Department, be requested to undertake the responsibility of all broadcasting services.[76]

The report itself reflected its hasty production. It was uneven and the reasoning on which its recommendations were based was tenuous or incomplete. Ashley, understandably, dissented. The report opened with the assertion that the Department's output was unimpressive and its expenditure unwarranted. It observed that the greater proportion of the material the Department supplied to the press was not used. The main matter published comprised ministerial statements and facts on war savings. These could be supplied by the Prime Minister's Department and Treasury's advertising section. The editorial background service was overrated, and the Prime Minister himself was a more appropriate source for the press and broadcasting stations. There was considerable duplication of services supplied by other departments. The Services publicity officers could do this work as well, without departmental assistance. There was disappointment that the Department continued to operate from Melbourne. The report offered little in support of its recommendations. It did not consider what improvement, if any, in the quality of co-ordination of publicity its recommendations would have. It was an organizational paper bereft of any organizational objective beyond cost-cutting.

In the event, a compromise was reached. On 9 June 1942, Cabinet decided that the Treasurer and the Minister for Information

> should confer with regard to budget estimates and endeavour to reach agreement on a reduced scale of functions and expenditure. The Department should run on this amended basis for three months when the matter should be raised again.[77]

The political sensitivity of the issue was reflected in Curtin's press statement of 10 June, which omitted reference to the envisaged reduction in functions and talked only of a "substantial revision".[78]

The press rallied to the ailing Department. *Smith's Weekly*, a journal previously not known as a strong supporter of the Department, published a long article critical of the Scullin-Lazzarini report:

> They were reporting upon the editorial section of the Department without having any personal knowledge of what that

section should do to give the greatest service to the public; they were looking into films and broadcasting sections without any intimate knowledge of the public needs in either of these sections.[79]

The article speculated that the report may have been a sop to the emergence of the Army Public Relations Directorate and other growing publicity sections in the Services. *Smith's Weekly* preferred to have the Department, limited as it was, to all these new and expanding, uncoordinated sections. Richard Hughes of the Melbourne *Herald* wrote similarly:

> The Committee's recommendations are of course no more than a fantastic evasion of a problem no Australian Government has yet tackled with any semblance of courage, intelligence and realism . . . Whatever the reasons however, the Department has never had a chance. Designed to inform it had no information. Designed to lead it had no authority. Designed to illume public policy it never had a policy. Designed to create ideas it had never the money or encouragement to allow its ideas to function.[80]

Meanwhile, a less publicized review of the Department's role by another committee was taking place. This was the Prime Minister's Committee on National Morale. It was chaired by A.A. Conlon and comprised: J. Stone, R.M. Crawford, S.H. Deamer, A.K. Stout, R.I. Hogbin, W.E.H. Stanner, R.D. Wright, and E.D. Roper,[81] all already becoming leading and influential academics or professionals in their respective fields.

The official historian described the Committee as "a curiously-composed body" and said of it: "it is difficult to discover what standing this Committee had. It is easy to discover that it had no influence. Official records do not support claims that have been made in public that this Committee played a significant role in this [national morale] or any other matter."[82]

Such strong criticism of such a small committee raises more questions than answers. A committee with such little effect, little standing and the recipient of such criticism surely deserves more attention, especially in the context of the Department of Information. The Committee was officially styled the *Prime Minister's* Committee on National Morale. It had its own annual budget of some £2,000. Its members served in an honorary capacity and it was purely advisory. Its terms of reference were: to study matters of civilian morale, to advise government on matters of policy concerning morale, to consider the co-ordination of adult education, physical fitness and other agencies for defence purposes.

The origins and scope of the Committee's work remained veiled in some mystery, however it appears its formation sprang from a paper presented to Curtin on 4 April 1942 on aspects of morale. Those associated with the paper were Dr K. Barry, Dr. C.E.W. Bean, Professor I. Clunies Ross, S. Deamer, Dr I. Hogbin, Professor Julius Stone, Professor A.K. Stout and the chairman of the interim committee, Alfred A. Conlon. The paper appears to have been inspired in part by the outcry due to the recent "hate" campaign, as well as the noticeable lack of co-ordination in government policy on morale. The paper described aspects of morale and what needed to be done. Its chief recommendation was that a committee should be appointed, purely advisory in character, responsible directly to the Prime Minister and "consisting only of distinguished and disinterested minds".

Curtin approved, and requested Conlon on 9 May 1942 to form such a committee, with Conlon as its chairman. On 18 June, Conlon convened Barry, Crawford, Deamer, Hogbin, Stone, Stanner, Stout, Wright and Roper to form a Committee of National Morale.[83]

The Committee's ideas about how the Department might be improved were influenced by the circumstances of similar agencies in Britain and the United States. News-clippings among the Committee's papers contain numerous articles arguing that the British Ministry of Information was no more adequate than its Australian counterpart. In contrast, the collection of American cuttings about the newly established Office of War Information and its chief officer, Elmer Davis, who reported direct to the President, were uniformly optimistic. The OWI was not the first agency to handle such functions, but was established to coordinate the plethora of public relations agencies created by each government department after Pearl Harbour.

On 26 August 1942, the Committee submitted an interim report to Curtin. It argued that the Department of Information had never enjoyed high prestige and that other government departments had built up their own public relations services, resulting in poor co-ordination generally. The Department lacked control of advertisements, publicity or research agencies employed by Treasury and other agencies. The splitting of censorship from the Department had not been effective. There was no research agency in Australia free of commercial links to properly survey public attitudes and the Department's main technique of using advertising was often unsuited to the real needs of propaganda.

The report recommended that Curtin take on the Information portfolio; that Censorship should be returned to Information, "to ensure what is not to be said and what is said should come under the same general direction"; that the Department should supervise all campaigns by government agencies and co-ordinate the unwieldy growth in the publicity sections and that a Director-General of Information be appointed. The Director-General shall be "a civil servant of high standing . . . a person of outstanding intellectual attainment, untrammelled as far as possible, by association with those commercial interests which it will be part of his duty to control and direct". The Director-General should have access to the War Cabinet. He should be assisted by advisory committees on press and radio, foreign affairs, social and economic trends, and morale problems. He should have a public attitude survey research organization. His staff should come from fields other than journalism, commercial advertising or radio. It was desirable that he be experienced in the impartial examination of sociological and psychological problems. Though the recommendations implied additional expenditure, the Committee felt the investment worthwhile.[84]

According to the official historian, the report had little

effect.[85] Nevertheless, fourteen months later, some of its recommendations were carried out with yet another reorganization of the Department, which came under a Director-General (Bonney), was integrated with Censorship and acquired some powers to co-ordinate publicity. In other respects, the Committee's report seemed to reveal a prejudice against journalists as administrators. It advocated leadership from the ranks of the disciplines of sociology and psychology. This was unlikely to convince former journalist, John Curtin. Although the Committee consisted of distinguished and diverse minds, it failed to acquaint itself with the workings of the Department, its main clientele, or the scope for introducing social science expertise. It did not appear to take account of the unfortunate "Cooper's Snoopers" row that occurred with the British Ministry of Information, when it had pressed for government sponsored public opinion surveys.

The Committee could not have known of the difficulties that would beset the OWI, on which it modelled some features of its proposals, and which was to come under continual fire. Congress insisted that the Domestic Branch (the local information section of OWI) be curbed. It was the Overseas Branch of OWI that was destined to be the largest and most successful of its activities.[86] The Committee saw little merit in commenting on overseas information policy. It may have regarded this as outside its brief. It seems to have felt the Department's main problem lay in its poor leadership, both at the ministerial and executive levels.

None the less, there was enough in the report for Curtin to want to ensure that it was given consideration, especially as the Department was due for its Cabinet review following the Scullin-Lazzarini report. On 10 September 1942, Curtin asked Scullin to discuss the report with Ashley and Lazzarini and report back on their views. As Scullin was ill, no action was taken until 27 November when Curtin asked Ashley for his reactions.

On 10 December, Ashley responded that there was little of use in the report: events had overtaken it. His department was functioning much better now and its prestige was increasing. It had a good reputation among the country press and was gaining improved acceptance from the city press. It had undertaken a number of important campaigns, such as those concerning rationing, food conservation and austerity, with satisfaction to client departments. It had good relations with Publicity Censorship and its films were acclaimed. Ashley agreed that the Department should co-ordinate all government publicity, with the exception of ministerial statements. He assured Curtin that the Department was operating efficiently and saw the Committee's report as adding little of benefit.[87]

By this time, both the Conlon Committee and Curtin had varied their ideas about the upgrading of the Department. On 19 December, Conlon chaired a meeting at the Hotel Canberra. Among those attending were Dr H.C. Coombs, Lt John Kerr (Conlon's assistant in his position as Army Directorate of Research), Vance Palmer and Brian Fitzpatrick (then publicity officer for Coombs' Rationing Commission). Under discussion was the unsatisfactory state of the Department of Information. Conlon informed those present that Curtin had asked the Committee whether there was any merit in transferring the Department of Information's functions to the proposed Department of Postwar Reconstruction. It is clear from the minutes of the meeting that the Committee had disowned its interim report. As Conlon put it, "I honestly don't see how it can be rehabilitated."[88]

Coombs was introduced as the future head of the Department of Postwar Reconstruction and was most hesitant to take on the Department of Information's responsibilities. He felt it was necessary to have policy and publicity closely attached, and doubted whether a single publicity organization could or should handle the publicity of all departments. More pertinently, he was sensitive to the adverse attitudes of other agencies to the Department of Information. He was concerned that the attitudes of those agencies towards his department might be coloured at the outset by what they knew of Information's functions and effectiveness.

The Committee agreed. Then Deamer suggested a new organization, the Commission for Public Relations, to take the place of the Department of Information. Coming from the ABC, Deamer was familiar with how responsive the ABC had been to political change. However, Coombs cast doubt on this suggestion also. Would it mean that departments would have to operate through such an agency to get their press or radio space? Coombs observed:

> I would like Mr Deamer to think about his Commission a little. Commissions tend to be drawn from outside Government circles, and balanced politically, whereas the function of this organization is to cover PR of a number of Departments with the broad principles underlying Government policy in mind, and this means that the organisation has got to be soaked with Government policy and take its attitude on detailed decisions from an interpretation of Government policy — that is why it would be better to have a Director, rather than a Commission.[89]

It appears that the Committee agreed with Coombs on the undesirability of the Department of Information's functions being transferred to Postwar Reconstruction, but differed on the Public Relations Commission. On 20 December 1942, Conlon informed Curtin it was inappropriate for Postwar Reconstruction to have central publicity functions, but stressed the need for an independent agency:

> A Public Relations Commission of five members responsible to the Prime Minister should be appointed with a Chief Executive Officer known as the Director of Public Relations. The functions of the Public Relations Commission and its officers should be substantially as set out in the Committee's interim report of 26 August 1942, and its internal organisation should be similar with the substitution of the Public Relations Commissioner for the Director-General of Information.[90]

No record of the note or a response appears in Curtin's files.

On 16 April 1943, Curtin postponed consideration of the Department's future until the budget estimates that year.[91] Perhaps the Conlon Committee's main influence was that it gave the Department time to recover from its loss of functions and time to consolidate the functions that remained.

It would be misleading to conclude that the Department went from strength to strength under Ashley. In fact, Ashley gave the Department little attention once the threat to his portfolio had been reduced. Matters such as the allocation of funds were left to the Department to sort out and bid for. This meant routine functions took precedence in the budget allocations. The Department's well regarded Film Division was to take the brunt of this neglect.

Damien Parer's case is illustrative. His films of 1942 and 1943 gained world-wide attention. They won applause from audiences and professional critics alike. His *Kokoda Front-Line* won the 1943 Academy Award for best documentary of the year with its simple but forceful portrayal of war in New Guinea. However, Parer was a perfectionist and his standards demanded more in resources such as films, cameras and travelling expenses that he was officially entitled to. Understandably, there was tension between Parer and administration headquarters. In 1943, Parer was ordered to Broome, in anticipation of a possible invasion. He resigned on 25 May.[92] War papers suggest the possibility of Parer being offered a position with the Army Public Relations Directorate. But this appears not to have been pursued.[93] Parer accepted employment with Paramount Films, but was killed in action on 17 September 1944 while filming American soldiers at the Palau group of islands.[94]

The fate of the Canberra Secretariat was happier. The Secretariat came to perform two functions. The material produced by Incoming Information — Local Press Digest, Overseas Press Digest — was distributed to Ministers, to brief them on the coverage given to the government's activities. The New York and London offices assisted in the compilation of these reports.

The second function was that of Outgoing Information. This section provided a background service to editors and overseas representatives, and prepared material for ministerial speeches. The background service for the local press ran into the problem of access to information from the beginning. McCauley reported in February 1942: "At the moment our sources of factual information are virtually non-existent."[95]

On 5 April 1943, the Secretariat moved from the Hotel Canberra to the old Community Hospital building. The conditions were less pleasant, but by then the Secretariat had established its role. In particular, it was working well in supplying information to overseas sources. McCauley observed:

> Apart from routine assignments and service to other departments emanating from Canberra, the work of the Secretariat during the last 12 months has been diverted along the lines of building up and strengthening overseas propaganda.[96]

The Department was returning to the policy that had established it in 1941. Again, what was required was a Minister who appreciated this policy and a Director to nurture its approach. This move was to come about in the following months, but the transition would not be a smooth one.

Notes

1. See P. Hasluck, *The Government and the People 1939-1941*. Canberra: Australian War Memorial, 1952, Appendix 1, pp. 571-80 for detailed information on all wartime ministries.
2. Much of this background was drawn from Don Whitington, *Ring the Bells: A Dictionary of Federal Politics*. Melbourne: Georgian House, 1956, pp. 6-7.
3. Melbourne *Argus*, 16 October 1941.
4. *CPD* (HR), 29 October 1941, p. 20.
5. *CPD* (Senate), 13 November 1941, p. 348.
6. Author's interviews with R.I. Horne, T. Hoey and W.M. Ball, 18, 16 and 18 February 1976.
7. Author's interview with G. Sawer, 20 April 1976.
8. Author's interview with I. Hamilton, 3 May 1976.
9. C. Edwards, *The Editor Regrets*, Melbourne: Hill of Content, 1972, p. 95.
10. L.D. Meo, *Japan's Radio War on Australia 1941-45*. Melbourne: Melbourne University Press, 1968, p. 161.
11. Hadley Cantrill (ed.), *Public Opinion 1935-1946*. Princeton: Princeton University Press, 1951, p. 704.

12. Ibid., p. 341.
13. Ibid., p. 816.
14. Quoted from Edwards, *Editor Regrets*, p. 96. According to Edwards, the article had been with the Melbourne *Herald* some days before anyone grasped its significance. The impassioned declaration could have been 'buried in the magazine pages'.
15. William Dunk, *They Also Serve*. Canberra: the author, 1974, p. 51.
16. Gavin Long, *MacArthur: As Military Commander*. Sydney: Angus & Robertson, 1969, p. 51.
17. Letter to Blamey, 15 March 1945; Blamey Papers, Australian War Memorial, File 136.1.
18. Gavin Long, *The Six Years War: A Concise History of Australia in the 1939–45 War*. Canberra: Australian War Memorial and Australian Government Publishing Service, 1972, p. 181.
19. F. Dixon, *Inside the ABC: A Piece of Australian History*. Melbourne: Hawthorn Press, 1975, p. 65.
20. Ibid.
21. Author's interview with W.M. Ball, 18 February 1976.
22. Melbourne *Argus*, 10 January 1942.
23. *Commercial Broadcasting*, 15 January 1942.
24. Bonney to Curtin, 15 December 1941; A.A., SP 195/1, File 71/1/10.
25. Bonney to Holmes, 22 December 1941; A.A., SP 109, Box 53, File 337.01A.
26. Bonney to Ashley, 12 January 1942; A.A., SP 109, Box 53, File 337.01A.
27. Background notes for ABC witness to Joint Committee on Public Accounts, 1968; ABC Archives copy, supplied to the author by the ABC Chief Archivist in 1976.
28. See minutes of meeting from Advisory War Council, 7 February 1941, A.A., CP 815/4, Item 87.
29. Melbourne *Age*, 19 January 1942.
30. *CPD* (Senate), 29-30 September 1942, pp. 1061-62. The official dates of the transfers were: Publicity Censorship to Defence Co-ordination, 1 March 1941; Advertising Division to Treasury, 2 April 1942; Shortwave Broadcasting to ABC, 1 July 1942; A.A., SP 109/6, Bundle 5.
31. "Committee of Review [The Pinner Committee], Civil Staffing of War-time Activities, 1945", internal government report on the Department of Information, p. 2.
32. A.A., CP 815/4, Item 51.
33. Melbourne *Argus*, 20 January 1942.
34. Statement of 26 August 1942; A.A., SP 109/6, Bundle 5.
35. *CPD* (Senate), 29-30 September 1942, pp. 1061-62.
36. See, for example, *CPD* (HR), 22 September 1942, p. 613.
37. Ian K. Mackay, "*Macquarie: The Story of a Network*" (1961), unpublished manuscript held in the library of the Australian Broadcasting Tribunal, Marland House, Melbourne, pp. 83-84.
38. Chairman's file on Miscellaneous Matters, A.A., SP 314/S1/B.5; and P. Mitchell, "The Development of ABC News Gathering 1932–42". Sydney: unpublished History IV (Hons.) thesis, University of Sydney, 1974, p. 51.
39. Mitchell, "ABC News Gathering", p. 50.
40. Ibid., pp. 51-52.
41. Dixon *Inside the ABC*, p. 78.
42. Ibid.

43. Mitchell, ABC News Gathering, p. 54.
44. Dixon, *Inside the ABC*, p. 80.
45. *CPD* (Senate), 6 March 1942, p. 224.
46. *CPD* (HR), 6 March 1952, p. 252.
47. Ibid., 19 October 1942, p. 1642.
48. Ibid., 15 March 1942, pp. 204-05.
49. Report to Prime Minister's Committee on National Morale (Conlon Committee), unsigned, c. late 1942, in Julius Stone Papers.
50. Ibid.
51. A.A., CRS A818, File 56/301/44.
52. Melbourne *Argus*, 8 April 1942.
53. *CPD* (HR), 7-8 October 1942, p. 1487.
54. Ibid., 19 October 1942, p. 1642.
55. Melbourne *Argus*, 15 December 1942.
56. Melbourne *Age*, 15 June 1942.
57. Ibid., 27 June 1942.
58. Tim Dare, "The War of Words". *Australian*, 7 December 1974.
59. Sydney *Truth*, 5 July 1942.
60. Melbourne *Age*, 29 June 1942.
61. *CPD* (HR), 3-4 June 1942, p. 2180.
62. McCauley to Ashley, 14 July 1942; A.A., SP 109/6, Bundle 5, Box 71, File 19/10/32.
63. Hawes to Ashley, 14 July 1942, A.A., SP 109/16.
64. From War Cabinet Submission by P.M. Forde, Minister for the Army, 1 July 1943; A.A., CRS A461, Item BP 6/1/1, Pt. 2.
65. Sydney *Daily Telegraph*, 9 July 1942.
66. Script (C. 1942), Central Administration Office of Assistant Secretary, General Correspondence, 1 May 1942-8 June 1943; A.A., SP 109/6, Bundle 5.
67. From the summary in Edwards, *Editor Regrets*, pp. 100-01.
68. C.A. Deputy Director of Information NSW, General Correspondence 1939-45, Item Anti-Japanese Propaganda; A.A., SP 109/16.
69. Melbourne *Argus*, 31 March 1942.
70. C.A. Deputy Director of Information NSW (from J. Rutledge, 7 April 1942), General Correspondence 1939-45, Item Anti-Japanese Propaganda; A.A., SP 109/16.
71. Ibid.
72. Ibid.
73. Australian Gallup Poll, nos. 41-46, May 1942.
74. *CPD* (HR), 27 May 1942, p. 1625.
75. Melbourne *Argus*, 13 May 1942.
76. A.A., CRS A461, Item BP 6/1/1, Pt. 2.
77. Ibid.
78. Ibid.
79. *Smith's Weekly* (Sydney), 27 June 1942.
80. Clipping (n.d.) in Julius Stone Papers.
81. *CPD* (Senate), 15 October 1943, pp. 638-39.
82. P. Hasluck, *The Government and the People 1942-1945*. Canberra: Australian War Memorial, 1970, pp. 398-99.
83. Julius Stone Papers.
84. Interim Report to the Prime Minister, A.A., CRS A461, Item BP 6/1/1, Pt. 2.

85. Hasluck, *Government and the People 1942-1945*, p. 399.
86. US Bureau of the Budget, Committee on Records of War Administration, War Records Section, *The United States at War: Development and Administration of the War Program by Federal Government*. New York: Da Capo Press, 1972, pp. 229-30.
87. A.A., CRS A461, Item BP 6/1/1, Pt. 2.
88. Julius Stone Papers.
89. Ibid.
90. Ibid.
91. A.A., CRS A461, Item BP 6/1/1, Pt. 2.
92. J. Hetherington, *Five to Remember*. Melbourne: Cheshire, 1960, pp. 177-78.
93. Correspondence, 18 September 1943; Australian War Memorial, File 773/4/90.
94. Hetherington *Five to Remember*, p. 180.
95. Memorandum, McCauley (Assistant Secretary) to Hawes (Secretary), 3 February 1942; A.A., SP 109/6, Bundle 5.
96. Ibid., 12 April 1943.

7

Bonney and Ball: Expression and Suppression outside the Department

"A man of manoeuvres"

For Australia, the deteriorating fortunes of war during 1942 and 1943 placed special pressures on the Department's two dispersed functions of shortwave broadcasting and censorship. This chapter traces the development of Shortwave Division, the activities of the censors and the values that underlay their policies. These values were to emerge in ideas on what impression Australia should present abroad to enemies and allies.

Until the end of 1941, the Shortwave Division had developed more or less unencumbered and unquestioned. Its broadcasts were beamed into countries also served by the BBC. However, in July 1941, coincidentally with the transfer of all operations to Melbourne, the broadcasts to Europe and South America ceased, partly for technical reasons and partly because of a desire to supplement rather than compete with the BBC transmissions. Transmissions to Asia were extended. Broadcasts in German, Italian and Spanish were eliminated, marking the first step in making Australian broadcasts an instrument of British Commonwealth and allied psychological warfare in the Pacific zone.[1]

Another development of significance in 1941 was the appointment by the Menzies government of the Joint Committee on Wireless Broadcasting, to inquire into all aspects of broadcasting and propose amendments to broadcasting legislation. The Gibson Committee, as it came to be called after its chairman, W.G. Gibson, examined shortwave broadcasting and questioned whether the Department of Information was an appropriate environment for the shortwave station. The Department handled overseas propaganda and yet its responsibility for a radio station seemed at odds with the responsibilities of the ABC. In the event, this was an area that the Gibson Committee failed to come to grips with. Its report misconceived Ball's integration of the shortwave staff in July 1941, regarding it as a move by the Department of Information to take responsibility away from the ABC. It believed, incorrectly, the ABC had been largely responsible for the shortwave operation to July 1942.[2]

The Committee asked Ball which was the best environment for the shortwave responsibility, the ABC or the Department? Ball hedged by suggesting that it all depended on what the necessary conditions for successful shortwave broadcasting were. He doubted whether the ABC's experience with radio made it an obvious candidate for running the service. The differences between medium-wave broadcasting and shortwave broadcasting were far greater than the similarities. He felt there was a need to monitor propaganda broadcasts and a need to have people with specialized knowledge of overseas countries. The ABC lacked this. Furthermore, the shortwave policy should remain under ministerial control.[3] In effect, Ball argued for the view that the Department should retain the shortwave responsibility. He may have felt he was in a better position with the Department's flexible Minister, Foll, and Principal Information Officer, Bateson. "I am satisfied to have the head of the Department as my supervisor."[4] He probably did not care at the time who was in charge of his division, provided he could continue to run it on his own terms.

His evidence may have irritated some of the Gibson Committee members. It was claimed that the output of the station discredited the Commonwealth. Sir Charles Marr, vice-chairman of the Committee, reported that he was disturbed that the station had broadcast such claims as, that Canberra was overrun by hares and that coastal areas were infested with rabbits. He felt only programs that definitely would benefit Australia should be broadcast.[5]

The Committee also was influenced by Sir Keith Murdoch, who advised that shortwave broadcasting was better placed with the ABC.[6] The position was complicated by the ABC's use of the shortwave facilities to reach outback areas. Demarcation disputes were frequent. The ABC, in addition to expressing concern about unnecessary duplication, argued for full responsibility for shortwave broadcasting in the following terms:

> We realise, of course, that the Department of Information must always suggest the main themes of talks or programs . . . but when all is said and done, we are experienced broadcasters and better able to devise interesting programs which, after all, are the foundation of all broadcasting.[7]

The debate took a new turn with the fall of the Fadden government. The new Minister for Information's portfolios embraced both the Department and the ABC. Following the Japanese attack in the Pacific, there were demands for changes to the Information portfolio, culminating in the Shortwave Division going to the ABC.

The transfer, however, was not as easy as was foreshadowed. The ABC baulked over the costs. Its general manager wrote to Ashley on 31 January 1942, requesting special funds since "it would seem clear that there should not be a charge against the normal licence fee". These negotiations delayed the transfer until 1 July. An interim funding arrangement was not agreed to until 18 July.[8] After July, Ball was relieved to see his division settle back into a routine. He wrote to Bearup, the ABC's general manager, in September 1942:

> Since the full transfer of this work to Commission control, the Commission and senior officers concerned have shown a most sympathetic understanding of our s.w. needs and

problems, and done a number of things to improve our conditions — such as the removal of salary anomalies and the provision of more accommodation and equipment. The cumulative effect of these actions, combined with the sense that we are working with an organisation with standards and aims that we can all respect, has produced a marked lift of spirits and a general increase in keenness and efficiency throughout the Department. I believe that the average quality of our work is remarkably higher than it was three months ago.[9]

Between March and August 1942, broadcasts to Asia were greatly extended and diversified, acquiring the character of political warfare. Malay, Japanese and Chinese were added to the transmissions, through the utilization of refugees who had arrived from Singapore and Java. The Netherlands East Indies Government Information Service was established in Melbourne in April and provided, gratis, translators, announcers and Listening Post monitors in Dutch and Malay. The British Ministry of Information provided a Japanese and Siamese expert. The Chinese Consulate in Melbourne made available a Chinese specialist. In June, the Prime Minister directed the Department of External Affairs to control the policy of the political warfare broadcasts.[10] A political warfare section was established within External Affairs to oversee this, and an Allied Political Warfare Committee, comprising British, American, Dutch and Chinese representatives, was created to advise the Minister for External Affairs on the work.[11] In practice, Ball found the Committee of little guidance. On 2 September 1942, he wrote to a colleague:

> Off the record, I get a bit annoyed with all these discussions about the right machinery for political warfare. We have in our own way, and often in a pretty poor and amateurish way, been carrying on political warfare for two and a half years. If we had waited till we had got the right machinery we would never have done anything.[12]

Where guidance was given, Ball tended to resist it if he disagreed with it. The Listening Post became prominent in 1942 when it began monitoring the Japanese broadcasts that identified prisoners of war. In October 1942, Ball chaired one of the subcommittees established by the Prime Minister's Committee on National Morale (the Conlon Committee). The most persistent issue before his subcommittee was government pressure to prohibit public listening to Japanese broadcasts, so that their propaganda value, laughable though this might be to most listeners, would have no chance to affect the morale of the populace. Ball cautioned that this would only encourage more direct listening, especially by relatives of POWs hoping to hear of their loved ones. Instead, Ball proposed that transcripts of all POW names be supplied to relatives, so that they would be assured that experts were listening on their behalf, and that therefore there was little need to make a special effort to listen in.[13]

Ball had even less enthusiasm for overt propaganda work. "We made some bad blunders in our wartime broadcasts to Asia," recalled Ball. For example, attempts were made to encourage resentment against the "quislings" as they were called. But for many Asian listeners, those who collaborated with the Japanese were patriots, protecting their community in difficult circumstances. They were not regarded as "quislings" when they collaborated with the British, Dutch or the French.[14] When asked what the worst aspect of the Shortwave Division was for her, Helen Ferber responded:

> How ghastly that we put out all that propaganda. Highly coloured pictures of Australia and the digger. A very favourable picture of Australia went out . . .[15]

Ball had chosen to organize his shortwave operation as one that provided truth via controversy, one that was capable of sophisticated analysis of international developments. He felt uncomfortable when having to impose overt propaganda guidelines on his broadcast staff and aimed for talks that built up morale in as subtle a way as possible.[16]

By mid-1943, the propaganda broadcasts began to form a smaller proportion of the Shortwave Division's daily schedule. For example, the broadcasts of 20 July showed that of the 9 hours and 15 minutes broadcast, only 2 hours and 35 minutes, a little more than a quarter, was devoted to political warfare to enemy-occupied territories. John De La Valette of the NEI government expressed his disappointment with Ball's lack of enthusiasm for the propaganda work.[17]

As the prospect of allied victory came closer, propaganda broadcasts tended to give greater emphasis to how good life would be after victory. The Dutch officials such as Valette naturally emphasized how good it would be for Indonesians to be returned to benevolent Dutch rule. However, Indonesian leaders felt differently about this and thus relations with the Dutch were sometimes delicate.

On the other hand, Ball's work in fostering links with the allies seemed well received. Broadcasts to North America had been made topical with the inclusion of interviews with American personnel. More than 200 medium-wave stations in the United States regularly picked up and relayed the Australian transmissions, and hundreds of special individual pick-ups also were arranged. Although messages from, interviews with or reports of Americans and American activities were the bait for these relays, it was possible at the same time to promote Australian achievements both in the war and on the home-front.[18]

Though his division flourished between June 1942 and August 1943 (when the Curtin government was re-elected), unresolved difficulties plagued the Division and the ABC. The first concerned its funding arrangement, which was never fully resolved. The money for running the Shortwave Division could not be taken from the ABC's regular revenue, but was appropriated from consolidated revenue by Parliament. The ABC had no regular account or dealings with the Treasury, and Treasury continued to regard the Department of Information as the ministry that had to certify to the propriety of expenditure. But the ABC was the body that had to secure increased grants as the importance of the shortwave broadcasting increased and the Division's activities expanded. This seemed unreasonable to both the ABC and the Department of Information. The former was unaccustomed to such negotiations and the latter had no effective control over the expenditure for which Treasury expected it to vouch.[19]

The second problem concerned broadcasting policy. The Department of External Affairs was responsible for communicating policy about political warfare direct to Ball. The ABC was anxious lest it be in any way responsible for carrying out such policies or should be regarded by the outside world as having a share in policy formulation. Subject to the Pacific First news policy, Cleary fought to retain the ABC's autonomy, yet one of his own divisions was subject to the policy of another government department. The Commission could not disassociate itself in practice from the activities of the Shortwave Division, for it had to face up to administration problems and the expenditure that the political warfare activities entailed. The Division's policy was not the ABC's, though the Commission had to accept responsibility for it.

The third problem was that Cabinet had not indicated which body was responsible for policy in transmissions that were not concerned with political warfare. As it had been taken for granted that Australian policy was British policy, little consideration had been given to this in the past. Though Ball's transmissions moved more and more into this ill-defined area, the ABC was reluctant to take responsibility for formulating policy.

The fourth problem was partly administrative. By mid-1943, Ball's contention, made before the Gibson Committee on the differences between medium-wave and shortwave broadcasting, was borne out by experience. Although the ABC's domestic organization should have been able to supply a good deal of material for shortwave broadcasting and, in practice, did supply some, the Shortwave Division was run in an essentially autonomous fashion. The ABC news bulletins proved unsuitable for general shortwave purposes. ABC features had to be rewritten for overseas audiences. ABC entertainment programs were used as fillers, with some effect. These could have been piped into shortwave transmissions whether the division was controlled by the ABC or not.[20]

There was some administrative advantage in drawing on ABC announcers and news writers, but generally by mid-1943 the ABC, like the Department of Information before it, found itself in charge of a very distinct and at times, financially troublesome division. Its controller, Ball, did little to discourage the evident separateness of shortwave broadcasting from the rest of the ABC.

On 29 June 1943, the ABC, the Department of Information, External Affairs, PMG's Department and the Shortwave Division prepared a report to Ashley for submission to Cabinet. The report's main point was that the Shortwave Division was becoming an expensive proposition. New transmitters costing £500,000, plus another £160,000 each year, were being planned, but who was to pay? The Division's budget of £28,400 was exceeded by some £15,000 for the year 1942-43. The estimate for 1943-44 was £58,780. Who would negotiate for the funds, the report asked, and on what basis?

The report recommended that the functions and responsibilities of the Shortwave Division should be more clearly defined and that "direction of policy be placed under Ministerial Authority"; that the policy for allied and friendly countries should be one that would achieve "an informed and intelligent understanding" of Australia and its war effort with the offensive and defensive political warfare against the enemy under ministerial direction; that authority be given to the ABC to pay off the excess expenditure for the year; and that for future funding purposes an interdepartmental committee comprising External Affairs, Information and the Postmaster-General's Department should advise the ABC.[21]

Ashley endorsed this report. However, it was not submitted for Cabinet consideration until 27 September, some six days after the appointment of the new Minister for Information.

With goodwill, these matters could have been resolved. The capital cost of the transmitters, for example, was buried in the Department of the Army's vote, because this was regarded as part of the national defence commitments.

But Ball's problems with the Censorship Division, now under Curtin, as Minister for Defence, began to upset the Department's activities. In particular, Bonney and Ball fought each other long and hard.

The struggle involved personalities, but it was not fundamentally personal in character. It rested on deeply-held differences about what was desirable in shortwave broadcasting propaganda. Ball wanted a shortwave service much like the BBC, which conceded the truth (subject to security constraints) even where it appeared to support some of the enemy's claims. He regarded this as good propaganda because it showed the enemy, allies and neutrals that democratic countries like Australia tell the truth even when it hurts. Bonney, by contrast, took the view that, in wartime, it was irresponsible not to be partisan about one's country and that broadcasting from the "Voice of Australia" should be supervised accordingly. Like other media, the Shortwave Division coped with the censorship regulations derived from the National Security Act, but it was expected to take special care since it was broadcasting direct to the enemy.

Ball encouraged his writers and commentators to take a fairly sophisticated view of their quarry. Propaganda broadcasts, where necessary, should be as credible as possible. He was inclined to favour talks that were frank, man-to-man discussions, in which matters of common knowledge were freely mentioned, not avoided. This approach featured where his targets were the Japanese, especially the Japanese monitoring service. (The Japanese people themselves were not permitted access to shortwave receivers.[22]) This meant that the Division transmitted some commentaries that seemed defeatist, or were not "tough" enough, when it conceded certain known allied military set-backs in order to lay the foundation for a credible commentary. The Publicity Censorship Division began to take an increasingly harsh line, cutting substantial portions of these talks. The cuts made the scripts so colourless that, in the view of Ball and his staff, the broadcasts almost certainly would be ignored.

A flash point in the conflict between Censorship and Shortwave derived from the backgrounds of the censors, many of whom were former newspaper men. Some of Ball's talks not only were being cut for security reasons but were being re-edited or partially rewritten before being approved by Censorship.[23] After one such cut, Ball complained to Bonney. Bonney, in reply, conceded that the censors might have gone too far, but reiterated the importance of censorship to morale:

> so far as the script you forwarded is concerned I think the censor improved your message with his five cuts. [One other] . . . seemed unnecessary and [another] was a borderline case.
>
> . . . The Censor's duty is clear. He should not permit publication of anything which contravenes our code of security . . . Especially in handling broadcasting material, it is necessary for the censor to consider the consequences of publication. Because propaganda affects morale — the enemy's as well as our own — this is an important function, even though as you point out, the Censor's control is negative in that he can only exercise it by making cuts . . .[24]

Indeed the censors increasingly became as keen to participate in propaganda formulation as they were to abridge. One censor took the opportunity to express to Bonney his low opinion of the work of Ball's division:

> So far as censorship of shortwave propaganda is concerned, my best information to date is that the bulk of this material is not really serving the purpose of propaganda, it is merely broadcast to keep open a channel that can be used on very rare occasions to put out some isolated item of real importance.
>
> This possibly explains why McMahon [sic] Ball is satisfied to have such poor material written by low-grade subordinates. This material is *not* prepared with care that should go into real propaganda and it is consequently obvious that it would not be safe to permit broadcasting without censorship . . .[25]

Bonney believed there was a clear connection between censorship and propaganda. In his view, Ball's approach to propaganda was half-hearted and potentially dangerous for morale. If the enemy were given certain information, this could lift enemy morale. If the material were then retransmitted back to Australia, this could depress ours. It might be all right to concede defeat in order to make the propaganda credible, but what would our allies in an enemy-occupied territory make of such concessions?

In the months before the re-election of the Curtin government, Bonney grew to regard Ball as being formidably and arrogantly independent in his control of the Shortwave Division. Ball, for his part, believed Bonney to be devious: a "man of manoeuvres".[26]

Ball was to be proved right. Bonney's handling of his Censorship Division during the height of the war bears adequate testimony to this. The surprise attack by the Japanese in the South Pacific influenced a change in ministerial responsibility for Censorship. Curtin took Censorship under his wing, possibly to discourage senior Service Ministers from improperly influencing Ashley, a relatively junior Minister, to the detriment of relations between government and the press. On 20 January 1942, Curtin forshadowed the possibility of some liberalization of censorship. Under the new arrangement, Bonney would occupy a "semi-judicial" position, arbitrating between the secrecy demands of the Services and the government's wish to pass on to the public all possible information about the war.[27]

Like other Information Ministers, Curtin was to qualify this promise of liberalization. On 10 February, Curtin summoned media representatives to a conference in Canberra, ostensibly to provide more sensitive background on the war. (This was the same conference that resulted in the fragile arrangement to continue the ABC's news-gathering role.) Curtin now argued that the press should withhold news from the enemy and guard against the publication of matters prejudicial to security or good relations with the allies. His government did not want to restrict the expression of opinion or criticism of policy, but it did expect that the government's own views "should be fully and adequately stated and should have priority of statement". Curtin expected the press to be conscious of its responsibilities to maintain national morale.[28]

Some members of the press took this as an attempt to stifle their freedom, in the guise of national security. Evatt's views on morale in particular may have disturbed them:

> The Prime Minister said that the truth must be told. There is no doubt as to the truth of enemy claims. The building up of morale does not consist simply of telling the truth to the people. If the news be bad, you have to counter it and make the people prepared to resist the enemy when he comes. The job of the press is not merely to give the news but also to prepare people to bear the impact of attacks when they come . . .[29]

Brian Penton, editor of the *Daily Telegraph*, believed Censorship was suppressing legitimate criticism. A censorship instruction prohibiting any reference to air raid precautions was given as an example where

> instead of being censored, much copy is merely edited by the censors for the purposes of preventing criticism of the Government, not because it contains information of value to the enemy or because of public morale. The "blanket" censorship opens the way to political censorship.

Bonney, who was in attendance, responded that criticism was allowable, "but giving the people the jitters is another matter". Penton retorted "it is difficult to criticise without causing some alarm".[30]

Curtin explained that he was not so much concerned with criticism that was disseminated locally, but he took strong exception to cabling stories *overseas*, in order to whip up opposition to the government's war legislation. Curtin was not alone in drawing this distinction in reporting, which was given added support on 5 March with the report of the Gibson Committee, which pressed for "banning from the air all matters which the enemy may use against democracies". Noting instances of Australian comment being reproduced on shortwave broadcasts from Berlin, Tokyo and Rome, the Gibson Committee recommended that:

> The Censor, or other authorities responsible, should vigorously prohibit the broadcasting from both national and

commercial stations of anything which the enemy can use, such as political party and individual quarrels and criticisms, industrial disturbances, interstate grievances . . .[31]

The promptness with which the enemy use local critical comment to its own advantage was an undeniable feature in Japanese propaganda tactics. In as little as eight hours from dispatch, one critical editorial in the local press was being rebroadcast over the enemy's radio to the Australian homefront and nearby battlefields.[32] The Advisory War Council agreed that even though some items had been published overseas, they might still "prejudice public morale" if they appeared in Australia. Cables to Australia were censored not only at the point of origin but in Australia as well.[33]

Guarding against "wrong impressions" continued to feature in censorship policies. On 6 May 1942, the *Daily Telegraph* was prohibited from distributing the day's issue overseas. Curtin explained that the paper was released in Australia but not overseas because the Censor decided that one article would adversely affect overseas opinion. The article in question was prejudicial to the efficient prosecution of war and cordial relations between Australia and the United States, and would be welcomed by the enemy. It in fact might make the Americans doubt the wholeheartedness of the Australian fighting effort. The article, which described politicians holding banners reading "Save Sydney but not San Francisco" and "Die for Darwin but why fight to resume Bataan", would convey the false impression that Australians let others fight for them, concluded Curtin.[34]

Another factor in the increasingly caustic relations between the Censor and the Sydney press, particularly the *Daily Telegraph*, arose from Bonney's reorganization of the Sydney office. Following his move to Canberra towards the end of 1941, Bonney became concerned that the Sydney office, run by H.A. Rorke (also a censor in World War I), had had more censorship decisions reversed than any other capital city. Rorke had developed good relations with the *Daily Telegraph* and the *Sydney*

Morning Herald, but his following of the new central office policy was poor. Some of his censors appeared to be working within 1914-18 rules.[35] Bonney decided the office had "lost touch with current events" and left too much to the discretion of assistant censors.[36] Rorke was replaced on 20 March 1942 with Henry Horace Mansell.[37] Mansell, a former campaign director of Evatt's, proved more satisfactory in the Sydney office, but failed to recapture the cordial relations Rorke enjoyed with the Sydney press. The press regarded Rorke's replacement as evidence of political censorship. Matters were not helped when Rorke's news statement on his resignation was partly suppressed by the Sydney office. The sentence, "Mr Rorke said there had been a trend in Censorship which he did not like" was purged, with the approval of Curtin, on the grounds that no censorship source would allow itself to be misrepresented by such a suggestion.[38]

To improve relations with the press, Curtin established the Press Censorship Advisory Committee on 9 April 1942, with J.H. Scullin as its chairman. The committee members were W.O. Fairfax (*Sydney Morning Herald*), H.A.M. Campbell (Melbourne *Age*), Sir Keith Murdoch (Melbourne *Herald*), and G.H. Sparrow (general president of the Australian Journalists Association). In late August, E.T. Kennedy (Sydney *Sun* and the chief executive of Associated Press) replaced Fairfax, who had resigned. In Curtin's view, the Committee was constituted

> so that newspapers as a body may express views to the Government rather than, as hitherto has been the case, by individual representatives of separate newspapers or press men associated with those newspapers taking a certain censorship order and harassing either the censor or the Government.[39]

Dissatisfaction with censorship treatment formed the agenda of these meetings. These and later complaints mainly concerned news of military operations, and particularly when questions of morale or overseas audiences were involved.[40] The official historian believes some good came of the Committee, mainly because of Scullin's competent chairmanship.[41] In effect, Scullin became the

Minister for Censorship. Bonney was to turn to Scullin for aid in much of his work during 1942.

Apart from differences with the press, the Censor had to cope with the censorship demands of both the American and Australian armed services. From the beginning, Bonney wanted to maintain his ultimate authority. The announcement of General MacArthur's arrival in Australia was first heard on the BBC, because the Americans insisted that the Australian announcement be embargoed. Bonney wrote to Scullin on 18 March 1942:

> Both the Government and Censorship have been given a very raw deal over the arrival of the American forces and General MacArthur . . . Once again . . . the BBC beats us very badly.

Bonney pressed Scullin to make the US Army's censorship role similar to that of the Australian Services — that is, purely advisory.[42] However, Curtin's determination to maintain good relations with America and MacArthur made him turn down Bonney's suggestion. MacArthur's advice continued to be binding. In the following months, MacArthur's communiqués formed the basis of censorship instructions:

> *17 April 1942*
> Editors are asked to play down suggestions of mystery or confusion concerning General MacArthur's position as Supreme Commander. They tend to bewilder the public and destroy the morale built upon General MacArthur.
>
> (Communiqués)
> War Communiqués must in future be published without amendment. Any sentence lifted for introduction must conform to the actual text.[43]

Other instructions prescribed that MacArthur's communiqués be fully adopted by the press and not be open to revision, comment or any speculation whatsoever:

> *27 June 1942*
> Publication is prohibited of any material calculated to undermine confidence in the accuracy of the War Communiqués issued in the SWPA. This does not prevent critical requests for more complete information. While it is in order to urge

that more war news be released it would be improper and against the terms of this instruction to state or even imply that communiqués are unreliable.[44]

The Censorship Advisory Committee began to turn its fire on the protection given to the MacArthur communiqués. The communiqués had to be more precise and their delivery more prompt. Scullin said he would press for "fuller and more colourful" communiqués, but only if these could be given with safety.[45]

More irritating for cordial relationships was the growth in the variety of censorship organizations. Because the military operations were occurring on Australian territory, it was possible for Australian journalists to visit and report on the area. This meant that Publicity Censorship was represented. Likewise, because the Americans were in charge of overall strategy, MacArthur had his own censorship at the field operation level; and because Australian troops were involved, the Army Public Relations Directorate had, theoretically, a separate censorship role to play as well.

Clearly, there was not room enough for three separate censorships, certainly as far as the journalists themselves were concerned. Thus on 6 July 1942, at a meeting of the Defence Committee representing both the Australian and American armed services in the South-West Pacific Area, Curtin decided that in questions of an operational nature affecting the fighting services, there would be "one transmitting authority" from the Services to the Chief Publicity Censor and this authority would be an officer at MacArthur's general headquarters. Only in emergencies were the Australian armed services to liaise with the Chief Publicity Censor.[46] In practice, the censorship function of the Army Public Relations Directorate was subject to consultation with GHQ SWPA or Publicity Censorship, for the sake of co-ordination. The Army was soon squeezed out of any substantial role in these matters, except for local Australian field operations.

The resolution of censorship demarcation did not ease press criticism. The press maintained its grievances about what it regarded as political censorship, especially where matters of morale appeared to be behind the Censor's decision. Bonney took the view at Censorship Advisory Committee meetings that it was his ultimate right, not that of the press, to determine such sensitive matters. In briefing Scullin in June 1942, Bonney wrote:

> It is our policy to release news of losses, but this does not mean we can safely ignore the manner in which it is first released ... Editors are better able to understand such obvious security matters as the departure of a troop ship than they are to appreciate questions of morale and therefore *more guidance* is needed in respect of morale than of military information.[47]

While the overwhelming bulk of censorship work concerned military information and its deletion, it was natural that the Censorship Advisory Committee's early meetings debated morale issues more than any other. The pressure of arbitrating on demands made by Bonney and the press apparently led to Scullin's resignation in November 1942.[48] The press continued to berate the government about what it viewed as political censorship. For example, reports of street fights between soldiers on leave were suppressed or only allowed to be published if they were placed together with an official statement by the military or civilian police. Curtin, now acting chairman of the Censorship Advisory Committee, regarded these as loose criticisms. Publication of such matters, in his view, could have a disastrous effect on morale, especially if the brawls involved white Australian soldiers and black American soldiers.[49]

In November 1942, the Australian Newspaper Proprietors Association passed a resolution regretting that censorship was being applied to news and opinion "beyond the requirements of security". Curtin denied this, claiming that censorship only was being used for security purposes — that is, under the National Security (General) Regulations.[50]

In contrast to the press, relations with broadcasting stations in 1942 remained cordial and co-operative. Minutes of a meeting between Hoey, the Victorian Publicity Censor, and radio station proprietors suggest that the stations were satisfied with the censorship arrangements:

> The Chairman (Hoey) asked all present to become familiar with the rules in order to ensure that they might check any tendency to permit unauthorized relaxations to creep in. He asked whether any station considered relaxations should be made in any direction. No relaxations were sought.
>
> Mr Dooley (AFCB) said that the rules appears satisfactory. Careful interpretation of them was the best means of ensuring fair and equal treatment to all stations also ensuring that there would be no breaches of security.[51]

By 1943, the immediacy of the Japanese threat to Australia had dissipated and Bonney's principal concern returned to guarding against false impressions overseas. In the first months of 1943, most complaints put to the Censorship Advisory Committee referred to the handling of *outgoing* overseas messages. One reason was that this was a responsibility jointly shared with the Chief US Military Censor.[52]

But Bonney's approach to censoring overseas messages also played a major part in this restriction. Overseas correspondents based in Australia claimed Censorship suppressed overseas stories critical of Australia.[53] Yates McDaniel (Associated Press, New York) argued that censors now not only cut sensitive material but occasionally subedited it as well:

> There has been a feeling that there has been a little too much of the sub-editorial point of view. Instead of censoring, censors have more or less put themselves up as sub-editors. Sometimes it works to our advantage. I know I have been picked up in slips in spelling and construction in messages, but I don't think censorship should assume the function of a sub-editor and change copy.

Bonney suggested that his censors were sympathetic to the work of journalists: "Nearly every censor in Australia is a former newspaperman." Most of his staff of seventy censors came from a background in journalism.[54] Apparently it had been a special kind of journalist that Bonney had sought: it was not the larrikin kind, thought to inhabit the environs of some sections of the Sydney press. The stories, argued Bonney, must be balanced. Criticism was only suppressed by censors when it was not "balanced" with praise:

> In writing a story . . . you should not just "knock" Australia and paint her blacker than any other country . . . My advice is to write in such a way that it will not lead people to believe that this country is not worth fighting for, or even with.

Yates McDaniel observed, "You seem to be touchier about certain aspects in your national life than in other countries." Replied Bonney, "It is a smaller place."

Bonney informed the correspondents that the actual cuts were far fewer than they imagined. Less than one per cent of stories were "killed", seventy per cent were passed without alteration, less than five per cent suffered major deletions. In his view, some ninety-four per cent got through. Dickson Brown (*News Chronicle*, London) felt there was more to it than that:

> I don't think that gives you a true picture of how censorship is applied, because some of us, including myself, often don't write stories because we feel that [sic] it has no chance of getting through censorship . . .

Bonney replied, "That is an easy way to earn money." But Brown insisted, "It is becoming a difficult way to earn your money if you cannot present a better picture than now." Bonney concluded the meeting by summarizing his basic policy:

> A story that presents both sides should not be stopped. The story that should be stopped is the one that presents only one side.

In his August 1943 circular to censors, on what was permissible for the election broadcasts, Bonney advised:

> In handling election scripts censors must distinguish between allegations designed to discredit any political party, and those which, based on half-truths or mis-statements, are calculated to *besmirch the good name of Australia, or belittle her war effort.*[55]

The distinction that Bonney sought to make was essentially a phony distinction. It could as easily be used for partisan purposes. Criticism of the good name of Australian inevitably meant the good name of the Labor government. As an example, in his circular Bonney showed how a script was amended by the Censor (the words deleted being italicized and those added appearing in parentheses):

> When Australia so magnificently co-operated with Britain in the early stages of the war — *when* it sent its Navy to fight with Britain in every ocean — *when* it sent its Airmen to fight over every Axis country, *when* its soldiers formed part of Wavell's wizards and Morshead's "Tobruk Rats" *then* the policy of Australia was the U.A.P. policy of co-operation. Since Labor came into power this policy has changed *from co-operation to isolation. Australia, like Southern Ireland, is now out of step with Britain — out of step with America.* It (the Labor Government) is adopting a narrow isolationalist policy confining its *fighting* (troops) to the Australian continent and narrow limits from its northern coast.

Bonney regarded the inclusion of the word "when" in three places as inferring that today our Navy, Air Force and Army were not free to fight in every ocean or Axis country. The further suggestion that Australia was not co-operating with Britain or America, indeed that it was out of step, or that it was restricted to a small area, was regarded as "likely to create a false impresson abroad. Thus the good name of Australia was involved."

By the end of August 1943, the Publicity Censorship Division had begun to take on some of the expressive functions of the Department of Information and the Shortwave Division. It was, indeed, more effective because it could influence directly the work of capital-city dailies, as well as overseas correspondents, through the censorship instructions and the cajolery of Bonney himself. Ironically, the importance of overseas propaganda and Censorship's increasing role came when the Japanese threat actually was in decline and when Australia's strategic value to the United States was considerably reduced. Roger Bell, in his survey of relations between Australia and the United States, observed that it was the war experience in the

South-West Pacific that prompted Australia to entertain new ambitions concerning control of the various island territories on its periphery.[56]

These ambitions entailed a more integrated approach to overseas propaganda. The Department of Information, with its principal activities now directed overseas, and a shortwave operation with its improved transmitters and censorship and its eye on false impressions abroad, had something in common.

Notes

1. "History of Overseas Shortwave Broadcasting Australia", Draft Report, ?1946 (unpublished ms., in Hoey Papers, author unknown, ?Tom Hoey), pp. 3-4.
2. *Report of the Joint Committee on Wireless Broadcasting* (Gibson Committee). Canberra: Commonwealth Government Printer, 25 March 1942, pp. 75-76.
3. W.M. Ball, evidence to Gibson Committee, 22 July 1941; ibid., pp. 88-89.
4. Ibid., p. 90.
5. *CPD* (HR), 2 June 1942, p. 1846.
6. Gibson Committee, *Report*, p. 75.
7. Alan Thomas "War and Radio: The ABC and the Australian War Effort 1939-45", unpublished History Seminar paper. Canberra: Australian National University, 1977.
8. Background notes for ABC witness to Joint Committee on Public Accounts, 1968; *ABC Archives* copy, supplied to the author by the ABC Chief Archivist in 1976.
9. Ball to Bearup, 10 September 1942; A.A., MP 272/3, File A/2A.
10. "History of Overseas Shortwave Broadcasting", draft report, p. 4.
11. Ibid., p. 5.
12. Thomas, "War and Radio", p. 6.
13. L.D. Meo, *Japan's Radio War on Australia 1941-45*. Melbourne: Melbourne University Press, 1968, pp. 169-70.
14. Ball in foreword to ibid., p. viii.
15. Author's interview with H. Ferber, 16 February 1976.
16. Ball to Helen Crisp, 10 October 1941, A.A., SP 109/11, Box 80, Bundle 1.
17. Valette to Ball, 29 July 1943, A.A., MP 272, Ball's General Files.
18. "History of Overseas Shortwave Broadcasting", draft report, pp. 5-6.
19. Ibid., p. 8.
20. Ibid., p. 6-7.
21. A.A., CRS A461, Item BP 6/1/1, Pt. 2.
22. Sawer to Ball, 10 November 1942; A.A., MP 272/1, Bundle 2.
23. Ibid.
24. Bonney to Ball, 10 November 1942; A.A., MP 272/1, Bundle 2.
25. A. Ingle-Hall to Bonney, 18 November 1942, A.A., SP 109, Box 57, File 341.08.

27. Melbourne *Argus*, 20 January 1942.
28. P. Hasluck, *The Government and the People 1942-1945*. Canberra: Australian War Memorial, 1970, pp. 404-5.
29. *Conference on Newspaper and Broadcasting Activities in relation to the War Effort held at Canberra, 10 February 1942*. Canberra: Government Printer, 1942, p. 16.
30. Ibid., p. 20.
31. Gibson Committee, Report, paras. 555-56.
32. Bonney to Scullin, 29 September 1942; A.A. SP 195/1, File 71/1/12.
33. Tim Dare, "The War of Words". *Australian*, 7 December 1974.
34. CPD (HR), 8 May 1942, pp. 1062-70. Francis Williams, *Press, Parliament and the People*. London: Heinemann, 1946, pp. 63-67, indicates that Churchill, for a period, pursued a similar policy and prohibited *outward* cables to the United States and the Dominions that were "likely to create a disharmony between ourselves or allied countries".
35. Bonney to Curtin, 20 February 1942, A.A., SP 195/1, File 71/1/10.
36. Ibid.
37. *Commonwealth of Australia Gazette*, No. 93 of 1942, 25 March 1942, p. 746.
38. CPD (HR), 5 March 1942, p. 200.
39. Hasluck, *Government and the People 1942-1945*, p. 407.
40. Ibid.
41. Ibid., p. 408.
42. Bonney to Scullin, 18 March 1942, A.A., SP 195/1, File 71/1/10.
43. T.C. Bray Papers, ANL, MSS 2519.
44. Ibid.
45. Hasluck, *Government and the People 1942-1945*, pp. 407-8.
46. Shedden, Secretary of Defence, File 10/301/85, Hoey Papers.
47. Notes from Censorship Advisory Committee Meeting, 16 June 1942; A.A., SP 195/1, File 72/26/3, emphasis added.
48. Bonney to Scullin, 3 November 1942; A.A., SP 195/1, File 71/1/12.
49. G. Long, *The Six Years War: A Concise History of Australia in the 1939-45 War*. Canberra: Australian War Memorial and Australian Government Publishing Service, 1972, p. 396.
50. Melbourne *Argus*, 13 November 1942.
51. Minutes of Conference called by State Publicity Censor at request of some state managers, held at Mr R. Dooley's office, 2.15 p.m., 6 November 1942, A.A., MP 272/1, Bundles 2-15/2.
52. Bonney to Curtin, 14 March 1943; A.A., CPC/6087, SP 195/1, File 71/1/15.
53. Minutes of conference between Bonney and journalists, 8 April 1942; A.A., CP 815/4, Item 46, from which various quotations have been taken.
54. "Committee of Review [The Pinner Committee], Civil Staffing of War-time Activities, 1945", internal government report on the Department of Information.
55. "Election Broadcasts" circular, 3 August 1943, Hoey Papers, emphasis added.
56. Roger J. Bell, *Unequal Allies: Australian-American Relations and the Pacific War*. Melbourne: Melbourne University Press, 1977, p. 146.

8

Transformation

"Every penny should be squeezed from Treasury for overseas propaganda purposes"

The period from August 1943 to the end of the war saw the Department of Information transformed from an agency concerned with information at home to that of information abroad. Its information policies rested on the government's desire to curb false or misleading impressions of Australia abroad. This laid the foundation for the Department's survival into the post war period.

On 21 August 1943, the Curtin government was given a rousing vote of confidence with a landslide election victory. On 21 September, Curtin appointed Arthur Augustus Calwell as the fifth Minister for Information in the Department's fourth year. Ashley kept the portfolio of Postmaster-General and was given the position of Vice-President of the Executive Council in place of the Information portfolio.

In the past, Calwell had disparaged the Department. In 1940, he saw the Department as an expensive "incubus", wasteful in the extreme.[1] In 1942, he pulled the Department to pieces for its "hate" campaign.[2] When the Department was the subject of the Scullin–Lazzarini Cabinet crisis, Calwell contended that "if ever there was a Department that ought to be abolished, it is that Department [of Information]."[3] His credentials for the portfolio, to say the least, were not founded on his advocacy of it.

By rallying Labor backbenchers against Curtin at caucus meetings, Calwell had been a thorn in the Prime Minister's side.[4] In December 1942 he moved that Labor should oppose Curtin's planned imposition of limited conscription outside Australia, but was defeated by 37 votes to 13.[5] But Calwell was not without influence. He clashed with Evatt, the Attorney-General, over the treatment of members of the Australia First Movement, then interned without a fair hearing:

> There is not a tittle of evidence to justify the incarceration of most of those who have been interned in N.S.W. . . . The holding of people without trial is opposed to everything for which the Labor Party stands and cuts across what every decent citizen believes to be a fundamental principle.[6]

At a time when the Japanese were still very much in the ascendancy, these were defiant words indeed. Calwell found few to support his cause, but the few who did proved influential. A review of the internment system eventually was agreed to and some 7000 of the 7500 citizens interned on the advice of Military Intelligence were freed.[7]

One incisive description of Calwell comes from a foe of his, Brian Penton, editor of the *Daily Telegraph*:

> Irish, irascible, with lots of ambition and lots of ability — especially in hot-headed, mudslinging debate — he was one of the leaders of Labor's isolationist, red-bogey-hunted, book-burning, church-ridden, anti-intellectual, anti-libertarian wing . . . He was always deadly, humourlessly, sincerely — the very archetype of the man with good intentions who hates his rivals and endows them with all the qualities of unmentionable evil because they propose to deprive the people of the benefit of his love and care. He never forgot a slight and never failed to repay one. Personal feelings, not abstract ideologies, were the dynamics of his political action.[8]

Calwell despised press proprietors such as Sir Keith Murdoch:

> When I see the sinister figure of Sir Keith Murdoch flitting

across the scene of Government activities I know that something detrimental to Australia is happening.[9]

He saw Murdoch as an arch-enemy of the working class. To Calwell, Murdoch typified the irresponsible and mendacious features of the anti-Labor press. His misgivings about the Department of Information may have reflected his suspicion that it was Murdoch's tool. Even after Murdoch's departure, Calwell believed, with some justification, that "Murdoch men" remained.

If Calwell hated hard, he also worked hard. He had been a productive backbencher and served with enthusiasm on the influential Joint Parliamentary Committee on Wireless Broadcasting (the Gibson Committee). The Deputy Prime Minister, F.M. Forde, commented:

> He seems very resourceful sometimes to the annoyance of some honourable gentlemen who wish to leave as soon as possible after the motion of adjournment has been moved. I have known him to rise at 1.00 a.m. with a bundle of papers in his arms and become eloquent. He is indefatigable, and he airs his grievances even at the risk of incurring the displeasure of some of his colleagues.[10]

When the abrasive Calwell gained his portfolio, few questioned his qualifications, but many wondered how he had achieved it — and with the one department he loved to hate. Archie Cameron kidded him in Parliament that his first task now should be to publish a pamphlet titled, "Labor Ministries and How to Get into Them".[11] Curtin's disappointment with Calwell's election to the ministry may have played some part. One employee recalls Calwell saying that Curtin was so angry, that he "tossed me the newspaper stand".[12]

The "newspaper stand" was the Department of Information. Significantly, Information now had a Minister it did not share with another department. With the exception of Foll, previous Ministers for Information would have deserted the Department for their other portfolio, if they had to choose between them. Now the Department need not compete with another department for the Minister's time. If the Minister was to make his reputation, he only had one department with which to do it.

A strong Minister is necessary to a department, but not sufficient. A more dynamic executive leadership was required, to match Calwell's ambitions. Edmund Garnett Bonney was appointed as his Director-General of Information on 13 October 1943. Bonney, like Calwell, was an outspoken man. "Ruthless" was the term Lionel Wigmore used. Bonney earned his reputation by a tough and uncompromising style as Chief Publicity Censor. He was suspicious of intellectuals and could attract strong loyalty from his staff. Furthermore, his coarse-grained manner did not handicap his appreciation of the requirements of public administration.[13] R.I. Horne of the Shortwave Division found him pleasant and well disposed to his division.[14] Likewise, Geoffrey Sawer summed up Bonney as a "fantastic administrator", strongly loyal to Calwell. Intrinsically, he seemed very able, with strong personal views. By training, experience and temperament, Bonney could identify himself with the particular ministerial and government outlook required by policy. Sawer, like Horne, recalls working with Bonney quite happily.[15] Someone as individual and forceful as Bonney inevitably invited hostility from some. His administration of Censorship was regarded unfavourably by the press.

> During his tenure of the post of Chief Censor, censorship . . . has earned itself an unenviable reputation of undue severity, not so much in the matter of military security, but in damping down criticism and unpalatable news, and, on occasions, of restricting matter politically opposed to the Government.[16]

Some staff members retained mixed feelings about Bonney's leadership. The following piece of doggerel was recalled by one:

My Bonney lies over the ocean,
  My Bonney lies over the sea,
And sometimes I get the notion,
  Bonney also lies to me.[17]

In his announcement of Bonney's appointment, Curtin

agreed to an expansion in the Department's functions. It would take over the Shortwave Division, formerly under the control of the ABC, and Censorship would become part of its functions once more. Bonney would retain his position as Chief Publicity Censor.[18]

From that day on, Calwell grabbed every piece of administrative action to nurture his new department. Although the Advertising Division remained with Treasury, Calwell proposed that his department be given additional co-ordination responsibilities. On 27 October 1943, Calwell suggested to Curtin that future government policy requiring publicity should be sent in advance to the Department, so that adequate coverage could be assured. On 8 November, Curtin agreed and sent a circular to all Ministers informing them of the new arrangement.[19] The following day, Calwell wrote a note to Curtin proposing "tentative machinery of co-ordination" to supplement the general promotion of forthcoming food and coal conservation campaigns. To avoid "ill-timed or injudicious" public statements that might divert attention from the central campaigns, Calwell suggested that his department should co-ordinate responsibility for these campaigns. He emphasized that he did not want to control the publicity "but merely to secure from the Ministers the best available news that will support the campaign, and to time its release so that the campaign will reap the maximum possible advantage". On 16 November, Curtin agreed and informed the other Ministers accordingly.[20]

Whereas, formally, Censorship once again came under the auspices of Information, the new arrangements actually meant that Information now came under the control of Censorship. Bonney now was both Chief Publicity Censor and Director-General of Information. Similarly, each State Publicity Censor became simultaneously Deputy and ex-officio Director of Information. As many censors were former journalists, the reorganization produced little friction, with the outstanding exception of the transfer of the Shortwave Division to Information.

Originally, Calwell had not intended the Shortwave

Division to form part of his portfolio. On 8 October 1943, he wrote to Curtin:

> After consideration, I recommend that the work of the Department of Information and of Publicity Censorship should be brought under one control in the interests of efficiency and economy, and that Mr C.E. [sic] Bonney should be appointed Director [sic] of the Department . . . [21]

It was in this form that Curtin gave his original approval.

Bonney had other ideas about the Shortwave Division. On 12 October, in a personal note to Hoey, the Victorian Publicity Censor, he expressed his concern about shortwave broadcasting presenting false impressions of Australia:

> . . . I will probably have more to say about the ABC s.w. in the near future when we will look at it closely to see how it is serving Australia . . . I would like you to scrutinise daily all s.w. material leaving this country and if you feel the job is being done badly then we can have a further talk . . . [22]

The following day, Curtin wrote to Calwell, approving both the transfer of Publicity Censorship and Bonney's appointment as "Director-General". An unexpected change found its way into Curtin's statement to the press:

> The Minister for Information [Calwell] has recommended to me that the amalgamation of the Department of Information, the Office of Publicity Censorship *and the Office of Shortwave Broadcasting to persons in enemy occupied territories* should take place immediately . . . [23]

Neither Curtin nor Calwell could explain the source of the addition. Curtin knew nothing of it until the statement was given to him for release.[24] The press was puzzled as to what was meant by "shortwave broadcasting to enemy occupied territories". Taken literally, it would have resulted in a bizarre arrangment: the Shortwave Division would need to be split in two. As only about a quarter of the transmissions now constituted such political warfare,[25] most shortwave broadcasting would remain the responsibility of the ABC. Broadcasts to enemy occupied territories were the policy responsibility of External

Affairs. If a genuine gap in policy responsibility loomed, it was with shortwave broadcasts to *non-enemy-occupied* territories.

Calwell glossed over this difficulty, to inform journalists that Curtin meant he was to run the entire shortwave service operated by the ABC. Ball, as controller of the Division, protested that neither the ABC nor External Affairs had been consulted about the change. It was, he said, "simply disastrous", and he succeeded in having Curtin call a meeting before the transfer took place.[26]

The issue of the shortwave broadcasting transfer festered and threatened to undo Calwell's empire. As he respected Ball's views, Curtin favoured shortwave broadcasting remaining with the ABC.[27] At the meeting with Ball, Curtin conceded that the announcement was a mistake. None the less, he thought the issue warranted further examination and referred it to a subcommittee comprising Calwell, Evatt and Ashley, to determine where Shortwave Division should go.[28]

Ball argued that his division should remain with the ABC. He stressed the value of sharing facilities with the ABC and warned of the decline in staff morale that the move would entail.[29] McCauley, the Assistant Secretary of the Department's Canberra Secretariat, briefed Calwell on the value of shortwave broadcasting coming under the Department's control. He rammed home the need to have journalists in charge of the Division.

> Although they have different purposes to serve the basis of all transmissions, whether Allied or to enemy occupied countries is news, and their treatment should obviously be under the direct control of men trained in the handling and presentation of news . . . [Although External Affairs may frame policy] . . . their application to treatment of the news is obviously a job for trained journalists . . . The only Government organization designed to put together all phases of this story is the Department of Information . . .

The need to co-ordinate overseas information policies also was raised:

> It seems farcical that, while we have the responsibility of backgrounding and directing the publicity policy of the [News

and Information] Bureau, we have no control over the selection or the angling of the spot news that our New York representatives have to distribute to and background for the American press . . . Finally [because the ABC is subject only to remote ministerial control, the Division does not have the daily contact that Information had], s.w. broadcasting is purely a propaganda and information service which obviously should be under the control of the Minister for Information, so that its activities can be co-ordinated with the general propaganda machinery of the Government.[30]

On 24 November 1943, the subcommittee presented its report to Curtin. It recommended that External Affairs be responsible for the policy of overseas transmissions, and that Information be responsible for the administration of shortwave broadcasting, and technical services supplied by the PMG, though the ABC would look after shortwave broadcasts within Australia.[31] Two days later, Curtin approved the report.[32]

Ball threatened to resign rather than work under Bonney. Calwell, anxious not to lose a valued officer and to avoid political embarrassment, persuaded Ball to remain pending further discussions with Curtin and Evatt.[33] Encouraged by this conciliatory move, Ball sought support from the ABC. On 3 December, he wrote to Boyer:

> Will the Commission just take it or will it fight back? . . . I personally feel very bitterly about all this . . . I hope very much your own moral indignation will be thoroughly aroused and that you will do everything you can, not as a personal favour to me, but simply in the interests of decency and public life, to get this decision restored . . . I do feel, quite bluntly, that in the main the fight has been left to me, and that I have been fighting almost single-handed what is in fact the Commission's battle, and what the Commission with a proper sense of its own responsibility would recognise to be its own battle and wouldn't leave the fighting to me . . .[34]

The ABC declined to fight. It went no further than to declare to the government that it considered:

> that in the interests of broadcasting it is inadvisable that a separate broadcasting department should be set up; and that the Chairman should confer with the Minister for Information the Hon. A.A. Calwell.[35]

Meanwhile, relations between Bonney and Ball deteriorated. Ball angered Bonney by warning him to stay clear of the Shortwave Division until a decision had been made. On 10 December, Bonney wrote to Ball:

> I do not intend to waste any further time writing to you. Your earlier letter was arrogant; the most recent one was impudent and hysterical . . . I will turn over to the Minister the whole of the correspondence that has passed between us, and tell him (preferably in your presence) what I think of your childish behaviour ever since it was announced that your division was to come under my administration.[36]

On 17 January 1944, Ball reminded Calwell of the need to clarify his division's status.[37] On 21 January, Bonney also pressed for clarification. Bonney's command of the struggle is illustrated in his advice to Calwell:

> Mr Ball apparently does not realise that it is not *proposed*, but it had been *decided* to transfer the administration of s.w. to your Department. I regard seriously his statement that such a transfer would only have a very bad effect on the morale and efficiency. This would only be the case if somebody had been moving round among the staff encouraging hostility against the Government's move . . . How nonsensical and heroic he is when he talks about the need for determining the future of s.w. in the interests of the country, instead of the plaything of personal ambitions. To whose ambitions does he refer — yours? He certainly cannot refer to me, because as you know, I have plenty of headaches without wishing to take over s.w. but if the Government instructs me to take it over, and instructs Mr. Ball to work under my direction, then we will be weaklings, if we let him carry on his antagonistic campaign one minute longer.[38]

It is a tribute to Ball's persistence that his position remained under discussion for a further two months. However, on 22 March 1944, Curtin announced that Shortwave Division would come under the control of Information: policy would come from External Affairs, technical services from the PMG and local transmissions from the ABC.[39] The transfer took place on 1 April.[40] Ball resigned. Four months later, he was back on the air in charge of a weekly ABC program "The Nation's Forum of the Air". It proved a fine vehicle for his ideas about broadcasting. In his foreword to the published transcript of the first program, Ball wrote:

> Most living issues are controversial and the Commission recognizes that if these sessions are to be pungent and real, they must be conducted in an atmosphere of frankness and freedom. No restrictions of any kind are imposed upon the speakers except those elementary restrictions necessary in wartime in the interests of security.[41]

With the transfer of the Shortwave Division to Information, Bonney assigned Lionel Wigmore to review its operations.[42] On 14 April, Wigmore reported on all aspects of the shortwave operations, including monitoring, news, special services, the Listening Post, and staff and their duties.

The staffing distribution had reflected Ball's priorities. Of 66 full-time staff and 15 part-time staff, 27 full-time and 6 part-time members were involved with Listening Post duties, 16 with the news room, 2 with political warfare, one with the US and UK armed forces services, one with French; there were 12 full-time and 2 part-time announcers/translators and one record librarian; the remaining 6 full-time and 2 part-time staff carried out general administrative work. Wigmore argued the need to make the Division a stronger part of the overseas publicity policy. After surveying a sample of news bulletins, he commented on the need for more references to Australia:

> As they are now written they contain references to Australia's part in the war only in so far as it fits naturally into the overall picture, but they might be made to carry some additional Australian news over and above this, as a means of pushing the Australian viewpoint.

Likewise, Wigmore suggested that Listening Post reports should be edited and prepared for the press as counter-propaganda material. Overseas broadcasts should be extended and the number of favourable references to Australia increased. To assist in allocating resources, he suggested that future funding shall fall within three programming categories: Australian national publicity, political warfare and general purposes. In practice, the Political Warfare programs continued to decline relative to other categories.

Wigmore was not asked to report on the morale of the organization, but it is safe to conclude that Ball's departure did affect morale. The identification of many of the staff with Ball, particularly those from the Listening Post, inevitably meant some turnover in staff. Helen Ferber was among those who felt unable to continue under the new regime. As she recalls, "I left shortwave in 1944 because Ball wasn't standing in between us and them."[43] Ball's position was never filled. The Division carried on to the end of the war without a Controller. As one person put it, "it had a lot of heads, but no single brain."[44]

The lack of a leader was aggravated by a continuing lack of official guidance on broadcasts. Despite the decision that External Affairs would provide such guidance, the broadcasting policy tended towards Australian national publicity as thought fit by Information. While the war continued, this posed no serious problem, since there were few distinctly Australian policies to advocate or defend, beyond solidarity with the allies and national publicity.

The consequences of this neglect were felt after the Japanese collapse in August 1945. From then on, unity among the allies rapidly disappeared. Australia had to develop its own policy on some matters and on others had to make a choice among the competing policies of other allies. The Department of External Affairs found itself illequipped to guide the policy of the Shortwave Division in the wider fields that opened up. Serious problems in news presentation also developed. During the war, news sources were controlled and censored by the various allied governments, so that major conflicts in news reporting did not occur, but after the Japanese collapse, news sources suddenly became diversified, expressing the divergent policies of different correspondents. The impossibility of "objective" news-reporting was demonstrated throughout this period by the wild contradictions and denials of previous reports that appeared in the newspapers and in such radio news services as those of England, the United States and Australia. Policy problems in relation to commentaries were similar. The experience of the period following the war was that policy control was necessary and that this was to become not less but more difficult.[45]

This difficulty was well exemplified in November 1945. In a series of commentaries on the fate of Indonesia, Geoffrey Sawer gave temperate support to the Indonesian Nationalists. He knew that both Calwell and Evatt distrusted the Dutch, and Sawer reflected some of this feeling in his commentary.[46] However, because he was not given explicit advice from External Affairs, his commentary caused official embarrassment and made front page news on 16 November. The broadcasts were repudiated by Prime Minister Chifley. Sawer's commentaries had accused "all the great powers" of hypocrisy and he had named Britain and the United States in connection with the Indonesian negotiations. A cartoon depicted Chifley demanding of a puzzled Calwell, "By the way, Arthur, what *is* our policy on Indonesia?"[47]

The funding issue also remained unresolved. In August 1945, an interdepartmental committee convened by the Department of Information, with representation from External Affairs, Postwar Reconstruction and the PMG, recommended that the cost of shortwave broadcasting be distributed between the PMG's Department, External Affairs and the Department of Information.[48] This did not prevent the 1946–47 budget for the Division's new transmitters being buried in the estimates of the Department of the Army's provision for buildings, fittings, etc., a total of £1,817,000.[49]

The transfer proved to be a much-needed stimulus for the Department. By September 1945, the shortwave staff had grown to a total of 95, including 22 journalists and 36 monitors, translators and checkers.[50] Bonney transferred many of his censors to shortwave broadcasting functions. By the close of the war, Tom Hoey, the Victorian State Censor, had become the Department's formal Controller.

Under Calwell and Bonney, the Department's information policy was overseas-oriented. This was not new. A similar policy had been pursued by Foll in 1941. However, the foundations for this policy were new. It emerged from Australia's new strategic and economic position. With the disappearance of the Japanese threat in late 1943, the status of the invaded Asian island territories and former colonies began to attract Australia's interest. The United States government was as conscious as the Labor government of the political implications of the Japanese defeats. The final battle campaigns in the Pacific tended to become wholly American in concept and practice. Australia, with New Zealand, found itself allotted minor roles in the Allied counter-offensives.[51] Australia needed to publicize its contributions to the war effort, if it were to claim an influential position in the post-war negotiations. A discouraging post-war slump also enhanced the need to promote Australia as a country worth trading with, worth visiting and worth settling in. The nature of Information's future contribution lay in increasing its overseas publicity services.

On 1 March 1944, Calwell announced an increased budget for the London office of the Department. The New York Bureau would expand its role with the establishment of a library devoted to Australian information. The Canberra Secretariat became central to consolidating the overseas information role. A special publicity unit was established in New Guinea, to stimulate publicity about the Australian war effort. Calwell foreshadowed a series of features, newsreels and brochures about key battles, to be produced in conjunction with the Army. *Home News*, a broadsheet for Australians in the Services, was published to inform on domestic developments.[52] Calwell hoped to open offices on the West Coast of America, and in Moscow and Chungking.[53] Overseas information expanded, spurred by the development of a distinctive Australian foreign policy rather than, as in the past, by a reaction to hostile press reception of the Department's local news role.[54]

Former Minister for Information, Senator Foll,

endorsed this in the Senate on 21 March 1944, when he moved for the early appointment of a Joint Parliamentary Committee to expand Australia publicity overseas. His motion was designed to assist the Department of Information. Conscious of the superior public relations facilities of the Americans, which swamped the Australian efforts, Foll urged the continuation of the Department's activities after the war. Expenditure on overseas publicity was insufficient. David Bailey and the Australian News and Information Bureau in New York had done fine work, but more needed to be done. Representatives were needed for the West Coast, the American Mid-West and the South American republics. Too much stress was placed on hand-outs and too little on reading-rooms and public libraries.[55] Senator Armstrong, among others, supported Foll's points: "every penny should be squeezed from Treasury for overseas propaganda purposes".[56] Foll withdrew his motion for the appointment of a committee, on being assured that more money would be spent.

For the first time in its five years, a consensus had emerged about what the Department *should* be doing. Senator Leckie, for example, was critical of the Department's expenditure on glossy promotion material, but was willing to revise his view if the expenditure was used for publicity *outside* Australia.[57] The press criticism of the Department shifted from attacking its amateurish local work, to despair that not enough was being done to let people *overseas* know of Australia's efforts.[58]

On his return from the United States in early 1945, opposition spokesman Percy Spender complained that Australian news there was still inadequate. A drastic overhaul was needed, to ensure that the ill-equipped and insufficiently financed Information offices were improved. He supported the need for an Information Bureau for the West Coast of America. Bonney responded that matters such as financing and equipment were for Spender to consider, as a member of Parliament, when the Department's estimates were due for discussion.[59]

"Why do you send all your publicity and propaganda to

America?" enquired Major H.L. Hall, secretary and director of William Heinemann Ltd, the London publishers, to a gathering of Australian booksellers. "Why not send some to England, because practically nothing is known there about you out there."[60] "The Government is proceeding too slowly," complained Senator Armstrong. "The war will be over soon in Europe."[61]

During 1944 and 1945, the Department appointed press attaches to Australian diplomatic posts in Ottawa, Delhi, Paris, San Francisco and Rio de Janiero. The Editorial Division became the central source for information material for the attaches. The government decided the Department of Information should undertake an extensive publicity campaign to attract post-war migrants.[62] Apart from the occasional pamphlet and some campaign work, the Department now had abandoned its local publicity output.[63] Its overseas output proved vast. In the six months beginning 1944, it produced the following:

Publication:	Print run
Know Australia	70,000
40 Facts about Australia's War Time Industry	20,000
30 Facts about Australia's Dairying Industry	30,000
40 Facts about Australia's War Time Agriculture	40,000
30 Facts about Health & Social Services	100,000
30 Facts about Repatriation	200,000
40 Facts about Australian manpower	300,000
South West Pacific	3,000
For This We Fight	250,000

In the year 1944, the New York Bureau dealt with 33,105 enquiries, distributed 25,000 photographs, arranged 115 lectures, 43 pictorial exhibits and press conferences, and distributed 38 films on sale or loan. In all, some 4 million copies of various publications were sold or distributed by the Department that year.[65]

Though difficult to assess the effectiveness of such efforts, the space commanded in the British press exceeded space devoted to other Dominions. In New York, the demand for the Department's monthly bulletin, *Australia*, averaged 12,000 copies per issue. Of the 2,270 photos of Australian troops released in a three-month period, over a third were published in American journals and dailies.⁶⁶ To stimulate the flow of news overseas, the government reduced the transmission rates for press cables.⁶⁷

In conjunction with these developments, Calwell saw that his Department took on more and more responsibilities suited to the post-war situation. In January 1944, Cabinet agreed to the establishment of an interdepartmental committee to co-ordinate government publicity. It is a testimony to the revived stocks of the Department that by January 1945 this committee recommended: "To avoid wasteful duplication, the Committee recommends that all new Government publications intended for public distribution or sale should be published in consultation with the Department of Information." Although this recommendation did not cover parliamentary papers or publications by the Armed Forces, it indicated an acceptance of the Department's work and potential from other sections of the bureaucracy.⁶⁸

In May 1945, following a round of conferences with Commonwealth and state agencies sponsoring documentary and education films, Cabinet approved the establishment of a National Film Board, chaired by the Minister for Information. The Board's duties were to expand, promote, assist and co-ordinate the production and distribution and importation of films for school and adult education, rehabilitation, social development, international understanding, trade, tourist and immigration purposes.⁶⁹

The Department now was geared on a post-war footing, though it had little official assurance of its continuation. Calwell energetically pressed his department's continuation. In February 1945, he declared:

> The work of the Department of Information was so important to the future well-being of Australia that the organization would not go out of existence when peace came . . . Much work remained . . . in telling the world about Australia's trade and tourist possibilities, and also in the campaign for migrants. This was a type of publicity which could not be carried out by any other Department.⁷⁰

The Department's fate still was not resolved by

mid-1945. Its dissolution seemed possible on 13 July, when Chifley, the new Prime Minister, gave Calwell the new portfolio of Immigration. It would have been a relatively simple matter to transfer many of Information's functions to the Immigration Department.

On 2 June, the government had appointed the Committee of Review into Civil Staffing Wartime Activities. Termed the Pinner Committee, after its chairman, the Acting Assistant Commissioner of the Public Service Board, it also included A.A. Fitzgerald, Director of War Organization of Industry in the Department of Postwar Reconstruction. Along with the head of each department, the Committee was required to review civil staffing of wartime agencies and advise which functions should remain. Departments were asked for information on possible staff economies that could be made as a result of the winding-down of war activity.

The Department and its complements of censorship staff were obvious targets. As it transpired, the Committee did not have the resources to independently assess the information supplied by departments and did not appraise the efficiency of the Department's staff or activities. It was content to adopt the information submitted by departments to form the backbone of its report.[71]

On 14 August, Bonney briefed Calwell of the approach he would take to minimize any possible dislocation due to the Committee's review:

> Although the Department of Information was set up primarily as a war-time organization to publicise the war effort both at home and abroad, to exercise war-time censorship, and to galvanise public support behind the war, it had during its six years of operation, had to extend its activities into the broad Australian publicity field, particularly overseas. As a result, when its purely war activities are stripped from it, there will remain an effective experienced and well-balanced publicity organization that can be adapted for the publicity approach that Australia will now have to make to the outside world, commensurate with the new international status that the country has achieved and the requirements of post-war trade and other international relationships . . .[72]

The Committee recommended that the Publicity Censorship and the Inter-Allied Relations Divisions be disbanded. The Editorial Division was to be reduced. However, the Shortwave Division was expected to continue and the Film and Stills photographic staff might even be increased in the future.[73]

Although there was an exhortation that the Department should be "progressively and substantially reduced", its overall size remained at the level of some 300 staff, its complement of 1944.[74] Bonney reassigned many of his censors to publicity duties. By the time of the Pinner Review, he already had disbanded his censorship apparatus. The Inter-Allied Relations Division never had comprised more than three officers at any time. By September 1945, the Department had 344 employees: 72 journalists, 61 typists, 36 monitors, translators and checkers, 28 messengers, 20 photographers and 125 others; 304 were stationed in Australia and 40 overseas.[75]

A firm assurance of the Department's continuation was not given until July 1946, when Chifley announced that as a matter of policy it had been decided that the Department of Information would continue.[76] Its work, said Chifley, was that of "high national importance" and its overseas publicity effort was costing considerably less per head of population than similar "progressive" countries.

In 1948, Bonney retired from his post of Director-General of Information to become Director-General of the Australian News and Information Bureau in New York. With the fall of the Chifley government in December 1949, H.E. Beale was appointed the Minister for Information and Minister for the Interior. In March 1950, the Department was abolished by Menzies, as it had been created: by an Executive Council Minute, No. 29.

Notes

1. *CPD* (HR), 12-13 December 1940, p. 1071.
2. Ibid., 27 March 1942, p. 560.
3. Ibid., 3-4 June 1942, p. 2127.

4. Don Whitington, *Ring the Bells: A Dictionary of Federal Politics*. Melbourne: Georgian House, 1956, pp. 26-27.
5. John Robertson, *J.H. Scullin: A Political Biography*. Nedlands: WA: University of Western Australia Press, 1974, p. 466.
6. *CPD* (HR), 3-4 June 1942, p. 2148.
7. Bruce Muirden, *The Puzzled Patriots: The Story of the Australia First Movement*. Melbourne: Melbourne University Press, 1968, p. 96.
8. Brian Penton, *Censored*! Sydney: Shakespeare Head Press, 1947, p. 58.
9. *CPD* (HR), 19 March 1941, p. 129.
10. Ibid., 29 April 1942, p. 638.
11. *CPD* (HR), 28 September 1943, p. 98.
12. Author's interview with T. Hoey, 16 February 1976. In his memoirs, Calwell provides few clues. On his account, he made "peace" with Curtin before the election and was informed he might be elected to the next Ministry. See A.A. Calwell, *Be Just and Fear Not*, Hawthorn, Vic.: O'Neill, 1972, p. 56.
13. Author's interview with L. Wigmore, 12 April 1976.
14. Author's interview with R.I. Horne, 18 February 1976.
15. Author's interview with L.G. Sawer, 20 April 1976.
16. *Sydney Morning Herald*, 14 October 1943.
17. The verse was supplied to the author on the condition that its source was not identified. Proof of the informant is recorded on cassette.
18. Calwell to Curtin, 8 October 1943; Curtin to Calwell, 13 October 1943; A.A., CRS A461, Item BP 6/1/1, Pt. 2.
19. A.A., CRS A461, Item B 301/1/2, Pt. 3.
20. Ibid., Pt. 4.
21. Ibid., CRS A461, Item BP 6/1/1, Pt. 2.
22. Hoey Papers.
23. Curtin to Calwell, 13 October 1943; A.A., CRS A461, Item BP 6/1/1, Pt. 2, emphasis added.
24. Ball to Calwell, 17 January 1944, Ball Papers.
25. John De La Valette to Ball, 29 July 1943; A.A., MP 272.
26. F.A. McLaughlin file minute, 13 October 1943; A.A., CRS A461, Item BP 6/1/1, Pt. 2.
27. Ibid., 15 October 1943; A.A., CRS A461, Item BP 6/1/1, Pt. 2.
28. 15 October 1943, Ball Papers.
29. Ball submission to ministerial subcommittee, 25 October 1943; A.A., CRS A461, Item BP 6/1/1, Pt. 2.
30. McCauley to Calwell, 25 October 1943; A.A., SP 109/6, Bundle 5.
31. Subcommittee report to Curtin, 24 November 1943; A.A., CRS A461, Item BP 6/1/1, Pt. 2.
32. Ibid.
33. "Shortwave Do I Diary", Ball Papers.
34. Ball to Boyer, 3 December 1943, Ball Papers.
35. "Background Notes for ABC Witness to Joint Committee of Public Accounts, 110th Report, 1968", 10-12 January 1944.
36. Bonney to Ball, 10 December 1943, Ball Papers.
37. Ball to Calwell, 17 January 1944, Ball Papers.
38. Bonney to Calwell, 21 January 1944, A.A., SP 109, Box 76.
39. *CPD* (HR), 22 March 1944, p. 1753.
40. "Background Notes for ABC Witness to Joint Parliamentary Committee on Public Accounts 110th Report, 1968".

41. Ball foreword to *The Nation's Forum of the Air* (broadcast on the ABC national network, 2 August 1944, vol 1, no. 1 "Freedom or Control in Industry"; A.A., SP 109, Box 47, File 318.71.
42. The reports are in Wigmore Papers.
43. Author's interview with H. Ferber, 16 February 1976.
44. Author's interview with T. Hoey, 16 February 1976.
45. "History of Overseas Shortwave Broadcasting in Australia", Draft Report, ?1946 (unpublished ms., in Hoey Papers, author unknown, ?Tom Hoey), pp. 9-10.
46. Author's interview with G. Sawer, 20 April 1976.
47. Melbourne *Argus*, 16 November 1945. Sawer's script of 5 November read: "Australia cannot be blind to the fact that 40 million Indonesians in our near North may well, in the long run, be more important to our security, not to mention our trade and commerce, than a few thousand Dutch who have hitherto controlled that area, and whose control is now disputed . . . There is a certain element of hypocrisy in the policy towards Indonesia which has hitherto been followed by all the Great Powers. The USA has attempted like Pontius Pilate to wash its hands of the matter . . ."
48. "Committee of Review [The Pinner Committee], Civil Staffing of War-time Activities, 1945", internal government report on the Department of Information, p. 5.
49. *CPD* (Senate), 5 December 1946, pp. 1061-62.
50. Pinner Committee "Report", p. 3.
51. T.R. Reese, *Australia, New Zealand and the United States of America: A Survey of International Relations*. London: Oxford University Press, 1969, p. 24.
52. *CPD* (HR), 1 March 1944, pp. 717-18.
53. Ibid., 7 March 1944, pp. 1059-62.
54. F. Alexander, *From Curtin to Menzies and After: Continuity or Confrontation?*. Melbourne: Nelson, 1973, pp. 12-13.
55. *CPD* (Senate), 29 March 1944, pp. 2122-27.
56. Ibid., p. 2133.
57. Ibid., 2 March 1945, p. 267.
58. *CPD* (HR), 15 March 1944, p. 1324.
59. Melbourne *Argus*, 15 and 16 February 1945.
60. Ibid., 5 April 1945.
61. *CPD* (Senate), 20 September 1944, p. 1047.
62. Pinner Committee "Report", p. 2.
63. *CPD* (HR), 15 March 1944, p. 1324.
64. Ibid., 19 July 1944, p. 251.
65. A.A. Calwell, "Telling Australia's Story to the World", *Labor Digest* 1, no. 6 (August 1945): pp. 29-33.
66. *CPD* (HR), 15 March 1944, pp. 1321-24.
67. Reese, *Australia, New Zealand and the United States of America*, p. 28.
68. "Notes on Interdepartmental Conference convened by Advisory Government Publicity Committee at Canberra, January 11, 1945" (mimeographed internal government report), p. 4.
69. *CPD* (HR), 1 May 1945, p. 1252.
70. Melbourne *Argus*, 9 February 1945.
71. G.E. Caiden, *Career Service: An Introduction to the History of Personnel Administration in the Commonwealth Public Service 1901-1961*. Melbourne: Melbourne University Press, 1965, pp. 289-90.

72. Bonney to Calwell, 14 August 1945; A.A., CP 815/4, Item 51.
73. Pinner Committee "Report".
74. See *CPD* (HR), 30 June–1 July 1949, p. 1903, for manpower statistics.
75. Pinner Committee "Report".
76. *CPD* (HR), 3-4 June 1946, p. 2169.

9

The Censorship Row of April 1944

"No paper can be permitted to adopt a law-breaking policy"

If there is anything for which the Department of Information is remembered, it is the incident that culminated in the suppression of the major Australian newspapers in April 1944. Apart from a brief account by the official historian, and Brian Penton's rushed though lively book, little has been written of the incident. Penton's account, though illuminating, is misleading and contains numerous errors.[1] Among other lapses, he gives the impression that a High Court injunction disposed of the matter and he also mistakenly read the numbering system of censorship instructions for the actual frequency of the instructions. Calwell, in his memoirs, not only adds little to what is known, but he confuses the incident with a later one concerning the suppression of news about the Cowra Japanese POW breakout.[2] His biographer, Colm Kiernan,[3] also confuses the issue further by mistaking an earlier High Court interlocutory injunction with a High Court decision, concluding, in effect, that Calwell and Censorship had lost the case, when, in fact, a compromise was reached, with shared costs.

As there is considerable significance in the incident, it is surprising there has been no attempt to independently review it. It can be examined from many perspectives —

legal, constitutional, personal, social and moral. The present account treats the incident as exemplary, albeit unusual, of the consequences of using censorship to support the Department's policy of fostering favourable impressions of Australia abroad.

The incident probably had its origins in the replacement of Curtin as Censorship Minister by Calwell, the most junior Minister in the government. The newspapers had tolerated the problems of the Censorship Advisory Committee, because Curtin lent it prestige acting as its chairman. It was the last straw to have the Minister most critical of the press chairing the Advisory Committee.

Curtin advised Calwell that the Chief Censor always should be supported by the Minister. In particular, he warned Calwell never to let himself be placed in the position of being an appeals authority for aggrieved press proprietors.[4] It is unlikely, in any case, that Calwell would have sought this role.

The newspaper editors attempted to persuade the new Minister to take a more liberal attitude to censorship. Unfortunately, at the same time, the *Daily Telegraph*, in defiance of Censorship instructions, published comments on the coal strikes.[5] In response, Calwell authorized Bonney to place the paper under the first order-to-submit issued since 1940. The order, which was sent to the editor, Brian Penton, on 30 November 1943, was accompanied by a note from Bonney:

> The deliberate flouting by your paper of a censorship instruction last night has left us with no alternative but to serve upon your paper a total order-to-submit . . . During my term of Office as Chief Censor your paper has been one of the most consistent offenders against Censorship. Our files show that many warnings have been administered following repeated bad breaches. Obviously no paper can be permitted to adopt a law-breaking policy . . .[6]

The order-to-submit operated from 30 November 1943 to 1 February 1944. Penton wanted to challenge the legality of the order, but eventually the matter was settled out of court.[7]

The incident did not endear the newspaper proprietors to the Censorship Advisory Committee chaired by Calwell. On 31 January 1944, Sir Keith Murdoch, Warwick Fairfax and Eric Kennedy wrote to Calwell of their intention to withdraw from the Committee, challenging him to justify the Committee's value, given the differences between the government's determination to censor and the press hostility to such censorship. Calwell replied on 7 February, that their boycotting of the Committee implied that "any form of censorship, no matter how important to the safety of the nation is to be regarded by them as galling and oppressive and unwarranted interference in their money-making activities." This inflamed the proprietors and effectively ended the Censorship Advisory Committee.[8]

Henceforth, Censorship was subject to openly provocative jibes from the press. Newspapers argued they were patriotic enough to practise self-censorship.[9] Calwell dismissed such an idea as "impudent". Penton's editorials continued to prick at Calwell. That of 17 December 1943 was typical: "We challenge Mr Calwell to take the Editor of this paper into court and to prosecute him for any breach of censorship he thinks we have committed." Calwell attacked such criticism as being "insincere and unpatriotic".[10]

Calwell was no stranger to clashes with Penton. In 1942, he asked Curtin to prevent Penton from going on a lecture tour in America. He criticized Penton's articles and books, and accused him of having housed a noted Nazi propagandist, Kurt von Stutterheim, before he was interned.[11] Penton was no innocent bystander either. His booklet *Think or Be Damned* displayed his penchant for conflicts. Its preface read:

> You will find this homily ill-mannered, unpatriotic, subversive and destructive. It is intended to be. It is written in a mood somewhere between horror, fear, anger and irrational faith in the future of this continent.[12]

As editor, Penton was not above distorting the news. His paper frequently was accused of cabling misleading impressions of Australia to readers abroad. Locally, the

AJA Ethics Committee recommended Penton's expulsion for distorting Eddie Ward's press statements. On 16 December 1942, the *Daily Telegraph* quoted Ward, as Minister for Labour and National Service, as saying: "There is neither need nor justification for the people to pay in sweat, blood and tears while the war lasts." Ward had actually said:

> "There is neither need nor justification for the people to pay in sweat, blood and tears while the war lasts, and when peace comes, to be burdened with interest payments condemning them to perpetual misery, poverty and degradation."

The deletion was deliberate and made by Penton personally,[13] according to the Ethics Committee.

The flash-point was to come from far afield, however. In October 1943, the government decided to bring back some Australian troops from the frontline to carry out work in Australia, assisting with the production of food and materials needed for the war and with some post-war preparation. On 8 April 1944, the Minister for the Army, Frank Forde, announced that there would be a reduction in the strength of the Australian Military Forces of 90,000 men in the next twelve months. Reports were cabled by correspondents to the United States, where Forde's announcement was criticized by three US Senators. They pounced on the reduction in strength of any army at war as "shocking" and "unbelievable". This was precisely the kind of incident that Bonney feared. The statement had been blown up — a false impression had been made abroad.

On 11 April, Forde explained that his statement did not indicate any change in the Army policy decided the previous October, and that the only special releases agreed to had been for 20,000 men for essential industry. The total of 90,000 men was made up by including normal wastage and discharges for other causes. In reply, the papers wondered why Calwell's department had not made this clear. On Thursday, 13 April, Calwell attacked the Sydney papers for suggesting that his department had misled the American people about Forde's original statement.[14] The chairman of the Australian Newspaper Proprietors' Association, and general manager of the *Sydney Morning Herald*, R.A.G. Henderson replied to the criticism.[15] On Friday, Calwell retorted by charging Henderson with inaccuracy and untruthfulness.[16] Calwell was in his element, and the punches were flying. Then the press hit below the belt.

In a further reply, Hendeson quoted examples of "political censorship". His action cut across paragraphs 11(e) and (f) of the Press and Broadcasting Censorship Order issued under the National Security (General) Regulations:

> A person shall not print or publish in Australia . . .
> (e) any matter in such a way as to show that any alteration, addition or omission, has been made by or under the direction of a publicity censor;
> (f) any statement to the effect that publication of any matter has been forbidden by the publicity censor.

Henderson's statement was submitted to Censorship in Sydney on Friday night, 14 April. The Censor deleted his references to the specific acts of censorship. Frank Packer contacted Henderson and encouraged him to leave blank spaces in the *Sydney Morning Herald*, to challenge the Censor. Henderson declined. Instead, he refused to publish Calwell's rejoinder. However, the *Daily Telegraph* decided to carry out the challenge. Assured by legal counsel that the Censor had gone too far, Penton published the 15 April issue of the *Daily Telegraph* with blank spaces in its report of Henderson's statement, implying censorship deletions.[17]

H.H. Mansell, the NSW State Publicity Censor, then served an order-to-submit on Consolidated Press Ltd, the owners of the *Daily Telegraph* and *Sunday Telegraph*, so that all matter intended for publication had to be cleared by the Censor. The *Sunday Telegraph* submitted all its proofs to the censor but flouted Censorship by leaving blank spaces in its issue of Sunday, 16 April. In compliance with the directions, the editor of the *Sunday Telegraph* made deletions to the editorial concerning the Calwell-Henderson controversy and omitted the whole of the editorial, but left blank spaces in the first two columns on the front page and a blank column on page three. In the two columns of space on the front page were photos of Henderson and Calwell, and a box containing the following words in large type:

> A Free Press—?
> The Great American democrat Thomas Jefferson said,
> "Where the press is free and every man able to read, all is safe."

As soon as the first edition appeared on the streets, Mansell warned the *Sunday Telegraph* that, unless the blank spaces were filled with type, he would take action to prevent further distribution of the paper. This warning was ignored, and at 11.20 p.m., the Commonwealth Peace Officers, on instruction from Mansell, went to the newspaper offices and prevented further distribution. There was no violence.[18]

The next morning, approximately 300,000 readers of the *Sunday Telegraph* had to do without their paper.[19] By prior agreement, the rival Sunday papers did not increase their print-runs to take advantage of the shortfall. An attempt was made to explain the reasons for the suppression by Sydney's commercial radio stations. A paragraph of the announcement was censored.[20]

On the afternoon of the 16 April, at 2.30 p.m., the managers of the *Daily Telegraph* and *Sunday Telegraph*, and *Sydney Morning Herald*, Associated Newspapers, the *Sun*, *Truth* and *Sportsman*, and the *Daily Mirror* met with Henderson. Armed with legal advice that the Censor had gone too far, Henderson and Fairfax agreed that the issue should be fought collectively. Ezra Norton of the *Daily Mirror* and the *Truth* was inclined to demur at first about breaking the law, but was persuaded that they were only "testing" it and agreed to join them. The conference concluded with Penton preparing a common statement for publication in each of the represented newspapers.[21]

Bonney became aware of the rebellion around 2 a.m. Monday morning, 17 April, and received Calwell's concurrence to suppress the publications.[22] Commonwealth

Peace Officers prevented the bulk of the morning papers from being distributed. One officer was photographed brandishing a pistol.

The incident provided high melodrama for the afternoon press, the *Sun* and *Daily Mirror* and the Adelaide press, though outside Sydney the barricades were manned less vigorously. The Melbourne *Herald* maintained hourly contact with Tom Hoey, the Victorian Censor, so that only the final copies of the last edition incurred prohibition. Hoey seized those copies and then adjourned, with the staff of the paper, for drinks.[23]

However, the incident was not taken lightly. Hoey discussed the Sydney cuts with Gilbert Mant, the State Censor for South Australia. "We were horrified, both of us."

The Melbourne *Age* of 18 April commented in its editorial that the dispute appeared to be peculiar to Sydney:

> In Melbourne there has been generally a spirit of co-operation and good-will between the two parties [Censorship and the press]. In Sydney these qualities have been less conspicuous.[24]

Hoey had his suspicions about the incident. Part of the problem, he believed, was in the personality of the Sydney censor, Horace Mansell. There was the possibility that Evatt, for whom Mansell acted as campaign director, may have pushed him into being tough with the Sydney press. As Hoey put it,

> I suspect that Evatt had been on Horrie's back — "Don't let the papers get away with this sort of stuff — You're the censor. Cut it out . . ." Now I've got no proof that Doc Evatt did this . . . but I know the way Horrie spoke to me. Doc Evatt . . . was Attorney-General. He was a senior member of Cabinet. He liked to throw his weight around, and he lived in Sydney, and he knew Horrie Mansell very well . . .[25]

Penton's account supports the view that Evatt was less than friendly to the press. When asked by Penton to intervene in the dispute, Evatt replied, "Why don't you just fill up the blanks, then everything will be all right." He said he was sympathetic to the papers' plight, but this did not stop him from flying down to Tasmania to give a talk.

Mansell generally was a tougher censor than Hoey. For example, he kept a closer eye on incoming cables that might be objectionable to the Polish government in London, whereas Melbourne censorship, in Mansell's words, "once or twice have beaten us to the pistol and released such messages".[26]

The papers had struck a fine first blow. Public reaction to the incident culminated with some 2,000 university students marching through the streets of Sydney in protest. It was not as great an outrage — judging by letters to the editor and independent protests — as the Murdoch "expression" regulations of 1940 or the storm of abuse that greeted the "hate" campaign of 1942. The public was tired of being outraged. Penton conceded as much in his own account:

> the greater number of newsreaders did not understand exactly what it was the censor did not want them to read. Perhaps the newspapers were trying to publish something they oughtn't publish — something that might help the enemy.[27]

On the afternoon of 17 April, the newspapers applied to the High Court for, and were granted, an interlocutory injunction restraining the Censor from forbidding publication of the material at issue. Consequently, the later editions of the *Sun* and the *Daily Mirror* appeared on the streets unencumbered.

The High Court hearing[27] that day was lively. The hearing was meant to be a procedural one, in the sense that the decision before the Court was whether the case should be heard immediately, without restraining the Censor's action, or to hear it only after the Censor was restrained. However, Justices Starke and Williams seemed anxious to discuss matters other than the procedural ones. "What have the articles to do with the safety of the Commonwealth?" asked Justice Williams. Counsel for the Commonwealth quite properly did not want to debate the substantive matter, partly because it was not appropriate and partly because they were not briefed on the aspects of the case. The feeling among the judges was that the articles were not of a nature that would harm the country, and on the condition that the defendants did not publish any matter prejudicial to public safety, defence of the Commonwealth or the official prosecution of war, and by a majority of 3 to 2, granted the injunction restraining the Censor to 21 April 1944.

An injunction is an interlocutory and discretionary matter. The Court can grant it or not grant it on conditions as it pleases, without making any necessary presumption of what the ultimate finding is going to be.[29] One of the justices who voted for the injunction was related to one of the defendants, Fairfax. Justice Sir Dudley Williams' mother-in-law was a daughter of Ross Fairfax, youngest son of the founder of John Fairfax and Sons and a partner in the same company. The other two in favour of the injunction, Sir Hayden Starke and Sir George Rich, were not enamoured of Evatt, and in later years saw to it that they stayed on the Bench until Menzies was returned into government, for fear that Evatt might replace them with Labor-oriented appointees.[30]

Evatt probably had cause to be a little perplexed about the injunction outcome as well. In 1919, Evatt had assisted T.J. Ryan in a libel action against the *Argus*. The same Justice Rich was on the High Court Bench and Justice Starke was appearing for the *Argus*. The judgement had gone against Ryan at the time.[31] In later speeches, Evatt was to recall that Justice Rich said, "You can't censor the censor."[32]

Likewise, Geoffrey Sawer remains hesitant about the correctness of the injunction decision. On a technical basis, he believed the Crown was putting a strong case for not restraining the action of the Censor:

> the solicitor for the Censor was putting the right point. It was a point that could well have persuaded a somewhat differently constituted court, for example presided by Isaacs as Chief Justice, to go on the other tack and say *no*. We decline to interfere with this in this summary fashion. It is the responsibility and the ultimate judgement of the State for national morale . . .[33]

The injunction was a strategic victory for the press. Penton's account misquotes and distorts the context of the proceedings, suggesting that the substantive matter had been settled also.[34]

Penton concluded his account of the incident at this point. However, from then on the struggle became complicated for all parties. The hearing itself was unusual and requires some appreciation of the legal technicalities to understand its outcome.

The interpretation of constitutional law has to be qualified by the Defence power in time of war. The precedents were not favourable for the press. In Farey v. Burnett (1916) 21 CLR 433, the High Court laid down that any measure which "in the opinion of the Executive Government was conducive to better organization of the nation for war was within the Defence power of the Commonwealth". In wartime, those in whom security is entrusted were the sole judges of what security measures were required. The 1929 Royal Commission on the Constitution concluded that Australia should be regarded as an unitary state in war times. And despite some modifications, the High Court had expressed its adherence to the principle established in 1916.[35] It only required the government to be satisfied that what was said was "likely to be prejudicial" to the war effort for the case to go against the defendant. In 1942 and 1943, the power of the Defence Act was affirmed by the High Court in the cases of the Australia First Movement and Jehovah's Witnesses' appeals. In the former case, the High Court indicated that the wartime defence power enabled the Commonwealth to vest "absolute discretion, uncontrollable by the Courts", in Ministers in such matters as the internment of persons suspected of endangering security. In the latter case of 1943, the High Court indicated that the guarantee of freedom of religion in Section 116 of the Constitution *did not prevent* the dissolution of a religious body on defence security grounds, if the teaching of a church were prejudicial to the war effort. Geoffrey Sawer concluded:

> The majority [of the High Court] adhered to the orthodox

view that once a reasonable potential connection between economic and social organization and the conduct of the war was shown, the wisdom and expediency of the measure was *not* a matter for judicial decision.[36]

Thus although the decision that the censorship regulation was a conclusive power, and by 1944 was an arguable issue, the High Court still was bound by the precedents of the Great War, amounting to giving the government absolute discretion in matters such as censorship during wartime.

The legal wild-cat injunction decision was about to be tamed. The pendulum was bound to swing away from the press when the parties stood before the Bench on 21 April 1944. A packed court-room featuring a large array of senior counsel engaged in the case witnessed some odd exchanges. Mr Weston, K.C., on behalf of Consolidated Press, argued that the injunction had effectively disposed of the issue and that all that was required was the matter of costs. Chief Justice Latham disabused him of this view and asked him what his motion was. Mr Barwick, K.C., (for the Commonwealth) suggested that it would be appropriate for the injunction motion to be dismissed on the grounds that Mr Weston actually had not moved his motion for the injunction at the previous hearing. The Bench differed and insisted the matter *now be proceeded with substantively*. J. Barry, K.C., for Mansell, appeared as bemused:

> "It is impossible to understand just what is the nature of the order that was made on Monday."

> Replied the Chief Justice,
> "The terms of the Injunction were quite clearly stated and I think all parties understood."

> Barry replied:
> "I can only say we were definitely under the impression that the matter which had been dealt with was an application for adjournment, and that the terms were imposed in connection with that."

> Justice Starke responded:
> "You have been wrongly informed."[37]

This irked both the press and Censorship. Eventually, on

Weston's insistence, the matter of costs was decided in the Court of Petty Sessions. This case was adjourned, pending the High Court decision, but costs at that stage were awarded to the *Daily Telegraph*.[38]

The papers contended that Section 11(e) of the order was invalid because it was not necessary for the efficient prosecution of the war. Censorship contended it was vital for its proper working that the newspapers should not be allowed to indicate that censorship material submitted had been disallowed.

On the first day of the substantive hearing, the origin of the censorship row was conceded in the editorial from the most hostile of the anti-Calwell press, the *Daily Telegraph*. Though it attacked Censorship, Penton softened the tone to conclude:

> One good thing may come of it, however. Seeing what a bad press this wild rampage got Australia, Mr Curtin may feel more inclined to do something about his Cabinet when he returns from overseas. He will be able to check at first hand in America the cause from which the current conflict between Mr Calwell and the newspapers arose. This was the failure of our Department of Information — inadequately staffed, inadequately financed and lead from this end — to interpret to the American people, Australia's wartime policies including the decision to transfer a number of men to the other No. 1 priority work.[39]

The High Court hearing continued into May 1944. Bonney was on the witness-stand for many days. Although subject to sustained cross-examination, he never conceded that the Censor may have acted improperly. At most, he allowed that in some censorship cases there may have been an error in judgment, but insisted his action in suppressing the papers' publication was not only proper but necessary.[40]

Eventually, on 5 May, Chief Justice Latham intervened. After hearing legal argument, he pressed Censorship and the press to resolve the matter out of court. As an incentive to negotiate, he hinted that Censorship was on fairly strong legal ground:

It must be recognized that whatever the decision of the Court may be as to the validity of the regulations affecting Censorship, there must, in time of war, be some control, actual and potential, over the publication of matter in the press, but whatever form of censorship might be introduced, if these provisions are held to be valid, or even if present provisions are held to be valid and continue in operation, differences of opinion as to the form of administration of censorship are almost certain to arise.[41]

On 18 May, the negotiations gave birth to "a code of censorship principles" which were added to the Press and Broadcasting Censorship Order. These directions read:

(Powers of Publicity Censors)
12A Every direction, order of prohibition issued, given or made under this Order by a Publicity Censor in relation to the publication of any matter shall be issued, given or made solely by reference to the requirements of defence security, as they exist at the time of publication or proposed publication of the matter in question.

(Limitation of Power to Seize)
12B The Power conferred on a Publicity Censor by paragraph 12 of this Order to authorize the seizure of copies of a newspaper, periodical or other publication may be exercised only in cases where immediate and obvious danger to defence security is likely to arise from the circulation of the newspaper, periodical or other publication.

(Power of Supreme Court to Order Suppression)
12C—(1) Where a person is convicted under paragraph 11 of this Order, the Commonwealth may, within seven days after the conviction, make application to the Full Court of the Supreme Court of the State in which the conviction takes place for an order directing that during the period specified in the order the newspaper or periodical in relation to which the conviction took place shall not be published.

(2) Notice of such application shall be served upon the proprietor of the newspaper or periodical.

(3) The Full Court of the Supreme Court of the State shall have jurisdiction to hear and determine the application.

(4) On the hearing of the application the Court shall take into consideration the seriousness of the contravention in respect of which the conviction took place and the extent to which previous contraventions have occurred in the case of the newspaper or periodical.

(5) The Court may at any time vary any such order upon

further application either of the Commonwealth or of the proprietor or publisher of the newspaper or periodical.

(General Principles of Censorship)
12D In the Administration of this Order the following general principles shall be applied:-
"Censorship shall be imposed exclusively for reasons of defence security. Owing to the many and changing phases of the war, 'defence security' cannot be exhaustively defined. Primarily 'defence security' relates to the armed forces of all the Allied Nations and to all the operations of war. It covers the suppression of information useful to the enemy. It may at times include particular aspects of Australia's war-time relationship with other countries. Censorship shall not be imposed merely for the maintenance of morale or the prevention of despondency or alarm. Censorship shall not prevent the reporting of industrial disputes or stoppages. Criticism and comment, however strongly expressed shall be free. Mere exaggeration or inaccuracy shall not be a ground for censorship. 'Defence security' shall be the governing principle of every application of censorship."[42]

The press hailed the amendments as a victory against the censors. Penton was so absorbed in his account of the incident, that he forwarded advance galley drafts of his book on the censorship row to Mansell and Bonney before these codes were agreed to. Bitterly critical of the manuscript, Bonney faulted Penton on matters of fact and interpretation. In any case, he insisted the book should not be published, since it was counter to the spirit of co-operation that was implied by the code.[43]

On 29 May, Penton wrote to Bonney denying, any undertaking to withhold publication of his book as a condition of the settlement. To add insult to injury, he asked Bonney to clear the publication:

My company does not propose to withdraw this book voluntarily. You are therefore to treat the copy as a Censor, and you will naturally bear in mind the new regulations under which censorship is to be imposed.[44]

Bonney advised Calwell that inclusion of censorship instructions within the book might constitute an offence against the Crimes Act, but there was little he could do as Censor but warn Penton of this. If the publication could not be stopped, Bonney asked Calwell for the right to publish a rejoinder and probably to sue the company for libel.[45]

Penton then relented, saying the book would not be published, but he insisted it still be treated by Censorship. Bonney, realizing the absurdity of the request, gained Calwell's agreement to steer clear of this queer fish.[46] While Evatt advised Mansell that if Censorship refused to treat Penton's book, Penton might have an action for a writ of *mandamus* to compel treatment of Penton's proofs,[47] no further action on the draft was taken.[48]

Penton's book finally was published, in an expanded though still uncorrected version, in 1947. Bonney did not publish a rejoinder or sue for libel.

Today, there remains the impression that the Government "lost the case".[48] In fact, legal costs arising from the row were settled on the basis that each party would pay its own. No payment of costs was made by the government on behalf of the press or others concerned.[49] A contrary case could be made for the Censor winning on points. It was generally overlooked that the new code applied only to the press section of the Press and Broadcasting Censorship Order. The Attorney-General's Department's advice to Bonney was that "the powers of the Censor have not been greatly affected by the new code".[50]

The regulations were more symbolic than substantive. Section 12B did not cut down the powers of censors, since it was assumed that the Censor had always exercised his power for the purposes of defence security. The main effect of 12C was to clarify the legal machinery. 12D laid down seven main principles of censorship. The reference to "morale" imposed less restrictions than might be apparent. Morale alone could not be the determining factor. The legal advice was that "morale" meant "civilian morale" and not the morale of troops, which was "clearly a defence security matter".

On the question of civilian morale, Regulation 17(2), which banned "anything likely to cause . . . public alarm or despondency", had to be taken into account. Thus the press still would have to guard against publicity material that might have this effect.

The reference to "industrial disputes or stoppages" was seen mainly as a qualification about *reporting*, not censoring. The word "prevention" meant absolute prevention, not a qualified prevention. The term "mere exaggeration" stressed the qualification "mere". This did not refer to *any* exaggeration but to "mere" exaggeration.

In short, it is difficult to regard the new code as the unqualified victory the press (and historians) had asserted it to be. The press had the resources to proclaim that the code favoured its views and interests, but in practice, Censorship maintained its powers.

For example, the rest of the press did not join the *Daily Telegraph* when it defied Censorship over the reporting of the Cowra Japanese POW breakout. The security principle, that if the Japanese got word that their POWs had been killed, Australian POWs might be slain, though tenuous, was accepted. In the event, although the *Daily Telegraph* defied the censorship instruction once, it deferred publishing the later stories, along with other papers, admittedly only after Curtin personally wrote to Penton on 19 August 1944 that the lives of many Australian POWs might be prejudiced if any hint of the breakout reached the enemy.[51]

In later months, censorship was liberalized. The number of censorship instructions became fewer. Finally, on 31 August 1945, the eve of termination of hostilities with Japan, Calwell announced that local censorship had been lifted. Radio and cable censorship continued a further twelve days.[52] By then, the Censorship staff had been redeployed by the Department.

In concluding the history of the Censorship Division, it is worth asking whether it was generally as repressive as some historians have suggested. One conclusion, by Roger Bell,[53] that Australian censorship was so repressive that the press was transformed into a propaganda arm of the government, remains arguable. Bell cites the views of frustrated overseas correspondents. This can be balanced with examples of frustrated overseas correspondents in other allied countries such as the United States, United Kingdom and New Zealand:

> It is not easy to get through messages which are at all critical or uncomplimentary regarding the set-up here. Newspapermen who filed out of war-time London to the US and who are now filing out of war-time NY or Washington to Britain say flatly that the American censorship is stricter than Britain's ever was.[54]

> The [UK] Government's political censorship is closing round newsmen's necks like a noose.[55]

> New Zealanders were being steadily stripped of rights of free expression and criticism and that censorship was being operated for purposes not connected with military security.[56]

Furthermore, there was some favourable reaction by overseas correspondents in Australia to censorship. The chief Australian correspondent of the London *Times*, R.L. Curthoys, wrote to the Chief Publicity Censor on 4 March 1943:

> my relations with your staff in Melbourne have been consistently happy. I have not agreed with every decision rendered in reference to my despatches, but I have tried to accept each one in the spirit in which it has been given . . . I have found your people consistently fair, courteous and helpful . . .[57]

Bell may be correct in his conclusion that the press became a propaganda arm for the government, but he overstates the dissatisfaction that the press and radio may have had with Censorship. Dissent from censorship was uneven and mainly came from the Sydney press, especially the *Daily Telegraph*. At the height of the censorship row of 1944, the *Age* leader commented:

> In Melbourne there has been generally a spirit of cooperation and good-will between the two parties [Censorship and the press]. In Sydney these qualities have been less conspicuous.[58]

The radio stations always had been in accord with censorship policies. In 1940, one censor reported:

We have had very little trouble here. I have been impressed by the control of their own organization of the "B" [Commercial] class stations. Their rules for their own conduct are probably more rigid than censorship could demand.[59]

In 1942, Mr Dooley of the Australian Federation of Commercial Broadcasters indicated that he sought no relaxation in the censorship.[60]

To judge the repressive nature of censorship, quantitative yardsticks such as the number of censorship instructions issued and the degree of cuts are required. Bell refers to an average of eight instructions per day being issued by the censor. First cited in Brian Penton's *Censored!*,[61] this estimate is incorrect. As has been said, despite its publication date, Penton's book was a rush job, conceived and largely written as early as May 1944. Penton's estimate of the number of censorship instructions issued was arrived at by confusing the numbering of instructions with the numbering of the Censor's correspondence. His confusion was understandable. It is difficult to pinpoint the number of instructions issued. A system for *numbering* censorship instructions was introduced only on 1 May 1942, when every instruction issued for telephoning to the press was given a serial number for identification. Previously, there was no numbering of instructions conveyed by phone. Judging by Penton's figure of 10,214 instructions over the period September 1939 to July 1943, it is obvious he confused this figure with the *letter* numbering system. Every letter from the Sydney censor was given a unique number until a change was introduced on 19 July 1943, when a new numbering system was brought in. The last letter sent out under the old letter numbering system was designated SPC 10,231. It was addressed to a private individual.[62]

As both censors and their critics seem to agree that the actual frequency of instructions is a reasonable indication of suppression under the various regimes,[63] the number of censorship instructions issued each month from 1940 to 1945, drawing on the various incomplete sources, is estimated in Appendix B. This suggests that throughout the war, some 2,272 instructions were issued. The overall monthly rate was 33.4, however, the rate of instructions varied considerably throughout the war period. The more intense the war effort, the more instructions issued. The monthly rate of instruction per year was 35.8 (1940), 41.4 (1941), 56.3 (1942), 35.0 (1943), 17.1 (1944) and 5.5 in the declining war period of 1945. The monthly rate of instructions issued under the United Australia Party government was 39.1. Under Labor, it was 30.9, from October 1941 to August 1945. The average during 1942–44 was 36.1 per month.

Likewise, the actual censorship treatment statistics suggest the overwhelming majority of copy submitted was untouched. Treatment of 1943 federal election broadcast scripts showed no more than 0.4 per cent of scripts "killed"; 3.6 per cent incurred some deletion or amendment and 96 per cent were aired without alternation.[64] Overseas dispatches were treated more severely, owing to the danger of the material coming into enemy hands; no more than 1 per cent of stories were "killed" and 5 per cent suffered major treatment, leaving some 94 per cent of copy to be sent more or less as it was written.[64] The censorship of cables also reflected light censorship treatment. From March to October 1944, 63,377 inward cables were received, 30 suffered some deletion (i.e. 0.047 per cent). In the same period, 7,398 outward cables were submitted for treatment. Of these, 93 (i.e. 1.3 per cent) had some deletions made.[66]

Evaluation of Australia's experience with censorship is quite unrealistic unless some account is taken of the complexities Australia faced both strategically and internationally. To comment on the basis of anecdotal examples, that the Curtin government was more repressive than the Menzies government, seems inadequate. The Menzies government suppressed the media itself, not just its stories. Four radio stations associated with the Jehovah's Witnesses and nine newspapers associated with Communist League were outlawed at a time of comparative low threat for Australia. Under Curtin, Australia and its territories were attacked and remained under threat for at least two years. This certainly would encourage more aggressive censorship. Even so, the monthly number of instructions issued during Curtin's reign was lower than those of Menzies.

After Pearl Harbour, Australia was restrained by not one, but three different censorships. MacArthur had his field censorship, the Australian Army's Public Relations Directorate exercised field censorship in the Territories, and finally there was the general publicity censorship of the Department of Information.

The censorship of the Cowra POW massacre, raised by Bell as typical of Australia's political censorship, also is arguable. It could as easily be understood as resulting from a concern that reports of the massacre would prejudice the lives of Australian POWs through enemy retaliatory action.

There was political censorship under both administrations, though the political goals varied. Under Menzies, censorship tended to be used to delay reports of embarrassing such incidents as administrative bottleneck in organizing for the war, under the guise of withholding information that could be of value to the enemy. This delay was implemented by requirements that any statement about the Navy, for example, had to be submitted to the Admiralty for security clearance, as well as cleared by the Censor. This delay allowed the Navy Minister time to prepare his own statement on the matter, to be issued simultaneously with the release of the Censorship-treated copy. The intention was to neutralize political damage to the government.

Under Curtin, censorship policy reflected the growing need to project Australia's position as an ally in its own right, initially to encourage assistance from the Americans following the entry of the Japanese into the South-West Pacific, and later to support Australia's bargaining role when the decisions on post-war arrangements were in view in 1944–45. Censorship was integral to Australia's foreign policy and its main effect was to suppress unfavourable publicity about Australia or its war effort being received overseas. Bell correctly notes that foreign correspondents were the first to be affected by this policy, but unnecessarily generalizes the effect to cover all areas of censorship.

Radio and cables always were censored more heavily than the local press because of the fear that the messages would provide a poor picture of Australia as an ally. Copies of one edition of the *Daily Telegraph* were barred from shipment overseas because it was believed that the articles and editorial provided a misleading picture of Australia. For that matter, the censorship row of 1944 can be traced back to a conflict between the Department of Information and the press about the best way to publicize Australia's war effort.

Notes

1. B. Penton, *Censored!: Being a True Account of a Notable Fight for Your Right to Read and Know, with Some Comment upon the Plague of Censorship in General.* Sydney: Shakespeare Press, 1947. Most secondary accounts of the incident, including Peter Coleman's *Obscenity, Blasphemy, Sedition* and R.S. Whitington's biography of Sir Frank Packer, draw on Penton as the source.
2. A.A. Calwell, *Be Just and Fear Not.* Hawthorn, Vic.: O'Neill, 1972, p. 90.
3. Colm Kiernan, "Arthur A. Calwell's Clashes with the Australian Press, 1943–45", *Historical Journal* (University of Wollongong Historical Society) 2, no. 1, (March 1976): 91.
4. Calwell, *Be Just and Fear Not,* p. 90.
5. Penton, *Censored!,* pp. 58-59.
6. Bonney to Penton, 30 November 1943; A.A., W. 17126.
7. File note, 1 February 1944; A.A., SP 109/5, Box 66.
8. A.A., SP 109/5, Box 66. This also is dealt with by Kiernan, "Calwell's Clashes . . .", pp. 83-84.
9. *Sydney Morning Herald*, 17 December 1943.
10. Kiernan, "Calwell's Clashes . . .", p. 81.
11. CPD (HR), 21 May 1942, pp. 1458-61; 27 May 1943, pp. 1616-19.
12. B. Penton, *Think or Be Damned.* Sydney: Angus & Robertson, 1941.
13. CPD (HR), 26 February 1943, p. 1056.
14. *Sydney Daily Telegraph*, 13 April 1944.
15. *Sydney Morning Herald*, 14 April 1944.
16. *Sydney Daily Telegraph*, 15 April 1944.
17. Penton, *Censored!,* p. 13.
18. *Sydney Morning Herald*, 17 April 1944.
19. Penton, *Censored!,* p. 13.
20. *Sydney Morning Herald*, 17 April 1944.
21. Penton, *Censored!,* pp. 72-74. See Appendix C in this volume for full text of the statement.

22. Calwell, *Be Just and Fear Not*, p. 90.
23. Author's interview with T. Hoey, 16 February 1976. With some pride, Hoey showed the author a photo of the incident. All were smiling for the camera.
24. Penton, *Censored!*, pp. 70-71.
25. Author's interview with T. Hoey, 16 February 1976.
26. Mansell to Bonney, 23 March 1944, A.A., SP 109, Box 53, File 337.09.
27. Penton, *Censored!*, p. 76.
28. CPD (HR), 29 November 1944, pp. 2321-28.
29. Author's interview with G. Sawer, 20 April 1976.
30. At retirement, they were aged 72 and 81 respectively. See Eddy Neumann, *The High Court: A Collective Portrait 1903-1970*. Occasional Monograph No. 5. Sydney: Department of Government & Public Administration, University of Sydney, 1971, pp. 26, 48.
31. Melbourne *Argus*, 11 October 1919.
32. CPD (HR), 29 November 1944, p. 2328.
33. Author's interview with G. Sawer, 20 April 1976.
34. Penton, *Censored!*
35. G. Sawer, "The Defence Power of the Commonwealth in Time of War". *Australian Law Journal* 20 (December 1946): 295.
36. G. Sawer, *Australian Federal Politics and Law 1929-1949*. Melbourne: Melbourne University Press, 1963, pp. 152-53.
37. Melbourne *Argus*, 22 April 1944.
38. Melbourne *Age*, 5 May 1944.
39. Sydney *Daily Telegraph*, 21 April 1944.
40. Melbourne *Argus*, 29 April 1944.
41. Ibid., 6 May 1944.
42. Publicity Censorship Directions, issued under the amended Press and Broadcasting Censorship Order, with the relevant National Security Regulations and Orders; see Appendix A.
43. Bonney to Calwell, 16 May 1944; A.A., SP 109/3, Box 53, File 323.41.
44. Penton to Bonney, 29 May 1944, ibid.
45. Bonney to Calwell, 1 June 1944, ibid.
46. Bonney to Calwell, 6 June 1944, ibid.
47. Bonney to Calwell, 17 June 1944, ibid.
48. See Kiernan, "Calwell's Clashes . . .", p. 91.
49. CPD (HR), 29 September 1944, p. 91.
50. Report of the Censorship Conference 7-8 June 1944; A.A., SP 109, Box 51, File 325. 14.
51. Kiernan, "Calwell's Clashes . . .", pp. 97-98.
52. CPD (HR), 31 August 1945, p. 5070.
53. Roger Bell, "Censorship and War: Australia's Curious Censorship Experience, 1939-1945". *Media Information — Austrlia* 6 (November 1977): 1-3.
54. *World Press News*, 26 February 1942.
55. Eric Baume, London *Daily Mirror*, 21 September 1942.
56. Sydney *Sun*, 8 October 1942.
57. A.A., SP 195/2.
58. Melbourne *Age*, 18 April 1944.
59. A.A., SP 109, Box 72, CPC 2/1/40.
60. A.A., MP 272/1.
61. Penton, *Censored!*, p. 35.

62. For example, Senator Ashley, the Minister for Information tendered as evidence of his permissive approach to censorship the fact that censorship instructions over his first months of administration had been 60 per cent fewer than in the corresponding period in the year before. See Melbourne *Argus*, 3 December 1941. Also Chief Publicity Censor, Bonney had advised Ashley on 7 October 1941 that his approach to censorship was liberal by arguing: "in the four weeks preceding my appointment on 9 April 1941, 48 censorship instructions, etc . . . were issued to Press and Broadcasters. In the four weeks ended last Saturday, however, there were only 14 . . ." See A.A., SP 195/1, File 71/1/11. Finally, Brian Penton (*Censored!*, p. 35) attacked censorship by estimating (wrongly) that it issued eight instructions each day to the press.
64. Tom Hoey Papers.
65. A.A., C815/4, Item 46.
66. These were calculated from figures contained in A.A., SP 106/9.

Conclusion

It was Max Weber who first systematically described the features of bureaucracies.[1] He distinguished bureaucracy from other organizations of authority in that it had a "rational-legal" basis. He expected bureaucracy to predominate as an institutional form in modern society because it was hierarchical, rule-based, impersonal and potentially formidable:

> Once it is fully established, bureaucracy is among those social structures which are hardest to destroy. Bureaucracy is *the* means of carrying "community action" over into rationally ordered 'societal action'. Therefore as an instrument for "societalizing" relations of power, bureaucracy has been and is a power instrument of the first order — for the one who controls the bureaucratic apparatus.[2]

The question of who controls the bureaucracy has remained a live and difficult one. The Department of Information had been created as an auxiliary to the war effort, and was destined for extinction at the return of peace. It remained generally unpopular, and its functions were dispersed to other agencies by the incoming Labor government in 1941, mainly to settle political scores. However, the Department not only survived but prospered beyond the end of the war. The Department of Information can be seen as an example of an agency created for a vague and by no means widely accepted role, which found and nurtured its own constituency and policy area in order to survive. In serving political ends, the Department had itself become a political creature.

This study shows that the process of acquiring this political leverage was an uncertain one. It did not come from any demonstrable superiority in the Department's efficiency or rationality of organization. Its administration was sometimes incoherent, or capricious, and was occasionally bizarre, as the Shortwave Division's shuttle between the ABC and the Department discloses.

The Department of Information was really a department of journalists who were expected to perform propaganda and censorship activities in the framework of a public service agency. This study has shown that the professional backgrounds of these journalists came to exercise a profound influence upon the Department's policies and activities. Censors tended to concern themselves with overall information policy as much as did the formally assigned promotion and editorial staff. Censors had the legislative clout to follow through where the other information areas only could request co-operation. Bonney transformed his censors into editors. The suppressors became the expressors. However, public service procedures did produce the need for the expressors to develop a consistent and politically acceptable policy for their activities during a period of declining threat for Australia. In turn, this led to a search for a consistent Australian culture fit for promotion overseas. Is it only coincidental that to this day, Americans and Britons retain a stereotype of kangaroos in Pitt Street?

At the same time, its co-ordination of government information proved difficult to achieve and contributed to the failure of the Department's local news service being used by the metropolitan media. The reluctance of other government agencies to use the Department for such functions also forced the Department to find a more acceptable role for itself.

Three reasons emerge to explain the Department's survival at the end of 1945. First, by virtue of its diverse functions, the Department developed a momentum of its own, once it had been established. The lack of systematic overview of government administration during World War II contributed to the expansion of the Shortwave Broadcasting Division. The entry of the Japanese into the war increased the need for censorshp, yet the Department's enlarged staff continued to operate long after the principal security threat to Australia had disappeared by the end of 1943. The Censorship Division cultivated a new mission for itself: protecting the "good name of Australia". The Editorial Division of the Department began to concentrate on overseas promotion, because it made little progress at home.

Secondly, and more importantly, the backgrounds of the Department's staff exercised an important influence on its organization and policies. The conflicts between the Censorship and Shortwave Divisions reflected the divergent views and backgrounds animating the staff. The censors led by Bonney were primarily journalists. They had come from a craft that stressed the "story" — the primacy of the headline and the need to marshall the facts to support the theme. Conflicting or diverting "angles" were out of place and needed to be edited out. This approach contrasted with that of the more academically oriented Shortwave Division, led by Ball. His broadcasts, especially those directed to the Japanese, were experimental and tentative. "Good" and "bad" news of Australia's war effort was broadcast, to enhance the station's credibility in the eyes of the enemy. This was in harmony with Ball's belief that credible communication explored differeing points of view. To the journalists on the Censorship staff, this smacked of defeatism and a lack of professionalism. It blurred the line they wanted to promote, that Australia and its allies were winning. Ball's Listening Post was regarded by these journalists as a luxury, irrelevant to the task at hand. For Ball, it was fundamental to framing his broadcasts. In developing his commentaries, Ball stressed the need to interpret the "enemy's line".

Thirdly, the Department's relationship with the media remains fundamental to understanding how and why the Department came to develop its mission, ethos and priorities from local morale-boosting to being that of promotion of Australia abroad. Consistently unsympathetic reception by the metropolitan press to the Department's local news efforts and its censorship function stimulated the growth of the Department's overseas promotion and Shortwave Broadcasting Division, yet it was the press that in mid 1942 defended the Department's existence. In part, this reflected a fear that the Department's demise would stimulate other government information units, especially in the Armed Forces, to interfere with local news-gathering.

How journalists accommodated to their seemingly antithetical censorship functions remains central to this case-study. Journalists were pleased to become censors because the experience of World War I suggested that if censorship was necessary, it was better for them, rather than for quasi-military officials, to undertake this sensitive task. In addition, implementing censorship regulations bore some resemblance to the discipline of editing.

These journalists saw little conflict between writing stories and being censors. In times of war, discretion in journalism was agreed to on security grounds. In practice, the journalists who joined the Department differed from those who continued to work in newspaper offices. The censor-journalists became more sensitive to the demands of "responsible" journalism: a perceived duty not to degrade the standing of Australia's war effort; a need to present Australia to the world as a nation equal to if not better than its allies. These censor-journalists were to rally round the cause of protecting "the good name of Australia" — an attempt to evolve a bipartisan new role for censorship.

For other journalists and editors in the press, such censorship amounted to the suppression of legitimate criticism of the Australian government. The Department recruited journalists as censors who maintained a favourable orientation to reporting the Australian war effort. In so doing, it unwittingly may have added to the hostilities between journalists inside and those outside the Department by effectively polarizing the "responsible" and the more "larrikin" journalists at a time of general manpower shortages.

The Department's censorship function impelled it to relate to the media and its dominantly journalist staff tended to reinforce its orientation. Notwithstanding experiments with Group Committees and the "hate" campaign, the Department settled down to conducting its expressive functions in close liaison with the media. Had the Conlon Committee's recommendations to broaden the expertise available to the Department along social science lines been agreed to, the Department may have fostered more direct links with the public and evolved along more community development/citizens advice bureau lines.

If the media became the main point of action for the Department, it is also true that the Department came to influence the media organizations. While the metropolitan press ignored the offerings of the Department, the provincial and suburban press welcomed it and may have flourished because of it. In radio, the Department's influence was indirect though considerable, since the rationing of newsprint increased the importance of radio. The ABC's news efforts, reluctantly tolerated by the press, were aided by the Department's withdrawal of its local news services in 1941. Commercial stations found themselves in need of an authoritative and cheap news service in early 1942. The ABC's offer to provide its news service gratis in place of the Department's brought the commercial and national stations together, allowed the government to inject its "Pacific first" theme into all news sessions, and avoiding the protests of news management that had plagued Sir Keith Murdoch earlier, allowed the commercial listening public to hear ABC news and laid the foundations for the public and political acceptance of a national news service after the war.

While the means by which the Department and its staff

developed a political role is highlighted, there are implications to be drawn about ministerial/departmental relations. This case-study has not upset seriously the conventional Westminster model for analysing government administration, nor was it intended that it do so. One might summarize the case-study as illustrating the waxing and waning of interest by different Ministers and their governments in propaganda and censorship. However, it has shown that Ministers can become as dependent on their departments as departments can on their Ministers. The Department survived the war with the most junior Minister and one with a history of antagonism to the Department's existence. Calwell's advocacy for his department owed at least as much to his need to peform ministerially, whatever the portfolio, as to his hatred of the press proprietors. Other more senior Ministers for Information such as Gullett and Ashley were not as concerned that the Department should be seen to perform. They had other portfolios in which to shine.

Finally, the study has shed light on the nature and extent of censorship activities during the war. A statistical examination of censorship instructions issued from 1940 to 1945 suggests, if anything, that there was more censorship carried out by non-Labor than Labor governments. Political censorship was present under both regimes, but the political goals varied. Under Menzies, censorship came to be used to delay reports of embarrassing incidents under the guise of withholding information of value to the enemy. Under Curtin, censorship became obsessed with prohibiting "false impressions" abroad and "protecting the good name of Australia" under the guise of needing to project Australia as a worthy ally to overseas audiences, particularly the Americans. Indeed, the censorship row of 1944 was a consequence of this policy.

Are there any lessons in this six-year saga of propaganda and censorship? On the whole, the Department of Information model worked better than its para-military Great War progenitor. It got on well with the media, but it was not "captured", as so many other regulatory agencies were.

Many of its functions continue today — the Advertising Division, the Film Office, Radio Australia, the News and Information Bureau. However, the real issue is whether censorship should be grafted on to this reservoir of propaganda skills and, if so, what safeguards or safety valves should be instituted to protect the public, the media and even censorship? Is it really fair to have a general rule that references to censorship as such be censored? What role might there be for independent tribunals to ensure censorship regulations are not being abused?

If another war should provoke the Defence power and all its regulations, these questions must receive more attention and debate than they have in the past.

Notes

1. Max Weber, *From Max Weber: Essays in Sociology,* trans. and ed. H.H. Gerth and C. Wright Mills. London: Routledge & Kegan Paul, 1948, pp. 196-244.
2. Ibid., p. 228.

Appendix A

SECRET DOCUMENT
under the
National Security Act.

NOT FOR PUBLICATION.

COMMONWEALTH OF AUSTRALIA.

NATIONAL SECURITY (GENERAL) REGULATIONS.
REGULATION 16.

PRESS AND BROADCASTING CENSORSHIP ORDER.

PUBLICITY CENSORSHIP DIRECTIONS.
Issued on 31st October, 1944.

IN pursuance of the powers conferred upon me by the Press and Broadcasting Censorship Order, I, EDMUND GARNET BONNEY, Chief Publicity Censor, hereby issue the following Directions to each editor, printer and publisher of newspapers and other publications in Australia and to each owner or other person in charge of wireless transmitting apparatus in Australia.

PART I.—PRELIMINARY.

1. These Directions may be cited as the Publicity Censorship Directions.

2. The Consolidated Censorship Directions issued on 30th April, 1943, and all other censorship directions in force, are hereby cancelled.

3. The objects of these directions are to ensure that the enemy is not assisted by the publication or broadcasting of any matter that contravenes the requirements of defence security and that nothing is published or broadcast that is likely to prejudice the defence of the Commonwealth or the efficient prosecution of the war.

4. These directions apply to—
   (a) all newspapers and broadcasting stations;
   (b) all publicity media, such as periodicals, association journals, company reports, and matter issued to advocate a cause; and
   (c) all advertising, photographs and pictures, cinematograph films and all other matter that is not strictly a private communication between two persons.

5. Nothing in these directions shall derogate from the provisions of the Broadcasting Stations Standing Orders.*

PART II.—GENERAL DIRECTIONS.

6. The General Directions with respect to Press and Broadcasting Censorship are as follows:—

   (a) *Submission of Doubtful Matter*—
   Editors and broadcasters are obliged to reject material that is obviously inconsistent with censorship requirements. Doubtful matter must, in all cases, be submitted to a Publicity Censor. Copy, galley proofs or broadcasting scripts must be submitted in duplicate with headings.

   (b) *Re-submissions*—
   (i) Matter submitted to a Publicity Censor may be published or broadcast within one month after being passed for publication or broadcasting, but not thereafter unless it has been re-submitted and again passed. This applies particularly to photographs and pictures.
   (ii) Material prohibited by a Publicity Censor may be re-submitted when an editor or broadcaster feels that sufficient time has elapsed, or other circumstances have arisen, to render the material safe for publication.

   (c) *Published Matter Contravening Censorship Requirements*—
   Matter contravening Censorship requirements or conflicting with the essential principles of defence security, which has been published or broadcast, must not be re-published or broadcast without prior submission to and approval by a Publicity Censor. Matter which has been published or broadcast in breach of Censorship is not thereby released for use by other persons.

   (d) *Publicity Censorship and Service Authorities*—
   The Fighting Services or other authorities to which matter may be referred for advice are not Publicity Censorship authorities, and the fact that their approval or disapproval has been given to any material in no way signifies that a Publicity Censor has either passed or rejected that material.

   (e) *Official Statements Censorable*—
   Statements purporting to be official, made by recognized official sources, shall not be accepted as having been passed by, or as being immune from, Censorship, except where express provision is made in these Directions for exceptions in the cases of *official* statements by Ministers of State or by General Head-quarters. In all cases where official statements, other than those excepted, may contravene Censorship requirements they should be submitted to a Publicity Censor.

*NOTE.—Attention is particularly invited to sub-paragraphs (3.) and (4.) of paragraph 13 of the Broadcasting Stations Standing Orders which provide as follows:—
"(3.) All scripts concerning which the manager of any station is doubtful shall be submitted by him for censorship. Publication of an item in the press or elsewhere does not necessarily release it for broadcasting.
"(4.) Scripts of all news items, all news commentaries and all scripts relating to war operations, the fighting services, the conduct of the war, or the manufacture and maintenance of munitions and supplies shall be submitted for censorship before being broadcast."

(f) *Statements Likely to Cause Disaffection*—
No statement, cartoon, illustration or photograph, or other matter may be published or broadcast which—
  (i) evinces disloyalty, or is likely to encourage disloyalty or to cause disaffection;
  (ii) is likely to discourage enlistment in the Fighting Services or in any auxiliary service;
  (iii) is calculated to influence public opinion (whether in Australia or elsewhere) in a manner likely to be prejudicial to the defence of the Commonwealth or to the efficient prosecution of the war;
  (iv) is likely to prejudice His Majesty's relations with an Ally or with any Foreign Power with which he is at peace, or is likely to offend any such Ally or Foreign Power or any part of His Majesty's dominions; or
  (v) is likely to be, or is capable of being used to enemy advantage, or to the prejudice or disadvantage of British or Allied interests.

(g) *References to Armed Services and War Supplies*—
As defence security may be involved in reference to—
  (i) the leadership, organization or discipline of the Forces, or
  (ii) the production or methods of production of Munitions or other war materials for the use of the armed Services,
all such references relating to matter not previously released shall be referred to a Publicity Censor before publication.

PART III.—SPECIAL DIRECTIONS.

7. The Special Directions with respect to Press and Broadcasting Censorship are as follows:—

A.1. AIR RAIDS OR OTHER ATTACKS ON AUSTRALIAN TERRITORY.

1. Special instructions will be issued as soon as possible after an alert is sounded or an attack made by the enemy on an Australian city, district or area. Pending official relaxation Rule C.8 relating to Communiques will apply. All material referring to an alert or an attack must be submitted to a Publicity Censor.

2. There may be no reference to precise locations of A.R.P. control centres or particulars of secret code signals.

A.2. AIRCRAFT—OPERATIONS AND PERSONNEL.

Except with the consent of a Publicity Censor, no reference may be made to—
(a) ferrying of aircraft to or from Australia;
(b) embarkation, disembarkation, route, mode of travel, or other movements to, from or within Australia, of R.A.A.F. or Allied Service or Civil aircraft or personnel. (This applies also to suspension, diversion, or resumption of civil air services);
(c) re-fuelling particulars or movements of bulk fuel, stores, supplies and the like;
(d) new or experimental types of aircraft, or the production or assembly in Australia of any type of aircraft, aircraft engine or other aircraft part, the production or assembly of which has not been officially announced;
(e) the degree of production attained at any time with respect to any aircraft or aircraft engine or the details of construction or equipment of any aircraft or aircraft engine;
(f) the number, name, description, armament, equipment, performance or condition of any Allied aircraft used or intended to be used in operations; or the bases from which those aircraft are operating or may operate;
(g) the precise location or number of R.A.A.F. or Allied aerodromes or training establishments, the number of trainees, the time occupied in any phase of training, the attainment of any particular state of training or the methods of training, including paratroop training;
(h) the strength, establishment, location or operational organization of R.A.A.F. or Allied Air Forces, or any unit thereof;
(i) measures for defence of Air establishments or operational methods employed or to be employed by Service aircraft;
(j) the use or proposed use of gliders in the South-West Pacific Area;
(k) the exact location of air observers' posts;
(l) the fact that a member of any Allied Air Force is an Intelligence, Radio, or other special officer, or is engaged in any special duty; or
(m) R.A.A.F. signalling methods by wireless telegraph or otherwise, or interruption of those communications.

A.3. AIR ACCIDENTS.

No mention is permissible of any Service air accident in the South-West Pacific Area until details of the accident are released by the Service concerned. No photographs of those accidents may be published without the consent of a Publicity Censor. Evidence given at inquests into Service accidents must be submitted to a Publicity Censor.

A.4. AIRMEN'S BLACKOUT.

No reference to airmen's blackout or to any phase of activity directed towards remedying it is permissible without the consent of a Publicity Censor.

A.5. AIR SERVICES—OVERSEAS.

Except with the consent of a Publicity Censor, no reference may be made to the route, port of arrival or departure, or other information concerning any overseas air service, including air freight service, in being or contemplated.

A.6. ALIENS AND ENEMY AGENTS.

Except with the consent of a Publicity Censor, no reference may be made to—
  (a) the alleged presence or activities of enemy agents in the South-West Pacific Area;
  (b) the arrest or detention of, or other Military action dealing with, enemy aliens or alleged traitors;
  (c) plans or proceedings of the Aliens' Classification Committee or any similar body.

A.7. ARMY INFORMATION.

1. No information may be published concerning—
  (a) the numbers, location, armament or equipment of troops who are guarding military establishments and other places;
  (b) movements of troops connected with the manning of defence works, fortifications, or the furnishing of guards in places of defence importance;
  (c) the location or movements of troops or units, or their departure or return from overseas, *unless officially released*;
  (d) any measures for the defence or fortification of any place or area;
  (e) radio signal stations or the operation or condition of other means of telecommunication;
  (f) the Australian signal system, signal equipment, or organization of the Australian Corps of Signals;
  (g) protective measures taken by the Services through the provision of armed guards;
  (h) operational methods or tactics used by Allied or enemy forces;
  (i) the number of existing armoured units or possible expansion or reduction thereof; or
  (j) sources from which military information about the enemy has been obtained.

2. Except with the consent of a Publicity Censor, no reference may be made to—
  (a) the numerical or other designation of military establishments or of military units, their location, commanders, principal officers, strength, composition, armament, organization, equipment, morale, discipline, state of training, experience, or other information that may indicate the fighting value of any particular unit;
  (b) any measures of military assistance to Australia by friendly Powers or by Australia to them;
  (c) any diversion of road or rail traffic occasioned by the use of means of communication for military purposes, or as the result of enemy action;
  (d) any specific measures planned or adopted for beach or coastal defence;
  (e) the location or extent of any prohibited areas;
  (f) searches and raids for a military purpose;
  (g) the practice by Australian or Allied Forces of any technique of training new to Australia;
  (h) the composition of Forces, changes in boundaries of military districts, locations of head-quarters of armies, corps or divisions, or arrangements for their supply;
  (i) the objects and work of, and other information regarding, any technical or special unit of the Australian or Allied Forces;
  (j) the names of officers who have, or are supposed to have, received appointments in the Australian Forces;
  k) trials of army equipment, whether already in service or not; or
  (l) use or possible use of chemicals in war operations.

A.8. A.I.F., A.M.F., AND ALLIED UNITS.

1. Except with the consent of a Publicity Censor the identity of A.I.F., A.M.F., or Allied units, whether in Australia or abroad, must not be disclosed by publication of their identifying numbers. Such terms as "An infantry battalion" or "A Queensland artillery regiment" may be used. This direction does not prevent mention of the distinguishing numbers of military hospitals in Australia.

2. Identifying colour patches in photographs of Service personnel should be re-touched out before publication, unless a Publicity Censor considers that the identity of the units concerned is already known to the enemy.

3. Special attention should be paid to items in social, sporting and other sectional columns.

A.9. ATROCITIES.

Atrocity stories concerning Australians or relating to incidents in the South-West Pacific Area may not be published unless officially released under the name of a Commonwealth Minister, the Chief of Staff of the Service concerned, or by General Head-quarters.

A.10. ALLIED WORKS COUNCIL.

Material describing or locating Allied Works Council projects must be submitted to a Publicity Censor. Reasonable references to the magnitude and importance of works carried out by the Council will be passed, provided those works are not secret. Aggregate expenditure and employment figures for the Commonwealth as a whole, or a particular State or area south of the Tropic of Capricorn, will be allowed concerning works already completed.

B.1. B.B.C. BROADCASTS.

Notwithstanding any specific instructions to the contrary, the broadcast of a news item by the B.B.C. automatically releases that item for publication and broadcasting in Australia.

B.2. BROADCASTING STATIONS.

All radio stations and broadcasting stations must observe the Broadcasting Stations Standing Orders for the time being in force.

B.3. BROADCASTS OF OPERATIONS.

No information relating to operations or to the Defence Forces generally on matters affecting Military Security may be broadcast without prior reference to a Publicity Censor. This is to apply whether or not such information has already been published in the Press.

B.4. BOMB AND MINE DISPOSAL METHODS.

Except with the consent of a Publicity Censor, there may be no reference to the methods of disposing of or dealing with bombs, mines or booby traps.

CABLES.—PRESS.

See I.4. Incoming Press Cables.

C.1. CAMOUFLAGE.

There may be no reference to details, methods or location of camouflage. This restriction includes references to—

 (a) the demolition, removal or alteration in appearance of any well-known landmark ;
 (b) any other measures that may be proposed or undertaken to render out of date the enemy's knowledge of the appearance of Allied defences from the air ;
 (c) camouflage research ; or
 (d) dummy landing grounds and similar structures designed to deceive the enemy.

C.2. CASUALTIES AND CASUALTY LISTS.

1. No Service casualty may be announced before publication in an official casualty list, unless the announcement is authorized, in writing, by the next-of-kin, and does not identify the ship, unit or exact area in which the person was serving. Nothing in this direction shall authorize the announcement before publication in an official casualty list of the fact that an airman is missing.

2. Biographies of soldiers, sailors and airmen mentioned in casualty lists may be published but the units or ships in which persons were serving must not be disclosed unless included in an official Service announcement. The locality where the casualty occurred may be mentioned in general terms only, such as "the South-West Pacific Area", unless the locality has been otherwise specified in an official Service announcement. The prohibition against disclosure of a unit or ship extends to obituary notices in advertising columns of newspapers, but not to probate notices.

3. Broadcasting of casualty lists or references to casualties is prohibited, but subsequent to the issue of any casualty list broadcast reference may be made, subject to the consent of the Service concerned, to individuals whose records or deeds warrant special mention.

4. Summaries of casualties for particular Services, units, battles, dates, theatres of war, or specified localities may not be published, unless the subject of official release and passed by a Publicity Censor.

5. Reports of civil accidents in which Service personnel are concerned must be submitted to a Publicity Censor.

6. No figures relating to enemy casualties in any hostilities in the South-West Pacific Area may be published unless authorized by General Head-quarters.

C.3. CENSORSHIP—REFERENCES TO.

The Press and Broadcasting Censorship Order made under National Security Regulations prohibits the printing, publication or broadcasting of any statement to the effect that any alteration, addition or omission has been made to any matter by a Publicity Censor, or that publication of any matter has been forbidden. All references to specific acts of Censorship must, therefore, be submitted to a Publicity Censor.

C.4. CENSORSHIP UNIFORMITY.

When an Editor submits an item to a Publicity Censor, the item must, as a matter of course, be withheld from interstate correspondents and affiliates until the Censor's decision is given. Affiliated papers should be notified when items have been submitted to and passed by the Censor. The item may be transmitted by interstate correspondents only in the form in which it was passed by the Censor. This rule applies equally to Broadcasting Stations.

CHEMICALS.

See G.1. (Gas or Germ Warfare) ; M.1 (Munitions), and S.5 (Statistics).

C.5. CODES OR CYPHERS.

1. No mention or speculation is allowed as to the capture or compromise of any British or Allied code or cypher by the enemy or as to our capture or compromise of any of the enemy's.

2. Except with the consent of a Publicity Censor, there may be no publication of any matter which might identify any person employed on, or in connexion with, code or cypher work.

C.6. COMMUNICATIONS—SUSPENSION OF.

Except with the consent of a Publicity Censor, there may be no reference to the suspension for military reasons of postal, telegraphic, telephonic or cable communications.

C.7. COMMANDS.

Unless officially released for publication there may be no reference to—
 (a) changes or speculations about changes in Allied Commands in the South-West Pacific Area ; or
 (b) known or possible location or movements of any senior officer engaged in operational activities or associated with any operational or combat unit of the Australian or Allied Forces. (A "senior" officer is, in the Navy of or above the rank of Lieutenant ; in the Army, above the rank of Captain ; and in the Air Force, of or above the rank of Squadron-Leader.)

C.8. COMMUNIQUES AND SPECULATION.

1. No mention may be made of enemy or Allied operations in the South-West Pacific Area which have not been announced in an Allied Head-quarters communique. Comment on operations announced in communiques must be confined to the factual limits of the communiques. Discrediting of the reliability of communiques will not be permitted.

2. Speculation as to probable or possible enemy or Allied moves may not be published without the consent of a Publicity Censor.

3. All commentaries, reviews and letters to the Editor which refer to operational matters in the South-West Pacific Area must be submitted to a Publicity Censor.

C.9. COURT-MARTIAL PROCEEDINGS.

All reports of court-martial proceedings must be submitted to a Publicity Censor.

D.1. DISTURBANCES OR DISAFFECTION.

References to disaffection or indiscipline among members of Australian or Allied Forces or to riots or disturbances in which they take part must be submitted to a Publicity Censor. Publication is prohibited of anything likely to prejudice the training, discipline, or administration of the Forces or to affect Allied relations adversely.

E.1. ENEMY RADIO.

1. Enemy claims as received by cable or as broadcast by the B.B.C. of Allied losses in any specified action or series of actions or in any theatre of war in which Australians are operating, may be published. They must be presented in such a manner as to leave no doubt that the reports are of enemy origin.

2. Enemy radio claims or other announcements "picked up" by a newspaper or broadcasting station in Australia must in every instance be submitted to a Publicity Censor.

3. No reference may be made to radio announcements from Japanese or Japanese-controlled stations regarding Australian Service personnel whom the enemy claim to be holding as prisoners of war. (*See* P.2. Prisoners of War.)

4. No mention may be made either in a list or otherwise of the wave-lengths of enemy or enemy-controlled broadcasting stations, or of the times at which they broadcast.

E.2. ENEMY DOCUMENTS.

No reference is permissible to captured enemy documents, letters, diaries or photographs.

E.3. ENEMY SACRED OBJECTS.

Except with the consent of a Publicity Censor, there may be no reference to any object which is regarded by the Japanese as sacred and falls into the hands of Allied forces.

E.4. ESCAPE STORIES.

Except with the consent of a Publicity Censor, no publicity may be given to escapes from the enemy or from enemy-occupied territory of Service personnel or civilians.

E.5. EQUIPMENT—CONDITION OF.

Except with the consent of a Publicity Censor, specific allegations about any particular shortage of equipment or armament of the fighting forces may not be published.

F.1. FOOD.

Except with the consent of a Publicity Censor, there may be no reference to any research in connexion with foodstuffs for use for defence or Service purposes.

G.1. GAS OR GERM WARFARE.

Except with the approval of General Head-quarters, no reference is permissible to the actual or possible use of gas or germ warfare in the South-West Pacific Area, or to the training of Service personnel in the use of gas for the purposes of waging war or to research in relation to chemical warfare.

G.2. GOLD RESERVE.

Comment on the amount of gold reserve held against the Commonwealth note issue is prohibited. The actual figures officially announced at any time may be published, but previous statements must not be subjoined.

H.1. HOSPITAL SHIPS.

1. In interviews with, or stories about returning invalid Service personnel, reference may be made to the fact that they have reached an unnamed Australian port in a hospital ship. No indication may be given, by the use of a date line or otherwise, of the port of arrival or of the movements, whereabouts or identity of any hospital ship.

2. No such interviews and no photographs of any such personnel may be published or transmitted by a newspaper to any affiliated newspaper until they have been passed by a Publicity Censor in the capital city where the interviews and pictures were obtained. All clues to the identity of a ship or port must be eliminated from photographs of invalids taken on any ship or wharf.

3. No advance publicity is permissible regarding the expected arrival of invalids at any Australian port or regarding plans for their reception.

H.2. HEALTH OF FORCES.

Except with the consent of a Publicity Censor, no reference may be made to—
    (a) the existence of ill-health or disease among, or the deterioration of the physical or mental condition of, the Forces or any of them, or as to the extent of any such ill-health, disease or deterioration ; or
    (b) the details of the measures taken by Service authorities in the South-West Pacific Area to control or prevent malaria or other diseases.

IMPORTS AND EXPORTS.
See S.5. Statistics.

I.1. INVENTIONS.
Except with the consent of a Publicity Censor, no reference may be made to any novel kind of fighting machine or to any invention for use in the manufacture of munitions or equipment or in warfare.

I.2. INTERNEES.
All material relating to internees, former internees, or internment camps in Australia must be submitted to a Publicity Censor.

I.3. INTELLIGENCE PERSONNEL.
1. Except for official releases, no reference is permissible to the identity or activities of Intelligence personnel, particularly those who are or have been engaged on secret work in Japanese occupied territory or Pacific Islands.

2. No reference is permissible to persons engaged in interrogating enemy prisoners-or-war or in translating captured enemy documents. It is particularly important that it be not disclosed that American-born Japanese (Nisei) are engaged on this work.

INTERVIEWS WITH SERVICE PERSONNEL.
See S.7. Service Personnel.

I.4. INCOMING PRESS CABLES.
Voluntary Censorship, as applied by the Press to news received from internal sources in Australia, will also apply to Press, cable and Beam messages from overseas. Editors should therefore submit to a Publicity Censor any doubtful messages received from the United Kingdom or elsewhere.

L.1. LEAFLETS (PROPAGANDA).
Propaganda leaflets used in the South-West Pacific Area, whether distributed by the enemy or by the Allies must not be quoted or reproduced without the consent of a Publicity Censor.

LETTERS FROM SERVICE PERSONNEL.
See S.7. Service Personnel.

M.1. MUNITIONS.
Except with the consent of a Publicity Censor, there may be no publication of—
- (a) photographs which show munitions factories, annexes or contractors' workshops as a whole;
- (b) material that gives descriptions of work carried on in any such establishment;
- (c) any indication of the exact nature or quantity of munitions produced or to be produced in any particular establishment;
- (d) the locations of—
    - (i) munition factories, annexes or contractors' workshops, in particular machine-tool factories and bomb-filling and shell-filling centres;
    - (ii) optical instrument factories;
    - (iii) marine mine and torpedo manufacturing centres;
    - (iv) ammunition, explosive, fuel, armament and supply stores or dumps; or
    - (v) radio location instrument factories;
- (e) references to new types of munitions, munitions production, armaments, guns, tanks or transport vehicles, existing or projected.

M.2. MAN-POWER.
Unless approved by the responsible Minister or the Chief of the General Staff, publication is prohibited of figures analyzing, grouping or classifying the man-power available for the Australian Armed Forces or for war purposes.

MALARIA.
See H.2. Health of Forces.

MEDICAL RESEARCH.
See A.4 (Airmen's Blackout), F.1 (Food), and H. 2 (Health of Forces).

MINING AND MINERALS.
See S.5. Statistics.

MISSING SERVICE PERSONNEL.
See S.7. Service personnel.

N.1. NAVAL INFORMATION.
1. There is no restriction on the publication of overseas reports of naval actions, or reports of the dispositions of ships which have already been passed by the Censorship Authorities in the United Kingdom or other British Dominions, or in Allied countries.

2. In general, photographs of types of ships mentioned in copy passed for publication are allowed, provided those photographs do not reveal details of their construction, equipment, or armament. All new photographs of ships must, however, be submitted to a Publicity Censor. Photographs incorporated in "Jane's Fighting Ships" may be taken as a guide of the type of photographs which are permissible.

3. Except for official releases, publication of the following matters is prohibited:—
   (a) Any reference, direct or indirect, to the location, disposition or projected movements of—
      (i) Allied naval vessels of any description;
      (ii) hospital ships (See H.1.)
      (iii) British, Allied, or neutral merchant ships (including coastal vessels and oil tankers);
      (iv) enemy naval vessels of any description;
      (v) enemy merchant ships;
   (b) Reports of concentrations of war or merchant vessels in a specified locality;
   (c) The movements and duties of naval personnel or the appointments of naval officers;
   (d) Security measures taken to exercise surveillance over potential enemy vessels, or to restrain prospective enemy persons;
   (e) Any information regarding naval munitions, materials, establishments, technical apparatus or equipment, the arming or fitting out of vessels, or the construction or erection of naval buildings and dockyards, including graving and floating docks. (See P.5. Ports and Wharves);
   (f) Reports of, or survivors' stories of, encounters between merchant vessels and enemy raiders, submarines or aircraft;
   (g) Loss of or damage to war vessels or merchant ships, whether as the result of enemy action or accident;
   (h) Information about naval convoys and escorts or about transports associated with the conveyance of Australian, New Zealand, or Allied troops; and
   (i) Any reference to official sailing directions or orders referring to trade routes which have been issued by the Admiralty or the Navy Office.

N.2. NON-COMBATANTS.

No reference may be made to any non-combatant member of the forces, or to any person accompanying the forces, having been engaged in combatant activity.

O.1. OFFICIALS TRAVELLING ABROAD.

Except as officially released, no reference may be made, until after his arrival, to the actual or probable date of departure, route, means of transport, or progress of any Minister or Government officer travelling overseas.

P.1. PARLIAMENT—SECRET SESSION.

No reference is permissible to proceedings at secret sessions of Parliament.

P.2. PRISONERS OF WAR.

1. Except with the consent of a Publicity Censor, there may be no reference to—
   (a) the actual or contemplated employment of prisoners of war in connexion with any Service work;
   (b) alleged measures taken against enemy prisoners or to enemy persons, if the effect of the reference might be to provoke reprisals against our own personnel in enemy hands;
   (c) the interrogation of, or other particulars concerning, enemy prisoners-of-war, including statements made by them, their names, units or other intelligence derived from them.
   (d) mutinies, escapes or other happenings at prisoner-of-war camps, or to escaped prisoners.

2. There may be no publication of photographs of prisoners-of-war inside the confines of a prisoner-of-war camp, or while engaged, in the vicinity of a prisoner-of-war camp, as members of a working party. All other pictures of prisoners of war must be submitted to a Publicity Censor.

3. Members of the public may not be invited to correspond with named Australian prisoners-of-war in enemy countries.

4. No reference is permissible to broadcasts from any enemy-controlled broadcasting station by, or concerning, Australian prisoners-of-war. (See E.1. Enemy Radio.)

5. Without the consent of a Publicity Censor, there may be no reference to Australian or Allied Service personnel or to civilians taken prisoner, or allegedly taken prisoner, by the enemy.

6. No reference is permissible to any actual or contemplated exchange of prisoners of war or to any movement of prisoners for that purpose, unless the exchange or movement is officially announced in Australia or cabled from overseas.

P.3. PRISONERS' LETTERS.

Letters or extracts from letters written by Australian or Allied prisoners of war in enemy hands may be published only after submission to a Publicity Censor.

P.4. "PEN FRIEND" CORRESPONDENCE.

Except with the consent of a Publicity Censor, nothing may be published or broadcast inviting readers or listeners to engage in "Pen Friend" correspondence. This includes advertisements and invitations in letters to or from members of the armed forces or prisoners-of-war, and it applies to correspondence both within Australia and overseas.

P.5. PORTS AND WHARVES.

All references to wharf or other port facilities, built, being built or contemplated, to navigational conditions in any port in Australia, to the expansion of or alteration to those wharves or other facilities, or to work in connection with the navigational conditions of any port, must be submitted to a Publicity Censor.

P.6. POLITICAL WARFARE.

No material may be published giving or indicating any details of Allied political warfare activities or plans.

R.1. RADIO LOCATION AND RADAR.

All material dealing with radio location or Radar must be submitted to a Publicity Censor. Official recruiting announcements are excepted.

RAILWAYS AND ROADS.

See T.1. Transport.

S.1. SABOTAGE.

Except with the consent of a Publicity Censor, no reference may be made to reports of actual or alleged or attempted sabotage, malicious damage or other similar offences in any defence undertaking, public building or utility.

S.2. SHIPBUILDING AND LAUNCHINGS.

1. All references to the building or launching in Australia of naval or merchant vessels must be submitted to a Publicity Censor.

2. Subject to the consent of a Publicity Censor, the name, type, or tonnage of any ship launched, the place of launching and the dockyard at which it was built may be published.

3. Except with the consent of a Publicity Censor, there may be no reference to—
    - (a) the number of ships of any specified type launched or contemplated, or any other specific details of the Australian shipbuilding programme;
    - (b) the armament or speed of any naval vessel;
    - (c) the speed of any merchant vessel or the trade for which it is intended or is being used;
    - (d) the construction of lighters, barges or other types of small craft; or
    - (e) the expansion or number of slipways at a particular yard, or new slipways, docks, or other facilities, either built, being built or contemplated, for repairs to or maintenance of shipping in Australia, or to the expansion of existing establishments.

SHIPPING.

See N.1. Naval Information.

S.3. STRIKES AND LOCKOUTS.

It is important that in publishing material with respect to strikes or lockouts (existing or threatened), absenteeism, or any existing or threatened industrial dispute, editors and broadcasters should bear in mind the requirements of these directions as to specific matters and in particular the requirements contained in M.1, N.1, S.2 and S.5.

S.4. SUNSPOTS.

No publication is permitted of statements or forecasts relating to the effect of ionospheric activity (sunspots) on radio communications or to research connected with those matters. Speculation as to forthcoming ionospheric disturbances or research on those disturbances is forbidden, but references to past phenomena (e.g., Aurora Australis) may be published after reference to a Publicity Censor, provided no mention is made of any interference with communications.

S.5. STATISTICS AS TO SUPPLIES AND PRODUCTION.

1. Except with the consent of a Publicity Censor, there may be no reference to import or export of—
    - (a) munitions or fighting equipment;
    - (b) machinery for use in the manufacture of munitions, supplies or equipment for the fighting services;
    - (c) metals, minerals, chemicals or other raw materials used in the manufacture of munitions, supplies or equipment for the fighting services, other than coal or the base metals (such as iron), common chemicals or staple commodities such as wheat or wool; or
    - (b) gold, oil, petrol or rubber

2. Detailed statistics of imports or exports to or from India, the Middle East, the Near East or the Mediterranean Sea shall not include figures which may indicate, or from which may be deduced, the amount or route of shipping still in transit.

3. Except with the consent of a Publicity Censor, there may be no reference to—
    - (a) the production during the preceding twelve months or any part thereof of metals or minerals used in the manufacture of munitions, supplies or equipment for the fighting services other than coal or the base metals, such as iron;
    - (b) the quantities of those metals or minerals transported or delivered during such period; estimates of future production, stocks, labour engaged, or other data from which the quantity of production may be deduced; or
    - (c) discoveries of new deposits or the development of new sources of supply of those metals or minerals.
    PROVIDED that, with the consent of a Publicity Censor, production figures of an individual mine for the preceding twelve months may be published, but those figures shall not be published with other similar figures to show the total production of those metals or minerals for the Commonwealth or any State.

4. Except with the consent of a Publicity Censor, there may be no reference to—
    - (a) the quantities of munitions, supplies or equipment produced for the Fighting Services, or to any data from which those quantities may be ascertained or estimated;
    - (b) any shortage of any material, such as rubber or oil, used in the production of munitions, supplies or equipment for the Fighting Services; or
    - (c) anything which may reveal or indicate the stocks in Australia of any such material.

S.6. SECURITY SERVICE.

Apart from statements issued for publication by the responsible Minister or the Director-General of Security, all references to the Security Service or the activities of Security Officers must be submitted to a Publicity Censor.

S.7. SERVICE PERSONNEL.

1. All statements in relation to military matters by members of the Fighting Services must be submitted to a Publicity Censor.

2. Advertisements and other notices concerning missing Service personnel must not give their exact unit identity. The arm of the service to which a serviceman belongs may be given only in general terms, such as Infantry, Engineers or Ordnance. It is permissible to quote the missing man's Service number, rank and name.

3. Advertisements and other notices seeking information in respect of Service personnel may not be published without the consent of a Publicity Censor.

T.1. TRANSPORT.

Except with the consent of a Publicity Censor, there may be no publication of—
  (a) any material indicating the amount of traffic (goods or personnel) for war purposes passing at any time over any road or railway;
  (b) reports of extensive disorganization of road, rail, sea or air transport; or
  (c) information about the construction or proposed construction of strategic railway lines or roads of strategic importance.

W.1. WEATHER NEWS.

1. PRESS.—Press publication of meteorological information is generally permissible, but shall be subject to the following directions:—

  (a) *Forecasts.*—Weather forecasts, weather charts and weather synopses, except where applicable to the region west of 125 degrees East Longitude and north of 20 degrees South Latitude from the 125th to 138th degree East Longitude may be published without restriction provided they have been officially released for publication by a Meteorologist under the direction of the Director of Meteorological Services.

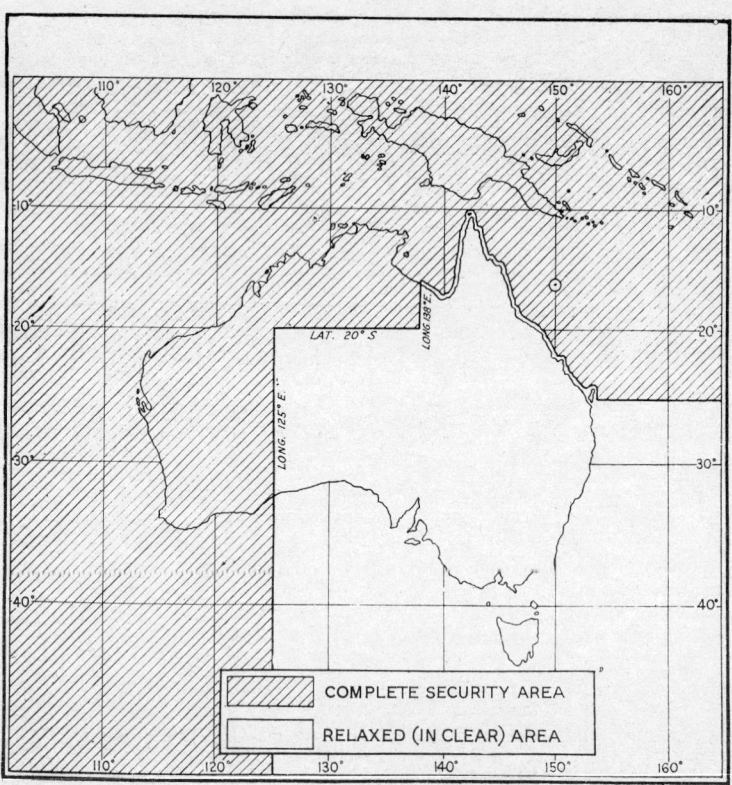

Appendix A **213**

10

(b) *Floods*—
  (i) Reports concerning floods anticipated or in progress north of 20 degrees South Latitude from the Western Australian coast to 138 degrees East Longitude shall be limited to necessary warnings that specific localities are in imminent danger. All such reports shall be submitted to a Publicity Censor.
  (ii) (1) Reports concerning anticipated floods, or of the progress of floods in other areas of Australia may be published.
    (2) Articles describing conditions in particular areas affected by floods and giving details of damage to local facilities in particular localities affected by flood waters may be published, provided no reference is made to any effect on military installations, establishments, or military movements or on strategic areas.
    (3) All news items referring to flood reports or rainfall conducive to floods, affecting or likely to affect military installations, establishments, or military movements or strategic areas, shall be submitted to a Publicity Censor.
(c) *Rainfall*—
  (i) Items relating to rainfall in the region north of 20 degrees South Latitude from the Western Australian coast to 138 degrees East Longitude should be limited to the fact that rain has fallen during the previous week in localities where its value is significant to primary industry and to the public. Publication of rainfall statistics for this area shall be confined to the weekly rainfall figures issued by Weather Bureaux.
  (ii) Rainfall information applicable to other areas of Australia may be published without restriction.
  (iii) News items in respect of the intensity or persistence of rainfall in Western Australia West of 125 degrees East Longitude shall be submitted to a Publicity Censor.
(d) *Special Weather Phenomena (such as Dust Storms)*—
  (i) Reports relative to these occurrences in the region west of 125 degrees East Longitude and north of 20 degrees South Latitude between 125 degrees and 138 degrees East Longitude may be published only with the consent of a Publicity Censor.
  (ii) Reports relative to these occurrences in other areas of Australia may be published without restriction.
(e) *Temperatures*—
  (i) Publication of temperature information in the region north of 20 degrees South Latitude between the Western Australian coast and 138 degrees East Longitude is not permissible until 24 hours after the time of observation.
  (ii) In other areas of Australia, temperature information may be published without restriction.
(f) *Bushfire Warnings*—Warnings of bush fire danger, including advice of the direction of surface wind in the area affected, may be published without restriction.
(g) *Conditions of Pastures, Stock and Crops, and Market Reports.*—Publication of information of this kind is permissible, except in respect of areas of strategic importance.
(h) *River Levels.*—Particulars in respect of heights of rivers issued by Weather Bureaux or by the State Water and River Commissions may be published without restriction.
(i) *Photographs*—
  (i) All photographs of damage caused by drought, storm, flood, or by other weather disturbances in the region west of 125 degrees East Longitude and North of 20 degrees South Latitude between 125 degrees and 138 degrees East Longitude shall be submitted to a Publicity Censor before publication.
  (ii) In other regions of Australia, only those photographs that disclose information of possible military value, in particular photographs showing strategic bridges or water installation need be submitted to a Publicity Censor.

2. **BROADCASTING.**—Broadcasting of meteorological information shall be subject to the following directions:—
  (a) *Forecasts.*—No weather forecast, direct or by inference, relating to S.W.P.A., and no weather notes or analyses interpreting weather systems or their anticipated developments, may be broadcast.*
  (b) *Flood Warnings and Reports*—
    (i) Broadcasting of information applicable to or originating in the region west of 125 degrees East Longitude and north of 20 degrees South Latitude between 125 degrees and 138 degrees East Longitude shall be restricted to warnings that specific localities are in imminent danger. Such warnings shall comply with the Broadcasting Stations Standing Orders.
    (ii) Information applicable to and originating in other areas of Australia may be broadcast without restriction, provided that no reference is made to the effects on military installations, military establishments, or military movements, and provided flood warnings other than those issued officially by a Meteorologist under the direction of the Director of Meteorological Services, comply with the Broadcasting Stations Standing Orders.
  (c) *Rainfall*—
    (i) Broadcasting of rainfall information from rainfall stations in the region west of 125 degrees East Longitude and north of 20 degrees South Latitude between 125 degrees and 138 degrees East Longitude shall be restricted to weekly, monthly, seasonal and annual rainfall figures officially issued from Weather Bureaux.
    (ii) Rainfall reports from stations in other areas of Australia may be broadcast without restriction.
  (d) *Special Weather Phenomena (such as Dust Storms)*—
    (i) Broadcasting of such information originating in or applicable to the region west of 125 degrees East Longitude and north of 20 degrees South Latitude between 125 degrees and 138 degrees East Longitude is prohibited.
    (ii) Such information originating in and applicable to other areas of Australia may be broadcast.

---
* NOTE.—There is no Security objection to the broadcasting of temperature figures and barometric pressures relating only to the "relaxed areas" provided that this information is not broadcast in such a manner as to conflict with the intention of sub-paragraph (a) of paragraph 2.

Appendix A

(e) *Frost and Bush Fire Warnings—*
    (i) In the region west of 125 degrees East Longitude and north of 20 degrees South Latitude between 125 degrees and 138 degrees East Longitude broadcasting of frost information is restricted to official warnings issued by a Meteorologist under the direction of the Director of Meteorological Services. Bushfire warnings may be broadcast provided that they comply with the Broadcasting Stations Standing Orders.
    (ii) Frost information originating in and applicable to other areas of Australia may be broadcast without restriction but bushfire warnings shall comply with the Broadcasting Stations Standing Orders.

(f) *Conditions of Pastures, Stocks and Crops and Market Reports—*
    (i) The broadcasting of such information originating in or relating to the region west of 125 degrees East Longitude and north of 20 degrees South Latitude between 125 degrees and 138 degrees East Longitude is prohibited.
    (ii) Such information originating in and relating to other areas of Australia may be broadcast without restriction.

(g) *River Heights.*—Bulletins issued by Weather Bureaux may be broadcast without restriction.

Dated this 31st day of October, 1944.

E. G. BONNEY,
Chief Publicity Censor.

APPENDIX A.
NATIONAL SECURITY (GENERAL) REGULATIONS.

Attention is directed to the following National Security (General) Regulations :—

National Security (General) Regulation 17—

"17.—(1.) Subject to these Regulations, a person shall not, in any manner likely to prejudice the defence of the Commonwealth or the efficient prosecution of the war—
  (a) obtain ;
  (b) record, communicate to any other person, or publish ; or
  (c) have in his possession any document containing, or other record whatsoever of,
any information being, or purporting to be, information with respect to—
    (i) the number, description, armament, equipment, disposition, movement or condition of any of the forces, vessels or aircraft of the King or the Commonwealth ;
    (ii) any operations or projected operations of any of those forces, vessels or aircraft ;
    (iii) any measures for the defence or fortification of any place on behalf of the King or the Commonwealth ;
    (iv) the number, description or location of any prisoner of war ;
    (v) munitions of war ; or
    (vi) any other matter whatsoever information as to which would or might be directly or indirectly useful to the enemy.

"(2.) A person shall not make any false statement, or spread a false report, whether orally or otherwise, or do any act, or have any article in his possession, likely to be prejudicial to the defence of the Commonwealth or the efficient prosecution of the war, or likely to cause disaffection to His Majesty or public alarm or despondency or to interfere with the operations of any of the Forces of the King or the Commonwealth or the Forces of any foreign power allied or associated with His Majesty in any war in which His Majesty is engaged.".

National Security (General) Regulation 19 (1.) (c)—

"19.—(1.) Subject to any exemptions for which provision is made by order of the Minister, a person shall not, except under the authority of a written permit granted by or on behalf of the Minister—
  (c) make, or have in his possession, any photograph, sketch, plan or other representation—
    (i) of a prohibited place, or of any part of or object in a prohibited place ;
    (ii) of, or of any part of or object in, any area specified by order of the Minister, being an area in relation to which the restriction of photography appears to the Minister to be expedient in the interests of the defence of the Commonwealth ; or
    (iii) of a place, person, thing or occurrence of any description specified in any order made by the Minister, or of any part of such place, person, thing or occurrence.".

National Security (General) Regulations 41 (1.), 41A and 41B—

"41.—(1.) A person shall not—
  (a) endeavour to cause disaffection among any persons engaged (whether in Australia or elsewhere) in the service of the King or the Commonwealth, or in the performance of essential services, or to induce any person to do or to omit to do anything in breach of his duty as a person so engaged ; or
  (b) with intent to contravene, or to aid, abet, counsel or procure a contravention of, paragraph (a) of this sub-regulation, have in his possession or under his control any document of such a nature that the dissemination of copies thereof among any such persons would constitute such a contravention.".

"41A. A person shall not by speech or writing advocate, encourage or suggest—
  (a) the use of force or violence as a means of advancing or carrying into effect any political cause, measures, policies or proposals ; or
  (b) the use of sabotage or the destruction of or injury to property.

"41B. A person shall not—
  (a) print, publish, distribute, circulate or, without lawful excuse (proof whereof shall lie upon him), have in his possession, any book, periodical, pamphlet, ' dodger ', circular, hand bill, card or newspaper ; or
  (b) broadcast by means of wireless telegraphy any message or other communication,
containing any matter advocating, encouraging or suggesting—
  (c) the use of force or violence as a means of advancing or carrying into effect any political cause, measures, policies or proposals ; or
  (d) the use of sabotage or the destruction of or injury to property.".

National Security (General) Regulation 42 (1.) and (4.) (a)—

"42.—(1.) A person shall not—
  (a) endeavour, whether orally or otherwise, to influence public opinion (whether in Australia or elsewhere) in a manner likely to be prejudicial to the defence of the Commonwealth or the efficient prosecution of the war ; or
  (b) do any act, or have any article in his possession, with a view to making, or facilitating the making of, any such endeavour.

"(4.) In this regulation—
  (a) the expression ' public opinion ' includes the opinion of any section of the public.

APPENDIX B.
PRESS AND BROADCASTING CENSORSHIP ORDER.

WHEREAS by regulation 16 of the National Security (General) Regulations it is provided *inter alia* that, if it appears to a Minister to be necessary or expedient so to do in the interest of the public safety, the defence of the Commonwealth or the efficient prosecution of the war, or for maintaining supplies and services essential to the life of the community, he may by order provide for the censorship of newspapers and other publications and of broadcasting by wireless transmitting apparatus:

And whereas it appears to me, John Curtin, the Minister of State for Defence, to be necessary in the interest of the defence of the Commonwealth and the efficient prosecution of the war to provide for the censorship of newspapers and other publications and of broadcasting by wireless transmitting apparatus :

Now therefore I do hereby order as follows :—

PART I.—PRELIMINARY.
CITATION.

1. This Order may be cited as the Press and Broadcasting Censorship Order.

REPEAL.

2. The Press Censorship Order made on the fourth day of October, 1939, and published in the *Gazette* dated the sixth day of October, 1939, the Broadcasting Censorship Order dated the first day of March, 1940, and published in the *Gazette* dated the sixth day of March, 1940. and the Press and Broadcasting Censorship Order made on the fourteenth day of January, 1943, and published in the *Gazette* on the eighteenth day of January, 1943, are hereby revoked.

PARTS.

3. This Order is divided into Parts, as follows :—
   Part I.—Preliminary.
   Part II.—Press Censorship.
   Part III.—Broadcasting Censorship.

DEFINITIONS.

4. In this Order, unless the contrary intention appears—
   "Chief Publicity Censor" means the Chief Publicity Censor appointed by the Minister ;
   "Publicity Censor" means any Publicity Censor appointed by the Minister, and includes the Chief Publicity Censor, any Press Censorship Authority and any Broadcasting Censorship Authority appointed under any of the repealed Orders and holding office at the commencement of this Order ;
   "the Minister" means the Minister of State for Defence ;
   "the repealed Orders" means the Press Censorship Order made on the fourth day of October, 1939, and published in the *Gazette* dated the sixth day of October, 1939, the Broadcasting Censorship Order made on the first day of March, 1940, and published in the *Gazette* dated the sixth day of March, 1940, and the Press and Broadcasting Censorship Order made on the fourteenth day of January, 1943, and published in the *Gazette* on the eighteenth day of January, 1943.

EXISTING PRESS AND BROADCASTING CENSORSHIP AUTHORITIES.

5. Any Press Censorship Authority and any Broadcasting Censorship Authority appointed for the purposes of any of the repealed Orders and holding office at the commencement of this Order shall be deemed to have been appointed a Publicity Censor for the purposes of this Order.

PUBLICITY CENSORS TO BE PRESS CENSORSHIP AUTHORITIES.

6. The Chief Publicity Censor and each Publicity Censor shall be deemed to be Press Censorship Authorities for the purposes of regulation 16 of the National Security (General) Regulations.

POWER TO ISSUE DIRECTIONS.

7.—(1.) The Chief Publicity Censor or any Publicity Censor authorized by him may issue such directions as he considers necessary for the purpose of the censorship of newspapers and other publications, and of broadcasting by wireless transmitting apparatus.

(2.) Directions under this paragraph may be issued orally or in writing or by telephone or telegram—
   (a) in relation to the censorship of newspapers or other publications—to the editor, a sub-editor or the chief of staff of the newspaper or other publication or to a person nominated by the editor to receive such directions and approved by the State Publicity Censor of the State in which the newspaper or other publication is published or to the author or printer of the publication ; and
   (b) in relation to the censorship of broadcasting by wireless transmitting apparatus—to the manager of any wireless station or to a person nominated by the manager and approved by the State Publicity Censor.

PART II.—PRESS CENSORSHIP.
ORDER TO SUBMIT MATTER FOR PRESS CENSORSHIP.

8. A Publicity Censor may, by order in writing or orally, require the editor or printer or publisher of any newspaper or periodical, and the author or printer or publisher of any matter intended to be printed or published, to submit to him before publication all or any matter intended for publication, and, in particular, any matter intended for publication which contains any information or statement with respect to—
   (i) the number, description, armament, equipment, disposition, movement or condition, of any of the forces, vessels or aircraft of the King or the Commonwealth or of any Foreign Power allied or associated with His Majesty in any war in which His Majesty is engaged ;
   (ii) any operations or projected operations of any of those forces, vessels or aircraft ;
   (iii) any measures for the defence or fortification of any place in the Commonwealth or in any part of His Majesty's dominions ;
   (iv) the number, description or location of any prisoners of war ;
   (v) munitions of war ; or
   (vi) any other matter whatsoever information as to which would or might be directly or indirectly useful to the enemy, or prejudicial to the public safety, the defence of the Commonwealth or of any other part of His Majesty's dominions, the efficient prosecution of the war, or the maintenance of supplies and services essential to the life of the community.

POWER OF PUBLICITY CENSORS TO FORBID PUBLICATION.

9. A Publicity Censor may forbid the printing or publication of the whole or any portion of any matter submitted to him in compliance with any direction under paragraph 7 or any requirement under paragraph 8 of this Order, or may give directions as to the alterations to be made to any such matter before publication.

MATTER TO BE RE-SUBMITTED IF NOT PUBLISHED WITHIN ONE MONTH.

10. Where any matter passed for publication by a Publicity Censor is not published within one month after being so passed by that Censor, a person shall not publish that matter unless it has been re-submitted to and again passed by a Publicity Censor.

Persons to Comply with Directions of Publicity Censor.

11.—(1.) A person shall not print or publish in Australia—
  (a) any matter which is required by or under this Order to submit to a Publicity Censor, unless it has been submitted to a Publicity Censor and has been passed for publication (either with or without alteration) by that Censor;
  (b) any matter the printing or publication of which has been forbidden by a Publicity Censor;
  (c) in a form other than the form approved by the Publicity Censor, any matter which has been submitted to and censored by a Publicity Censor;
  (d) any statement to the effect, or from which it can be inferred, that any alteration, addition or omission has been made by, or under the direction of, a Publicity Censor;
  (e) any matter in such a way as to show that any alteration, addition or omission has been made by, or under the direction of, a Publicity Censor; or
  (f) any statement to the effect that publication of any matter has been forbidden by a Publicity Censor.

(2.) A person shall not lodge for transmission for printing or publication outside Australia any matter specified in sub-paragraph (1.) of this paragraph unless it has been passed for such transmission by a Publicity Censor.

(3.) A person shall not refuse or fail to comply with any direction or requirement issued by a Publicity Censor in pursuance of this Order.

(4.) The editor of every newspaper or other publication shall take such action as is necessary to ensure that all directions issued by a Publicity Censor are complied with by and in relation to the newspaper or other publication of which he is the editor.

Seizure of Newspapers, etc., Issued in Contravention of this Order.

12. Where any newspaper, periodical or other publication has been printed or published in contravention of this Order or of any direction issued by a Publicity Censor, or a Publicity Censor has reason to believe that any person is about to publish a newspaper, periodical or other publication in contravention of this Order or of any such direction, the Publicity Censor may, by writing under his hand, authorize the seizure of all copies of the newspaper, periodical or other publication, and thereupon any Commonwealth Officer or constable may seize such copies, and for that purpose may enter and search any premises, if necessary by force.

Powers of Publicity Censors.

12A. Every direction, order or prohibition issued, given or made under this Order by a Publicity Censor in relation to the publication of any matter shall be issued, given or made solely by reference to the requirements of defence security, as they exist at the time of publication or proposed publication of the matter in question. *Added by Order dated 18th May, 1944.*

Limitation of Power to Seize.

12B. The power conferred on a Publicity Censor by paragraph 12 of this Order to authorize the seizure of copies of a newspaper, periodical or other publication may be exercised only in cases where immediate and obvious danger to defence security is likely to arise from the circulation of the newspaper, periodical or other publication. *Added by Order dated 18th May, 1944.*

Power of Supreme Court to Order Suppression.

12C.—(1.) Where a person is convicted under paragraph 11 of this Order, the Commonwealth may, within seven days after the conviction, make application to the Full Court of the Supreme Court of the State in which the conviction takes place for an order directing that during the period specified in the order the newspaper or periodical in relation to which the conviction took place shall not be published. *Added by Order dated 18th May, 1944.*

(2.) Notice of such application shall be served upon the proprietor and publisher of the newspaper or periodical.

(3.) The Full Court of the Supreme Court of the State shall have jurisdiction to hear and determine the application.

(4.) On the hearing of the application the Court shall take into consideration the seriousness of the contravention in respect of which the conviction took place and the extent to which previous contraventions have occurred in the case of newspaper or periodical.

(5.) The Court may at any time vary any such order upon further application either of the Commonwealth or of the proprietor or publisher of the newspaper or periodical.

General Principles of Censorship.

12D. In the administration of this Order the following general principles shall be applied:— *Added by Order dated 18th May, 1944.*

"Censorship shall be imposed exclusively for reasons of defence security. Owing to the many and changing phases of the war, 'defence security' cannot be exhaustively defined. Primarily, 'defence security' relates to the armed forces of all the Allied Nations and to all the operations of war. It covers the suppression of information useful to the enemy. It may at times include particular aspects of Australia's war-time relationship with other countries. Censorship shall not be imposed merely for the maintenance of morale or the prevention of despondency or alarm. Censorship shall not prevent the reporting of industrial disputes or stoppages. Criticism and comment, however strongly expressed, shall be free. Mere exaggeration or inaccuracy shall not be a ground for censorship. 'Defence security' shall be the governing principle for every application of censorship.".

PART III.—BROADCASTING CENSORSHIP.

Order to Submit Matter for Broadcasting Censorship.

13. A Publicity Censor may, by order in writing or orally, require the owner or other person in charge of a wireless transmitting apparatus to submit to him for censorship all or any matter which it is proposed to broadcast, and, in particular, any matter which it is proposed to broadcast which contains any information or statement with respect to any of the matters specified in paragraph 8 of this Order.

Power of Publicity Censor to Forbid Broadcasting.

14. A Publicity Censor may forbid the broadcasting of the whole or any portion of any matter submitted to him for censorship, or may give directions as to the alterations to be made to any such matter before broadcasting.

Matter to be Re-submitted if not Broadcast within One Month.

15. When any matter passed for broadcasting by a Publicity Censor is not broadcast within one month after being so passed by that Censor, a person shall not broadcast that matter unless it has been re-submitted to and again passed by a Publicity Censor.

Persons to Comply with Directions of Publicity Censors.

16.—(1.) The owner or person in charge of a wireless transmitting apparatus shall not broadcast or authorize or permit the broadcasting of any matter specified in paragraph 11 of this Order, or any matter the broadcasting of which has been forbidden by a Publicity Censor, or refuse or fail to comply with any direction or requirement issued by a Publicity Censor.

(2.) The owner, manager or other person in charge of a wireless station shall take such action as is necessary to ensure that all directions and requirements issued by a Publicity Censor are complied with, by and in relation to the wireless station.

Dated this thirty-first day of July, 1943.

JOHN CURTIN,
Minister of State for Defence.

APPENDIX C.
CINEMATOGRAPH FILMS CENSORSHIP ORDER.

WHEREAS by regulation 16 of the National Security (General) Regulations it is provided, amongst other things, that if it appears to a Minister to be necessary or expedient so to do in the interest of the public safety, the defence of the Commonwealth or the efficient prosecution of the war, or for maintaining supplies and services essential to the life of the community, he may by order provide for the censorship of cinematograph films :

And whereas it appears to me, John Curtin, Minister of State for Defence, to be necessary in the interests of the defence of the Commonwealth and the efficient prosecution of the war to provide for the censorship of cinematograph films :

Now therefore I do hereby order as follows :—

CITATION.
1. This Order may be cited as the Cinematograph Films Censorship Order.

REVOCATION.
2. The Cinematograph Films Censorship Order dated the twenty-seventh day of June, 1940, and published in the *Gazette* on the third day of July, 1940, and the Cinematograph Films Censorship Order dated the fourteenth day of January, 1943, and published in the *Gazette* on the eighteenth day of January, 1943, are hereby revoked.

DEFINITIONS.
3. In this Order, unless the contrary intention appears—
"cinematograph film" includes—
    (a) the sound track or any other article on which sounds have been recorded for the purpose of their being reproduced in connexion with the exhibition of a cinematograph film ; and
    (b) any portion of a cinematograph film ;
"the Minister" means the Minister of State for Defence.

CINEMATOGRAPH FILM CENSORS.
4.—(1.) For the purposes of this Order there shall be such Cinematograph Film Censors as are from time to time appointed by the Minister.

(2.) All persons appointed, or holding office, as Cinematograph Film Censorship Authorities for the purposes of either of the Orders revoked by this Order, and holding office immediately prior to the making of this Order, shall be deemed to have been appointed Cinematograph Film Censors for the purposes of this Order.

CINEMATOGRAPH FILMS TO BE SUBMITTED TO CENSORS.
5. A person shall not—
    (a) publicly exhibit any cinematograph film in Australia ; or
    (b) export any cinematograph film from Australia,
unless the film has been submitted to a Cinematograph Film Censor and approved by that Censor for exhibition or export, as the case may be.

POWER TO REQUIRE SUBMISSION OF FILM FOR FURTHER CENSORSHIP.
6. Notwithstanding the fact that a cinematograph film has been approved by a Cinematograph Film Censor for exhibition and has been publicly exhibited, any Cinematograph Film Censor may, by order in writing, require the owner, lessee or person in possession of the film to submit the film to him for further censorship.

POWERS OF CINEMATOGRAPH FILM CENSORS.
7. A Cinematograph Film Censor may forbid the exhibition or export of any film submitted to him in accordance with paragraph 5 or paragraph 6 of this Order, or may give directions as to alterations to be made in any such film.

PERSONS TO COMPLY WITH DIRECTIONS OF CINEMATOGRAPH FILM CENSOR.
8. The owner, lessee or person in possession of any cinematograph films shall not refuse or fail to comply with any direction or requirement issued to him by a Cinematograph Film Censor in relation to the submission of the film for censorship or further censorship, the making of alterations to the film, or the exhibition of the film.

Dated this thirty-first day of July, 1943.

JOHN CURTIN,
Minister of State for Defence.

APPENDIX D.
CONTROL OF PHOTOGRAPHY ORDER.

IN exercise of the powers conferred by regulation 19 of the National Security (General) Regulations, I, John Curtin, Minister of State for Defence, do hereby order as follows:—

CITATION.

1. This Order may be cited as the Control of Photography Order.

REVOCATION.

2. The Control of Photography Order made on the thirteenth day of August, 1941, and published in the *Gazette* on the nineteenth day of August, 1941, the Order amending that Order made on the third day of March, 1942, and published in the *Gazette* on the ninth day of March, 1942, and the Order amending that Order made on the fourteenth day of January, 1943, and published in the *Gazette* on the eighteenth day of January, 1943, are hereby revoked.

OBJECTS WHICH MAY NOT BE PHOTOGRAPHED WITHOUT A PERMIT.

3. A person shall not, except under the authority of a written permit granted in pursuance of regulation 19 of the National Security (General) Regulations, make any photograph, sketch, plan or other representation of places, persons, things or occurrences of the descriptions following, that is to say:—

    (a) Any fortification, battery, searchlight, listening post or other work of defence;
    (b) Any aerodrome or seaplane station;
    (c) Any assembly of any of the Naval, Military or Air Forces of the Commonwealth, or of any other part of His Majesty's dominions, or of any country which is allied or associated with His Majesty in any war in which His Majesty is or may be engaged;
    (d) Any barracks, encampment or building occupied, or in course of preparation for occupation, by any of the Naval, Military or Air Forces of the Commonwealth, or of any other part of His Majesty's dominions, or of any country which is allied or associated with His Majesty in any war in which His Majesty is or may be engaged;
    (e) Any munitions of war, equipment or supplies for use by the Naval, Military or Air Forces of the Commonwealth or of any other part of His Majesty's dominions, or of any country which is allied or associated with His Majesty in any war in which His Majesty is or may be engaged, or any arsenal, factory, magazine, store or plant used, or proposed to be used, in connexion with the manufacture or storage of such munitions of war, equipment or supplies;
    (f) Any wireless, telegraph, telephone, signal or cable station;
    (g) Any wharf, dock, caisson, dockyard, harbour, shipbuilding works, slipways or loading pier;
    (h) Any vessel of war, either complete or under construction, or any merchant vessel, or any vehicle engaged in the transport of supplies or personnel;
    (i) Any aircraft or the wreckage of any aircraft;
    (j) Any building, structure, vessel or other object damaged by enemy action or as a result of steps taken to repel action;
    (k) Any hospital or station at which casualties, whether civil or otherwise, are treated, any ambulance or convoy of injured persons, or any injured person;
    (l) Any electricity, gas or water works, or any gasometer or reservoir, or any oil store;
    (m) Any assembly of persons for the purpose of transport or evacuation, or any temporary camp or other accommodation or transport vehicles used for the purpose of evacuation;
    (n) Any riotous or disorderly assembly, or premises or other objects damaged in the course of such an assembly;
    (o) Any roads or railways or bridges exclusively connected with works of defence; or
    (p) Any area declared to be a protected area.

PUBLICATION OF PHOTOGRAPHS.

4. A person shall not publish in any manner any photograph, sketch, plan or other representation made under the authority of a permit granted in pursuance of regulation 19 of the National Security (General) Regulations unless and until it has been submitted to a Publicity Censor appointed or holding office for the purposes of the Press and Broadcasting Censorship Order and the publication of the photograph, sketch, plan or other representation has been approved by the Publicity Censor, and then only in accordance with such conditions or restrictions as are imposed by that Censor.

Dated this thirty-first day of July, 1943.

                                                        JOHN CURTIN,
                                                        Minister of State for Defence.

By Authority: L. F. JOHNSTON, Commonwealth Government Printer, Canberra.

Appendix B
Statistics: Censorship Instructions 1940-1945

There is no complete set of censorship instructions among the Department's files; nor were statistics systematically kept. Administrative changes, sloppy housekeeping and a general lack of interest in such statistics all have contributed to this unsatisfactory situation.

Nevertheless, there are several overlapping collections in existence. The most comprehensive of these comprise two separate sources of collected instructions: the T.C. Bray Papers (MSS 2519), deposited with the Australian National Library in Canberra, and a series of "Action Sheets" in the NSW State Publicity Censor's files (Australian Archives, SP 106/28).

The Bray collection of instructions spanned the period from January 1940 to December 1944. However, these are incomplete in that there are no instructions covering the latter part of 1943 or any during 1945, although several were issued during these periods.

The "Action Sheets" span the period 12 September 1942 to July 1945. An Action Sheet is notification of a specific matter to be censored or submitted to censorship. It records the date and time the instruction was issued, the authority, the subject to be censored, a list of all media that is to be notified, who is to be notified, and the time that person was notified. Originally, all such instructions were sent out as roneoed State Publicity Censor Instruction Sheets (or SPCIs). (See AA Series SP 106/4.) However, after December 1942, the frequency of issue resulted in the institution of a new system where all but major instructions were telephoned or telegrammed to the media. The latter method also increased the speed of receipt of instructions. While some of the sheets were missing from the files, the records of issue of the instructions remain, allowing some quantification of censorship trends.

There are difficulties in developing a series from the sources. For example, from an independent check of other sources, the Bray collection seems to underestimate the frequency of instruction before 1942. One reason may be that Bray, editor of the *Courier-Mail* in Brisbane, discarded the more transitional instructions or those dealing with interstate matters. (Annex 1 shows the raw counts of instructions for both sources.)

Fortunately, there is an overlap between the two sources of 21 of the months. This allows some statistical testing, to explore the relationship between the two series. A Pearson correlation coefficient between the two series is calculated in Annex 2. This shows high correlation of 0.90 between the series. The relationship between the two series was calculated to be as follows:

Monthly frequency of Action Sheets = 13.53 + 1.16 Bray (monthly figures).

Thus the best means of merging these two sets of data would be to adjust the figures derived from Bray by the factor of 13.53 + 1.16B (where B = Bray monthly figures derived from the papers). This was applied to all figures from January 1940 to August 1942 inclusive. Thereafter, the Action Sheet statistics are presented.

Therefore, a consistent estimate of the statistical series of the number of censorship instructions issued each month from January 1940 to August 1945 is as follows:—

	1940	1941	1942	1943	1944	1945
January	23	48	45	34	24	5
February	22	47	50	51	6	10
March	38	45	67	41	15	12
April	36	36	81	42	13	5
May	26	48	48	33	10	10
June	39	37	59	29	17	2
July	37	54	66	23	10	—
August	23	43	55	24	35	—
September	36	33	60	39	20	
October	47	37	59	30	23	
November	44	26	63	40	13	
December	59	43	27	24	19	
Totals	430	497	676	420	205	44 = 2272
Average/moth	35.8	41.4	56.3	35.0	17.1	5.5 = 33.4

Three independent checks available suggest the table to be reliable in terms of the overall extent of instructions and reasonably reliable on short-term trends:

(a) The average number of censorship instructions per day from May 1942 to May 1944 is put at 1.25, according to a paper in the Department's files (A.A., SP 109/3, Box 53, File 323.41). The total number of instructions issued during this 25-month period, according to the estimates in the table above, comes to 915 or 1.22 instructions per day.

(b) Senator Ashley claimed censorship instructions in September–October 1941 were 60 per cent of those issued during September–October 1940 (Melbourne *Argus*, 3 December 1941). The table above shows the figures to be 84 per cent of those issued during the previous year.

(c) Bonney wrote to Ashley on 7 October 1941 that "in the four weeks preceding my appointment on April 9 [1941], 48 Censorship instructions . . . were issued to Press and Broadcasters. In the four weeks ended last Saturday, there were only 14." (A.A., SP 195/1, File 71/1/11.) The figures from the table above relatively agree, but differ somewhat on absolute numbers. Bonney's figures for March 1941 and November 1941 were 48 and 14, whereas the table above puts this at 45 and 26 respectively.

Annex 1

Raw figures derived from count of instructions in Bray papers (B) and Action Sheets (A)

	1940 (B)	(A)	1941 (B)	(A)	1942 (B)	(A)	1943 (B)	(A)	1944 (B)	(A)	1945 (B)	(A)
Jan.	8	n/a	30	n/a	27	n/a	23	34	16	24	n/a	5
Feb.	7	n/a	29	n/a	31	n/a	36	51	3	6	n/a	11
Mar.	21	n/a	27	n/a	46	n/a	17	41	8	15	n/a	12
Apr.	19	n/a	19	n/a	58	n/a	14	42	3	13	n/a	5
May	11	n/a	30	n/a	30	n/a	21	33	—	10	n/a	16
June	22	n/a	20	n/a	39	n/a	n/a	29	6	17	n/a	2
July	20	n/a	35	n/a	45	n/a	n/a	23	2	10	n/a	—
Aug.	8	n/a	25	n/a	36	n/a	n/a	24	12	35	n/a	—
Sept.	19	n/a	17	n/a	29	60	n/a	39	12	20		
Oct.	29	n/a	20	n/a	41	59	n/a	30	3	23		
Nov.	26	n/a	11	n/a	29	63	n/a	40	4	13		
Dec.	39	n/a	25	n/a	13	27	n/a	24	—	19		

n/a = not available

Annex 2

Statistical relationship between the Bray estimates and Action Sheets

Pearson's correlation coefficient* is symbolized by the letter r. It is a means of quantifying a relationship between sets of variables. The numerical value of r may range from -1.0 through zero to $+1.0$. Both -1.0 and -1.0 are indicative of perfect correlation in a bivariate distribution.

The formula for Pearson's correlation coefficient for our purposes is

$$\frac{N \Sigma (BA) - (\Sigma B)(\Sigma A)}{\sqrt{[N \Sigma B^2 - (\Sigma B)^2][N \Sigma A^2 - (\Sigma B)^2]}}$$

where N is the total number of observations
B is the estimate from the Bray papers for each

where
    month

N	=	21
$\Sigma(BA)$	=	12,397
ΣB	=	292
ΣA	=	615
ΣB^2	=	6,974
ΣA^2	=	24,249
$\therefore r$	=	0.90

* John E. Peatman, *Introduction to Applied Statistics*. New York: Harper & Row, 1063, pp. 81-124.

The linear relationship between the Bray Papers and the Action Sheets is:

Action Sheets = $a + bx$ (Bray Papers)
where a, b are determined from the two equations:

      I $\Sigma(A)$ = $Na + b\,\Sigma(B)$
      II $\Sigma(BA)$ = $a\,\Sigma(B) + b\,\Sigma(B^2)$
i.e. I   615 = $21a + 292b$
     II   12,397 = $292a + 6,974b$

$$\therefore a = \frac{(615 - 292b)}{21} \quad \text{(from I)}$$

$$12,397 = \frac{292\,(615 - 292b)}{21} + 6,974b$$

(substituting into II)

$\therefore b = 1.16$
substituting into I
    615 = $21a + 292 \times 1.16$
    $\therefore a = 13.53$

Action Sheets = 13.53 + 1.16 x Bray estimates (substituting into I)

Appendix C
Joint Press Statement on Censorship, Sydney, 17 April 1944

The joint statement — containing the two suppressed statements of Mr Henderson — for publishing which, in defiance of the Censor, the Daily Telegraph, Sydney Morning Herald, Sun *and* Daily Mirror *were suppressed, reads as follows:*

The *Sunday Telegraph* was yesterday suppressed by the Censor.

The suppression followed the refusal of the *Sunday Telegraph* to comply with a censorship instruction ordering the Editor to fill in blank spaces on page 1 and page 3 from which matter had been deleted by the Censor.

This action was the culmination of a conflict of opinion between the Minister for Information (Mr Calwell), who controls censorship, and Mr R.A. Henderson (chairman of the Australian Newspaper Proprietors' Association).

At 11.20 on Saturday night, Commonwealth security officers served on the Editor of the *Sunday Telegraph* an order empowering them to seize all copies of the *Sunday Telegraph*. As a result, all except a few thousand copies of an early edition of the paper were confiscated.

ACCUSATIONS BY MINISTER

On Wednesday Mr Calwell defended his department by attacking newspapers. He said: "The hue and cry by some sections of the Sydney Press in particular, against the Department of Information and Censorship is being carried to absurd lengths.

"Because an extract from a statement by the Minister for the Army was torn from its context by some Australian correspondents and cabled overseas, where it created momentary misunderstanding, the Department of Information is blamed for not having kept the American people better informed.

"If the American people have not been kept accurately advised of events in this area, the metropolitan newspapers, with some few exceptions, must accept a large share of the responsibility, for a great many very mischievous messages to the United States have been based on partisan and inaccurate editorials published in the eastern States and in Adelaide.

"CANNOT BE QUOTED"

"If it had not been for the commonsense restraint imposed by censorship, the volume of anti-Australian propaganda would have been ten times as great.

"Many examples of unwise, if not vicious, propaganda have come under my notice, but they cannot be quoted at this stage for security reasons.

"The writers of some of these diatribes are little better than fifth columnists."

On Friday Mr Calwell attacked Mr Henderson who had stated that the Minister was diverting public attention from his own failures by making baseless charges against other people.

Mr Calwell accused Mr Henderson of untruthfulness and inaccuracy.

THREAT MADE

"Mr Henderson," he said, "makes a most inaccurate statement when he says that, because of censorship, most correspondents of American papers have been withdrawn from Australia. . . . Mr Henderson's additional statement that Australian correspondents have not been able to inform their papers truly of Australia's effort is also untrue."

Mr Calwell ended his attack by threatening to have Mr Henderson called before the Parliamentary Censorship Inquiry Committee, "where," said the Minister, "his and other wild, exaggerated statements will have to stand the test of cross-examination."

To these accusations, reflecting on his personal integrity, Mr Henderson replied. His statement covered five type-written sheets. The *Daily Telegraph* desired to publish both Mr Calwell's and Mr Henderson's statements in full, but this intention was frustrated by the State Publicity Censorship.

The Censor cut most of the matter in Mr Henderson's statement, but allowed the Minister's statement to appear complete. The passages deleted from Mr Henderson's statement were the most important, because, with dates and facts, they endeavoured to answer the essential points raised by the Minister.

Certain items cited by Mr Henderson were admittedly of a character which might possibly be argued as coming within the legitimate sphere of censorship, and if only these had been deleted the authorities' decision would have been accepted without demur.

But the bulk of Mr Henderson's reply didn't fall within this category, as the following quotations will show:

"My reply is to give the public a few examples of the manner in which censorship has been abused in this country:

"Here is a story of the tramway strike — another example of the censorship that is supposed to delete matter only on high grounds of national security. On Tuesday, 25 January, the newspapers were prevented from informing the public that Mr Curtin's order to the men to return to work was being defied, and that there would be no trams or buses running the following morning. Would Mr Calwell defend that instruction on the ground that the news contained information of value to the enemy?

"The South Coast miners on 5 March last decided not to return to work, and rejected a motion submitted to all meetings by the Central Council that work be resumed by all collieries in the southern district. The Central Council proposed that negotiations should be opened with the Government for the withdrawal of Army notices, and that, failing this, aggregate meetings should be called to consider a general stoppage. The Censor altered the word 'to consider a general stoppage' to 'to review the whole position'. This was a distortion of the motion. If a newspaper had made the change, it would have been accused — probably by Mr Calwell — of wilfully falsifying the report.

WORDS DELETED

"On 7 March in the Legislative Assembly, Mr W. Davies asked the Minister for Mines what method the Federal Government proposed to adopt to reopen the mines, in view of the difficulties that the Government has created for itself. The Censor deleted the words 'in view of the difficulties that the Government has created for itself'. This, Mr Calwell would have us believe, is non-political censorship.

"On 27 December, the New South Wales Publicity Censor forbade transmission of a cable by Reuter's, containing extracts from a leading article in a Melbourne newspaper dealing with Mr R.G. Casey's appointment as Governor of Bengal.

"On 25 November, the Censor forbade the despatch by Reuter's of a cable dealing with immigration generally, and including extracts from a speech by Dr Lloyd Ross.

"On 30 December, a cable reporting a speech by Dr Clunies Ross, prepared by the Sydney correspondent of the *Yorkshire Post*, dealing with immigration, was suppressed.

"A *Sun* despatch from Townsville was censored by the omission of the following words in a speech by Alderman Aitkens:

" 'The Nazi Minister for Misinformation Calwell, who banned the food broadcasts from Townsville.'

"The following words were deleted from a *Daily Telegraph* article dealing with Mr Calwell. The *Telegraph* said, after challenging him to take them to court and prosecute them for any breach of censorship:

ARGUE CAUSE

" 'Nothing would please us more than to argue the cause out before the people. That would give the public an opportunity to judge where the rights and wrongs of censorship lie. But such an appeal to the people is not likely to attract Australia's would-be Goebbels.'

"The paragraph in inverted commas was all censored.

"These are only a few of literally hundreds of examples that could be quoted."

The second paragraph of Mr Henderson's statement

said: "The answer I make to Mr Calwell is to set down briefly a few recent happenings so that the public may estimate the worth of his vicious attack." This sentence also was cut out.

To show that the censorship had intervened to prevent a fair presentation of both sides of the discussion, the *Daily Telegraph*, on Saturday, left 23 inches of blank space in columns three, four, and five, page three.

These blanks showed the extent to which the Censors had mutilated Mr Henderon's statement.

On Saturday afternoon Commonwealth Security Officers served on the Editor of the *Sunday Telegraph* (Mr Cyril Pearl) an order to submit all pages of the *Sunday Telegraph* before publication to the State Publicity Censor (Mr Mansell).

Complying with the order, the Editor of the *Sunday Telegraph* submitted a second statement which Mr Henderson issued on Saturday afternoon.

The Censor cut this statement entirely, headings and all.

The statement read:

NEWSPAPER PRESIDENT ANSWERS CALWELL

"Mr R.A. Henderson (president of the Australian Newspaper Proprietors' Association) yesterday made an additional statement on the attack made on him by Information Minister Calwell on Friday.

"Mr Henderson also commented on the censoring by the N.S.W Publicity Censorship authorities of his first reply to the attack, issued on Friday night.

" 'The censoring of my reply,' said Mr Henderson, 'is merely another example of the abuse of censorship in this country.

" 'Mr Calwell, who made the attack on me, is the Minister responsible for censorship.

" 'His concept of freedom is clearly shown to be freedom to do and say what he wants himself, but to deny that freedom to the other fellow.

" 'It is important that the public should know how a censorship that Prime Minister Curtin has laid down should be exercised only on grounds of national security is being carried out in practice by men like Mr Calwell.

" 'The facts of the present case are briefly as follows:

" 'Mr Calwell made a statement accusing the Australian newspapers, in effect, of engaging in anti-Australian, fifth-column activities in the U.S.A., to the embarrassment of the Government.

" 'When I sought to answer this vicious and untrue suggestion, he made a further attack on Australian newspapers, and a violent and personal attack on me, accusing me, in effect, of being a common liar.

" 'My obvious reply to this attack was to give some facts that would reveal to the public the truth of the statements I had made, so that they would be in a position to judge who was right.

" 'When this reply was submitted to Mr Calwell's officials, as is mandatory under present National Security Regulations, all the facts were ordered to be suppressed.

" 'Not one of the examples of censorship I gave in my reply had any remote relation to national security.

" 'They were all examples of political censorship.

" 'One or two of them were examples of criticism of Mr Calwell himself by public men, which were suppressed by his officials.

" 'Thus, Mr Calwell's officials permitted me to make some general statements in reply to his attack, but suppressed all the factual evidence that would have convinced the public of the truth of what I stated.

" 'Under present conditions I have to submit to this suppression, or else, by defying Mr Calwell, become a lawbreaker, and thus liable to the full penalties attaching to infringement of wartime regulations.

" 'With this weapon of wartime regulations up his sleeve, Mr Calwell is free to make venomous personal attacks on individuals, and then prevent them from giving the facts that would answer him.

" 'This comes from a man who, when the occasion suits him, prattles of democracy, freedom, and the rights of the individual.'

"Mr Calwell said yesterday: 'I don't propose to engage in an argument whether censorship should be exercised on Mr Henderson or not.' "

Subsequently the Editor of the *Sunday Telegraph* submitted a proof of page one, containing a two-column editorial, which read as follows:

DEMOCRACY IS BASED ON FREEDOM OF THE PRESS!

"Read what Prime Minister Curtin said on 14 December last:

" 'With the one stipulation that they cannot give information useful to the enemy, the Federal Government believes that newspapers should be free to treat all accounts of the war in the way their judgment regards as proper.'

"But Information Minister Calwell believes that newspapers should be free to treat news only as his judgment regards as proper.

"Mr Calwell's ambition to be Australia's No. 1 Censor and Newspaper Dictator isn't based on a disinterested passion for security regulations; it is rooted in a small-time politician's hatred of the Press.

"This hatred wasn't born when he became Minister for Information.

"It certainly became more bitter when newspapers revealed how he had bungled his job, wasted his time on vicious little feuds, instead of making Australia and her war effort better known.

"As a private member, Mr Calwell abused his parliamentary privileges to attack the Press as an institution, and to besmirch and vilify individual newspapermen.

"Now he is abusing his ministerial privileges to carry on his vendetta against the Press. His unconcealed aim is to shackle Australia's free, critical, democratic Press.

"**Mr Calwell's campaign reached a fantastic climax on Friday.**

"**Mr Calwell abusively attacked Mr R.A. Henderson, president of the Australian Newspaper Proprietors' Association, who had stated that the Minister was diverting public attention from his own failures by making baseless charges against other people.**

"**Yesterday's** *Daily Telegraph* **published Mr Calwell's statement in full — a statement which charged Mr Henderson with inaccuracy and untruthfulness.**

"The *Daily Telegraph*, having published Mr Calwell's statement, tried to give Mr Henderson the same facilities for reply.

"But Mr Henderson's reply, which answered every one of Mr Calwell's charges factually, was so mutilated by the State Publicity Censorship that it was utterly meaningless.

"The blank spaces on Page 3 of yesterday's *Daily Telegraph* showed how thoroughly the Censor did his job.

"We agree with Mr Curtin's statement on the function and limitation of censorship.

"Security was not involved when Mr Henderson protested against the use of censorship as a political bludgeon.

"Indeed, Mr Henderson was doing little more than underlining the words of Thomas Jefferson, that great American father of democracy: 'Where the Press is free and every man able to read, all is safe.'

"But that's not the end of the story.

"Yesterday the *Sunday Telegraph* received a demand from the State Publicity Censor (Mr Mansell) for submission of every page in this issue before publication.

"Everything, from the Russian war news to the Captain and the Kids, had to go to the Censor!

"When we pointed out that we had committed no breach of the regulations to warrant such repressive strong-arm action, Mr Mansell refused to comment.

"The truth is that the order to submit had no relation to security, to public morale, or to the prosecution of the war; it was imposed vindictively. It was simply Calwell-inspired persecution.

"The only purpose was to embarrass an organization serving 300,000 readers by imposing mechanical and editorial difficulties on a staff already heavily depleted by manpower requirements.

"Or — to put it bluntly — Mr Calwell has abused his Ministerial powers to persecute a newspaper because it has found it necessary to criticise him as a public man.

"Mr Calwell's concept of freedom, as Mr Henderson said yesterday, is 'freedom to do and say what he wants himself, but to deny that freedom to the other fellow. . . .

" 'This comes from a man who, when the occasion suits him, prattles of democracy, freedom, and the rights of the individual.'

"The latest and most scandalous example of Mr Calwell's methods shows how important it is to defend our free institutions against tinpot dictators.

"Democracy is based on the freedom of the Press. That is why Dr Evatt included a guarantee of this freedom in his Constitutional Alteration Bill.

"Dr Evatt, certainly, will find it hard to reconcile his own fine conception of a free and critical Press with the attitude of Mr Calwell."

The Censor returned this editorial severely mutilated. In the paragraph beginning "Now he is abusing his Ministerial privileges to carry on, etc. . . ." the words "abusing his Ministerial privileges" were cut out, and the sentence was altered to read, "Now as a Minister he is carrying on . . ."

The deletions made by the Censor are indicated in black type.

To indicate that censorship had mutilated Mr Henderson's statement and the editorial, the Editor left blank three-quarters of a column of space in column one, page three, and in the two columns of space on page one placed a picture of Mr Henderson, a picture of Mr Calwell, and a box containing the following statement in large type:

A FREE PRESS —?

The great American democrat, Thomas Jefferson, said —

"Where the Press is free and every man able to read, all is safe."

To frustrate the Editor's attempt to indicate that censorship had occurred, the Censor instructed him to fill up all blanks so that readers would be entirely ignorant of what had happened.

He refused to submit to this instruction, as he considered it an abuse of the Censor's powers.

The Censor immediately called in Commonwealth Security Officers to prevent the *Sunday Telegraph* from appearing on the streets, and the officers served on the Editor an order of seizure on the *Sunday Telegraph*.

At this time — close on midnight — bundles of papers were being loaded on lorries in the publishing room. Uniformed constables took up positions beside the trucks and refused to allow the papers to be moved. When one driver, acting on office instructions, attempted to drive his loaded car out, he was threatened with arrest.

The Censor made it plain to the *Sunday Telegraph* that if it agreed to conceal all evidence of the Censor's action by eliminating the blanks from pages one and three the paper could go on to the streets. He made it equally plain that if the *Sunday Telegraph* would not connive in covering up the Censor's tracks no papers would go out.

The *Sunday Telegraph* would not connive — and from that moment no papers left the building.

Those are the facts of the Minister's attempt to use censorship to prevent Mr Henderson from answering the Minister's charges and the newspapers from publishing criticism of Mr Calwell's administration.

STATEMENT CUT

Yesterday the *Sunday Telegraph* tried to explain over B class stations why its papers had not appeared that morning. The Censor cut from the announcement the following paragraph:

"Mr Calwell, over the past ten days, has criticised the Press of Australia.

"Mr Rupert Henderson (president of the Australian Newspaper Proprietors' Association) made a reply disputing the statements made by Mr Calwell. This reply was censored by Mr Calwell's own department, and was so cut that it ceased to be an answer to the charges levelled by Mr Calwell. The *Sunday Telegraph* refused to accept the cut copy, and left blank space in the paper where Mr Henderson's statement had appeared. The Censor ordered this space to be filled. The *Sunday Telegraph* refused, and he then sent Commonwealth Police and Peace Officers to seize all papers."

The editorial, suppressed by the Censor in the issue of 17 April, but printed next day under the High Court injunction, read as follows:

CALWELL CHALLENGES YOUR FREEDOM TO READ, THINK, WRITE

When yesterday you saw a placard announcing that the Censor had suppressed the *Sunday Telegraph*, you probably thought we had insisted on publishing information that would inform the enemy, weaken Australia's war effort, endanger national security.

You may be surprised to learn that this was not so — that the Censor objected to the *Sunday Telegraph*'s determination to publish on its front page a photograph of the president of the Australian Newspaper Proprietors' Association (Mr R.A. Henderson) alongside a photograph of the Minister of Information (Mr Calwell), in two columns of space, blank except for a panel containing the following words:

A FREE PRESS —?

"The great American democrat, Thomas Jefferson, said: 'Where the Press is free and every man able to read, all is safe'."

The *Sunday Telegraph* had intended to publish in these two columns an editorial criticising the censorship and Mr Calwell for using the censorship to further a personal vendetta against newspapers.

The editorial was emasculated — not because it contained any information of use to the enemy or endangered your national security, but because it attacked Mr Calwell.

You can see this for yourself by reading the editorial, which we print in full in the article on this page, with the deleted paragraphs shown in black type.

On page three of yesterday's *Sunday Telegraph* was another blank space.

In that space we had intended to print a reply from Mr Henderson to a vicious attack made upon him by Mr Calwell.

But this, too, the Censor killed to protect his Minister.

The *Sunday Telegraph* was determined not to abet the Censor by concealing this monstrous political censorship.

To let its readers know how Mr Calwell is using the censorship, it left these columns empty.

The Censor, backed by the security police and the vast powers of National Security Regulations, was too strong.

Mr Calwell turned a page in Australian history by using this power to suppress a newspaper which had dared to criticise his tinpot dictatorship and resist his officials.

We publish the simple facts of the crisis which now endangers the freedom of all the Press — and your freedom to think, write, read, and express your opinion as you wish within the limits of security — because we want the people to judge for themselves.

We are prepared to face any retaliation a spiteful Minister can invent — even suppression — because we believe the issue is far greater than any particular newspaper.

We believe that this issue is finely summed up in that phrase of Thomas Jefferson's which the Censor yesterday refused to allow the *Sunday Telegraph* to publish.

(Reprinted from Appendix 7 of Brian Penton's *Censored!* Sydney: Shakespeare Head Press, 1947, pp. 87-104).

Bibliography

Official Archives

Department of Information

All files of the Department, and practically all other files relevant to wartime information activities, were inspected in the course of the research.
 The main Australian Archives series files are:
CP 815/1-6 General Correspondence (including N. McCauley's personal papers), 1944-1950
SP 109/1-20 } General Correspondence, 1939-1949
SP 106/1-18
SP 195 Administrative History, Notes and Papers, 1939-1945

Prime Minister's Department

The Prime Minister's Department's files relevant to the Department are:
A 1606 Correspondence Files, Secret and Confidential Series, Third System, 1926-1940
A 461 Correspondence Files, Multiple Number Series, Third System, 1934-1950
CP 103/17 Commonwealth Publicity Officer, Correspondence Files, 1936-1940

Attorney-General's Department

The Attorney-General's Department's files relevant to the Department are:

A 472	Correspondence Files, "W" Series (War), 1939-1945
A 473	Number Registers, "W" Series, 1939-1945 (Control Records)
A 474	Subject Index Cards, "W" Series, 1939-1945 Item Box INA-JIN, Information Department of Control Records
A 816	Department of Defence III Correspondence Files, Multiple Number Series (Class 301) "C" Classified, 1935-1957

The ABC Archives relevant to the Department are:
MP 272, Series 1-5
SP 286/12
SP 314

Most of the above files are held in the Australian Archives repository in Canberra. However, the Australian Broadcasting Commission files are held by the Australian Archives Office, Melbourne, and a number of Department of Information files (especially SP 109/16) are held by the Australian Archives Office in Sydney.

Australian War Memorial, Canberra

The Australian War Memorial also has a selection of relevant files, particularly in the Blamey Papers collection.

These files are located at the Memorial, in Canberra.

Commonwealth Government Publications

Commonwealth Hansard 1901-1972: Its Establishment and Development. Canberra: Government Printer, 1975.
Commonwealth Parliamentary Debates, *Hansards* of the Senate and the House of Representatives, 1914-1952.
Commonwealth Year Books, 1939-1950. Canberra: Bureau of Census & Statistics.
Conference on Newspaper and Broadcasting Activities in relation to the War Effort held at Canberra, 10 February 1942. Canberra: Government Printer, 1942.

Department of Information: Summary of Activities for the Period ended 31st March 1940. Melbourne: Commonwealth Government Printer, 1942.
Public Service Board Annual Reports, 1940-1949.
Report of the Joint Committee on Wireless Broadcasting Gibson Committee). Canberra: Commonwealth Government Printer, 25 March 1942.

Manuscripts and Personal Papers

Ball, W. MacMahon, Papers. In possession of Emeritus Professor W.M. Ball, Eltham, Vic.
Bray, T.C., Papers. Australian National Library, Canberra. MSS 2519.
Hoey, T., Papers. In possession of the Hoey family, Hawthorn, Vic. (Papers contain a "History of Overseas Shortwave Broadcasting in Australia", Draft Report, ?1946; author unknown, ?Tom Hoey.)
Mackay, Ian K., "Macquarie: The Story of a Network" (1961). Held in the library of the Australian Broadcasting Tribunal, Marland House, Melbourne.
Murdoch, Sir Keith, Papers. Australian National Library, Canberra. MSS 2823.
Stone, Julius, Papers. In possession of Ann Conlon and family, Mosman, NSW. (Papers consist mainly of material on the Committee on National Morale.)
Wigmore, Lionel, Papers. In possession of L. Wigmore, Queenscliffe, NSW.

Unpublished Theses

Fewster, Kevin J., "Expression and Suppression: Aspects of Military Censorship in Australia during the Great War", Ph.D. thesis, University of New South Wales, Duntroon, 1980.
Kirkpatrick, Rod, "The Government Advocates", Journalism thesis, Canberra College of Advanced Education, 1975.
Mitchell, Pam, "The Development of ABC News Gathering 1932-42", History IV (Hons.) thesis, University of Sydney, 1974.

White, D.S., "The Government's Voice: A Study of Government Publicity and Information Services, with particular reference to their growth, functions and use in Queensland", B.A. (Hons.) thesis, University of Queensland, 1973.

Newspapers and Periodicals

Age (Melbourne) 1938-1950
Argus (Melbourne) 1914-1950
Australian Quarterly 1935-1946
Commercial Broadcasting 1938-1948
Daily Telegraph (Sydney) 1938-1948
Sydney Morning Herald 1938-1948
Sunday Telegraph (Sydney) 1938-1948

Recorded Interviews

The following interviews were recorded on audio cassette:
W. MacMahon Ball, Eltham, Vic.	18 February 1976
H. Ferber, Camberwell, Vic.	16 February 1976
H.S. Foll, Port Macquarie, NSW	10 February 1976
T. Hoey, Hawthorn, Vic.	16 February 1976
R.I. Horne, Malvern, Vic.	18 February 1976
C.E. Sayers, Dandenong, Vic.	17 February 1976
G. Sawer, Australian National University, Canberra,	20 April 1976
L. Wigmore, Queenscliffe, NSW	12 April 1976
R.D. Wright, University of Melbourne	18 February 1976

Unrecorded interviews with Ian Hamilton (3 May 1976), Stephen Alomes (10 May 1977) and Cliff Twelftree (4 September 1977) also were conducted in Canberra.

Books and Monographs

Alexander, F., *Australia Since Federation*. Melbourne: Nelson, 1967.
──────, *From Curtin to Menzies and After: Continuity or Confrontation?* Melbourne: Nelson, 1973.

Andrews, E.M., *Isolationism and Appeasement in Australia: Reactions to the European Crises 1935-1939*. Canberra: ANU Press, 1970.
Ball, W. MacMahon, *Japan: Enemy or Ally?* Melbourne: Cassell, 1948.
———, *Nationalism and Communism in East Asia*. Melbourne: Melbourne University Press, 1952.
———, "On Thin Ice", *ABC Annual*. Sydney: Australian Broadcasting Commission, 1939, pp. 155-57.
———, *Press, Radio and World Affairs: Australia's Outlook*. Melbourne: Melbourne University Press, in association with Oxford University Press, 1938.
Barrett, Edward W., *Truth is Our Weapon*. New York: Funk & Wagnalls, 1953.
Bell, Roger J., *Unequal Allies: Australian-American Relations and the Pacific War*. Melbourne: Melbourne University Press, 1977.
Benjafield, D.G., and Whitmore, H., *Principles of Australian Administrative Law*. Sydney: Law Book Co., 4th edn, 1971.
Berelson, Bernard, and Janowitz, Morris (eds), *Reader in Public Opinion and Communication*. New York: Free Press, 2nd edn, 1966.
Boelke, Willi A., comp., *The Secret Conferences of Dr Goebbels, October 1939-March 1943*. London: Weidenfeld & Nicholson, 1967.
Bolton, C.G., *Dick Boyer: An Australian Humanist*. Canberra: ANU Press, 1967.
Bramstead, Earnest Kohn, *Goebbels and National Socialist Propaganda 1925-1945*. London: Cresset Press, 1965.
Briggs, Asa, *The War of Words: The History of Broadcasting in the United Kingdom, Vol. III*. London: Oxford University Press, 1970.
Burchett, Wilfred, *Passport: An Autobiography*. Melbourne: Nelson, 1969.
Caiden, G.E., *Career Service: An Introduction to the History of Personnel Administration in the Commonwealth Public Service 1901-1961*. Melbourne: Melbourne University Press, 1965.
Calwell, A.A., "The Australian Labor Party and the Press: The Twenty-second Arthur Norman Smith Memorial Lecture in Journalism". University of Melbourne, 30 July 1959.

———, *Be Just and Fear Not*. Hawthorn, Vic.: O'Neill, 1972.
———, *Labor's Role in Modern Society*. Melbourne: Cheshire-Lansdowne, 1965.
Cantrill, Hadley (ed.), *Public Opinion 1935-1946*. Princeton: Princeton University Press, 1951.
Carroll, Wallace, *Persuade or Perish*. Boston: Houghton, Mifflin, 1948.
Catton, Bruce, *The Warlords of Washington:* New York: Harcourt, Brace, 1948.
Chakhotin, Sergei, *The Rape of the Masses: The Psychology of Totalitarian Political Propaganda*, trans. E.W. Dickes. New York: Alliance Book Corp., 1940.
Childs, Harwood L., and Whitton, J.B. (eds), *Propaganda by Shortwave*. London: Oxford University Press, 1942.
Choukas, Michael, *Propaganda Comes of Age*. Washington, D.C.: Public Affairs Press, 1942.
Christensen, Reo Millard, and McWilliams, Robert O. (eds), *Voice of the People: Readings in Public Opinion and Propaganda*. New York: McGraw-Hill, 2nd edn, 1967.
Clark, Sir Fife, *The Central Office of Information*. London: Allen & Unwin, 1970.
Coleman, Peter, *Obscenity, Blasphemy, Sedition: Censorship in Australia*. Brisbane: Jacaranda Press, 1962.
Coulthard-Clark, C.D., *The Citizen General Staff: The Australian Intelligence Corps 1907-1914*. Canberra: Military Historical Society of Australia, 1976.
Creel, George, *How We Advertised America*. New York: Arno Press, rep. 1972.
———, *Rebel at Large: Recollections of Fifty Crowded Years*. New York: Putnam, 1947.
Crisp, L.F., *Ben Chifley*. Melbourne: Longmans, 1960.
Crozier, M., *The Bureaucratic Phenomenon*. Chicago: University of Chicago Press, 1967.
Dalziel, A., *Evatt: The Enigma*. Melbourne: Lansdowne Press, 1967.
Davis, Elmer, and Price, Bryon, *War Information and Censorship*. Washington, D.C.: American Council on Public Affairs, 1943.
Deane, R.P., *The Establishment of the Department of Trade: A Case Study in Administrative Reorganization*. Canberra: ANU Press, 1963.
Dexter, L.A., and White, D.M., *People, Society and Mass Communications*. New York: Free Press, 1964.

Dixon, Frank, *Inside the ABC: A Piece of Australian History*. Melbourne: Hawthorn Press, 1975.
Dizard, Wilson P., *The Strategy of Truth: The Story of the U.S. Information Service*. Washington, D.C.: Public Affairs Press, 1968.
Doob, Leonard William, *Public Opinion and Propaganda*. New York: Holt, 1948.
Dovring, Karin, *Road of Propaganda: The Semantics of Biassed Communication*. New York: Philosophical Library, 1959.
Dumas, Lloyd, *The Story of a Full Life*. Melbourne: Sun Books, 1969.
Dunk, W., *They Also Serve*. Canberra: the author, 1974.
Dunn, Delmer, D., *Public Officials and the Press*. Reading, Mass.: Addison-Wesley, 1969.
Edelman, M., *The Symbolic Uses of Politics*. Urbana, Ill.: University of Illinois Press, 1964.
Edwards, Cecil, *The Editor Regrets*. Melbourne: Hill of Content, 1972.
Elder, Robert E., *The Information Machine: The U.S. Information Agency and Foreign Policy*. Syracuse, NY: Syracuse University Press, 1968.
Etzioni, A. (ed.), *Readings on Modern Organizations*. New York: Prentice-Hall, 1969.
Evatt, H.V., "Reconstruction and the Constitution", in *Postwar Reconstruction in Australia*, AIPS Seminar, ed. D.A.S. Campbell. Sydney: Australasian Publishing, 1944, pp. 238-90.
Farago, Ladislas (ed.), *German Psychological Warfare: Survey and Bibliography*. New York: Committee for National Morale, 1941.
Ferris, P., *The House of Northcliffe: The Harmsworths of Fleet Street*. London: Weidenfeld & Nicholson, 1971.
Fischer, Heinz Dietrich, *International Communication*, New York: Hastings House, 1970.
Fitzpatrick, Brian, *Short History of the Australian Labor Movement*, Melbourne: MacMillan, 1968.
Fraser, Lindley M., *Propaganda*, London: Oxford University Press, 1957.
Friedrich, C.J., *The Pathology of Politics: Violence, Betrayal, Secrecy and Propaganda*, New York: Harper & Row, 1972.

Galnoor, I. (ed.), *Government Secrecy in Democracies*, New York: Harper Colophon, 1977.
Gloag, John Edward, *Word Warfare: Some Aspects of German Propaganda and English Liberty*, London: Nicholson & Watson, 1939.
Gombrich, Ernst Hans Joseph, *Myth and Reality in German War-time Broadcasts*, London: Athlone Press in association with Oxford University Press, 1970.
Gordon, George N., *The Idea Invaders*, New York: Hastings House, 1963.
———, and Falk, Irving, A., *The War of Ideas*, New York: Hastings House, 1973.
Green, F.C., *Servant of the House*, Melbourne: Heinemann, 1969.
Hale, J., *Radio Power: Propaganda and International Broadcasting*, London: Elek, 1975.
Hardy, Alexander G., *Hitler's Secret Weapon: The Managed Press and the Propaganda Machine of Nazi Germany*, New York: Vantage Press, 1967.
Hasluck, Paul, *The Government and the People 1939-1941*, Canberra: Australian War Memorial, 1952.
———, *The Government and the People 1942-1945*, Canberra: Australian War Memorial, 1970.
———, *Telling The Truth in a Democracy: The 21st Syme Oration*, Sydney: Australasian Medical Publishing, 1958.
Havinghurst, Clark C. (ed.), *International Control of Propaganda*, New York: Oceana, 1967.
Henderson, John W. *The U.S. Information Agency*. New York: Praeger, 1969.
Hetherington, J., *Australians: Nine Profiles*, Melbourne: Cheshire, 1960.
———, *Blamey — Controversial Soldier: A Biography of Field Marshall Sir Thomas Blamey*, Canberra: Australian War Memorial and Australian Government Publishing Service, 1973.
———, *Five to Remember*, Melbourne: Cheshire, 1960.
Holden, W. Sprague, *Australia Goes to Press*. Melbourne: Melbourne University Press, 1962.
Keith Murdoch — Journalist, Melbourne: Herald & Weekly Times, 1952.
Kelly, Vince, *A Man of the People — From Boiler Maker to Governor-General: The Career of Rt. Hon. Sir William McKell*, Sydney: Alpha Books, 1971.

Klapper, Joseph T., *The Effects of Mass Communications*, New York: Free Press, 1960.
Klein, Herbert Arthur (ed.), *The War for Men's Minds: A Survey of Forces Shaping Attitudes and Actions*, Los Angeles: L.A. City College Press, 1940.
Knightly, P., *The First Casualty — From Crimea to Vietnam: The War Correspondent as Hero, Propagandist and Vigil-maker*, London: Deutsch, 1975.
Komisky, Morris, *The Hoaxers*, Boston: Branden Press, 1970.
Koop, Theodore T., *Weapons of Silence*, Chicago: University of Chicago Press, 1946.
Lake, Marilyn, *A Divided Society: Tasmania during World War I*, Melbourne: Melbourne University Press, 1975.
Lambert, Richard Stanton, *Propaganda*, London: Nelson, 1938.
Lasswell, Harold Dwight, *Propaganda Technique in World War I*, Cambridge, Mass.: MIT Press, 1971.
——— and Blumenstock, D., *World Revolutionary Propaganda: A Chicago Study*, New York: Knopf, 1939.
Lee, Alfred McClung, *How to Understand Propaganda*, New York: Rinehart, 1952.
Legg, Frank, *War Correspondent*, Adelaide: Rigby, 1964.
Lerner, Daniel (ed.), *Propaganda in War and Crisis: Materials for American Policy*, New York: George W. Stewart, 1951.
———, *Sykewar: Psychological Warfare against Germany, D-Day to V.E. Day*, New York: George W. Stewart, 1949.
Linebarger, Paul M., *Psychological Warfare*, Washington, D.C., Combat Forces Press, 1954.
Lockhart, Robert H. Bruce, *Come the Reckoning*, New York: Putnam, 1947.
Long, Gavin, *The Final Campaigns*, Canberra: Australian War Memorial, 1963.
———, *MacArthur: As Military Commander*, Sydney: Angus & Robertson, 1969.
———, *The Six Years War: A Concise History of Australia in the 1939-45 War*, Canberra: Australian War Memorial and Australian Government Publishing Service, 1972.
Lord Hill of Luton, *Both Sides of the Hill*, London: Heinemann, 1964.
Lyons, Enid, *Among the Carrion Crows*, Adelaide: Rigby, 1972.

McCarthy, Dudley, *South-West Pacific Area: First Year*, Canberra: Australian War Memorial, 1959.
Mackay, I.K., *Broadcasting in Australia*, Melbourne: Melbourne University Press, 1957.
McLaine, Ian, *The Ministry of Morale: Home Front Morale and the Ministry of Information in World War II*, London: Allen & Unwin, 1979.
McQueen, Humphrey, *Australia's Media Monopolies*, Camberwell, Vic.: Widescope, 1977.
Margolin, Leo J., *Paper Bullets: A Brief Story of Psychological Warfare in World War II*, New York: Froben Press, 1946.
Mahle, Walter A., and Richter, Rolf, *Communication Policies in the Federal Republic of Germany*, Paris: Unesco Press, 1974.
Mayer, Henry, *The Press in Australia*, Melbourne: Lansdowne Press, 1964.
────, and Nelson, Helen (eds), *Australian Politics: A Third Reader*, Melbourne: Cheshire, 1975.
Mendelssohn, Peter de, *Japan's Political Warfare*, London: Allen & Unwin, 1944.
Menzies, Robert, *Afternoon Light*, Melbourne: Cassell, 1967.
Meo, Lucy D., *Japan's Radio War on Australia 1941-45*, Melbourne: Melbourne University Press, 1968.
Mock, J.R., and Larson, C., *Words that Won the War*, Princeton, N.J.: Princeton University Press, 1939.
Mueller, Claus, *The Politics of Communication: A Study in the Political Sociology of Language, Socialization and Legitimation*, New York: Oxford University Press, 1973.
Muirden, Bruce, *The Puzzled Patriots: The Story of the Australia First Movement*, Melbourne: Melbourne University Press, 1968.
Munson, Gorham Bert, *Twelve Decisive Battles of the Mind*, New York: Greystone Press, 1942.
Murphy, D.J., *T.J. Ryan: A Political Biography*, St Lucia: University of Queensland Press, 1975.
Neumann, Eddy, *The High Court: A Collective Portrait 1903-1970*, Occasional Monograph no. 5, Sydney: Department of Government & Public Administration, University of Sydney, 1971.
Nicolson, Harold, "Propaganda", *BBC Handbook*, London: British Broadcasting Corporation, 1941.

Ogilvy-Webb, Marjorie, *The Government Explains: A Study of the Information Services for the Royal Institute of Public Administration*, London: Allen & Unwin, 1965.
Penton, Brian, *Censored!: Being a True Account of a Notable Fight for Your Right to Read and Know, with some Comment upon the Plague of Censorship in General*, Sydney: Shakespeare Head Press, 1947.
———, *Think or Be Damned*, Sydney: Angus & Robertson, 1941.
Perkins, K., *Menzies: Last of the Queen's Men*, Adelaide: Rigby, 1968.
Pratt, Carol Cornelius, *Psychology: The Third Dimension of War*, New York: Columbia University Press, 1942.
Pugh, D.S., *Organization Theory*, Ringwood, Vic.: Penguin, 1971.
———, Hickson, D.J., and Hinings, C.R., *Writers on Organizations*, Ringwood, Vic.: Penguin, 2nd edn, 1975.
Reese, T.R., *Australia, New Zealand and the United States of America: A Survey of International Relations*, London: Oxford University Press, 1969.
Riegel, Oscar Wetherhold, *Mobilizing for Chaos: The Story of the New Propaganda*, New Haven, Conn.: Yale University Press, 1939.
Robertson, John, *J.H. Scullin: A Political Biography*, Nedlands, WA: University of Western Australia Press, 1974.
Robson, L.L., *Australia and the Great War*, Melbourne: Macmillan, 1977.
Ross, Lloyd, *John Curtin: A Biography*, Melbourne: Macmillan, 1977.
Sawer, G., *Australian Federal Politics and Law 1929–1949*, Melbourne: Melbourne University Press, 1963.
Scott, E., *Australia during the War*, Sydney: Angus & Robertson, 1936.
Scott, William A., in collaboration with Scott, Ruth, *Values and Organisations: A Study of Fraternities and Sororities*, Chicago: Rand McNally, 1965.
Selznick, Philip, *Leadership in Administration*, New York: Harper & Row, 1957.
———, *TVA and the Grass Roots*, Berkeley, Calif.: University of California Press, 1949.

Seymour-Ure, Colin, *The Press, Politics and the Public*, London: Methuen, 1968.
Sigal, Leon V., *Reporters and Officials: The Organization and Politics of Newsmaking*, Lexington, Mass.: Heath, 1973.
Sington, Derrick, and Weidenfeld, Arthur, *The Goebbels Experiment: A Study of the Nazi Propaganda Machine*, New Haven, Conn.: Yale University Press, 1943.
Smith, Anthony (ed), *The British Press Since the War*, Newton Abbot, Devon: David & Charles, 1974.
Society for the Psychological Study of Social Issues, *Public Opinion and Propaganda: Book of Readings*, New York: Dryden Press, 1956.
"Special Operator", RAN, "The Story of FELO", *As You Were*, Canberra: Australian War Memorial, 1949, pp. 68-72.
Sorenson, Thomas C., *The Word War: The Story of American Propaganda*, New York: Harper & Row, 1968.
Spann, R.N., *Public Administration in Australia*, Sydney: NSW Government Printer, 1975.
_____, and Curnow, G.R. (eds), *Public Policy and Administration*, Sydney: Wiley, 1975.
Spender, P., *Politics and a Man*, Sydney: Collins, 1972.
Stanton, Alfred H., and Perry, Stewart E. (eds), *Personality and Political Crisis: New Perspectives from Social Science and Psychiatry for the Study of War and Politics*, New York: Free Press, 1951.
Sugarman, B., Stone, J., and McIntyre, N. eds, *Alfred Conlon: A Memorial by Some of His Friends*, Sydney: Benevolent Society of New South Wales, 1963.
Summers, Robert Edward (ed.), *America's Weapons of Psychological Warfare*, New York: Wilson, 1951.
Tennant, K., *Evatt: Politics and Justice*, Sydney: Angus & Robertson, 1970.
Thomas, Alan, *Broadcast and Be Damned: The ABC's First Two Decades*, Melbourne: Melbourne University Press, 1981.
_____, "War and Radio: The ABC and the Australian War Effort 1939-45" (unpublished History Seminar paper), Canberra: Australian National University, 1977.
Thompson, J., *Five to Remember*, Melbourne: Lansdowne, 1964.
Thomson, Charles A.H., *Overseas Information Services of the United States Government*, Washington, D.C.: Brookings Institution, 1948.

Thum, Gladys, *The Persuaders: Propaganda in War and Peace*, New York: Atheneum, 1972.
United States. Bureau of the Budget, Committee on Records of War Administration, War Records Section, *The United States at War: Development and Administration of the War Program by the Federal Government*, New York: Da Capo Press, 1972.
United States. Office of Censorship, *A Report on the Office of Censorship*, Washington, D.C.: US Government Printing Office, 1945.
United States. Office of War Information, *OWI in the ETO: A Report on the Activities of the Office of War Information in the European Theatre of Operations January 1944-January 1945*, Washington, D.C.: US Government Printing Office, 1945.
Viviani, Nancy, and Wilenski, Peter, *The Australian Development Assistance Agency: A Post Mortem Report*, National Monograph Series, no. 3, Brisbane: Royal Institute of Public Administration, 1978.
Warburg, James P., *Unwritten Treaty*, New York: Harcourt, Brace, 1946.
Weber, Max, *From Max Weber: Essays in Sociology*, trans. and ed. H.H. Gerth and C. Wright Mills, London: Routledge & Kegan Paul, 1948.
Weller, Patrick and Lloyd, Beverley (eds), *Caucus Minutes 1901-1949: Minutes of the Federal Parliamentary Labour Party, Vol. 3, 1932-1949*, Melbourne: Melbourne University Press, 1976.
White, Amber Blanco, *The New Propaganda*, London: Gollancz, 1939.
White, John Baker, *The Big Lies*, London: Evans, 1956.
Whitington, Don, *The House Will Divide: A Review of Australian Federal Politics*, Melbourne: Lansdowne Press, rev. edn, 1969.
———, *Ring the Bells: A Dictionary of Federal Politics*, Melbourne: Georgian House, 1956.
———, *The Twelfth Man*, Brisbane: Jacaranda Press, 1972.
———, *The Witless Men*, Melbourne: Sun Books, 1975.
Whitington, R.S., *Sir Frank: The Frank Packer Story*, Melbourne: Cassell, 1971.
Williams, Francis, *Press, Parliament and the People*, London: Heinemann, 1946.
Yanker, Gary, *Prop Art*, New York: Darien House, 1972.

Young, I.W., *Theodore: His Life and Times*, Sydney: Alpha Books, 1971.
Zald, Mayer, *Organisational Change: The Political Economy of the Y.M.C.A.*, Chicago: University of Chicago Press, 1970.
Zeman, Z.B., *Nazi Propaganda*, London: Oxford University Press, 1964.

Journal Articles

Ansell, R.D., "Advertising in Relation to the Public Service", Institute of Public Administration (Australia) Journal 6 (new series), no. 8 (December 1947):
Ball, D.J., "The Blind Men and the Elephant: A Critique of Bureaucratic Political Theory", *Australian Outlook* 28, no. 1 (April 1974): 71-92.
Ball, W. MacMahon, "The Australian Censorship", *Australian Quarterly*, no. 26 (June 1935): 9-14.
Bell, Roger, "Australian-American Disagreement over the Peace Settlements with Japan, 1944-46", *Australian Outlook* 30, no. 2 (August 1976): 238-62.
———, "Censorship and War: Australia's Curious Censorship Experience, 1939-1945", *Media Information — Australia* 6 (November 1977): 1-3.
Calwell, A.A., "Telling Australia's Story to the World", *Labor Digest* 1, no. 6 (August 1945): 29-33.
Dixon, M.F., "Bold Experiment in Nationally Owned News Service", *Meanjin Quarterly* 14 (1955): 115-20.
"External Shortwave Broadcasts — Work of Radio Australia", *Current Notes on International Affairs* 20, no. 7 (July 1948): 796-803.
Farago, Ladislas, "British Propaganda: The Inside Story", *United Nations World* 2, no. 9 (1948): 22-26.
Fried, Jacob A., "The OWI's Moscow Desk", *Public Opinion Quarterly* 10 (Summer 1946): 156-67.
Gosnell, Harold F., "Obstacles to Domestic Pamphleteering by O.W.I. in World War II", *Journalism Quarterly* 23 (December 1946): 360-69.
Hilvert, John, "More on Australia's Curious War Censorship Experience", *Media Information — Australia* 7 (February 1978): 41-44.

Jones, David, "Advertising Research: Myths, Legends and Realities", *Broadcasting and Television* 28, no. 1172 (16 March 1978): 39, 78.

Kiernan, Colm, "Arthur A. Calwell's Clashes with the Australian Press, 1943-45", *Historical Journal* (University of Wollongong Historical Society) 2, no. 1 (March 1976): 74-111.

Kris, Ernst, "Some problems of War Propaganda: A Note on Propaganda New and old", *Psychoanalytic Quarterly* 12 (July 1943): 381-99.

Lyford, Joseph P., "A Proposal: Journalism in Government", *Centre Magazine* 7, no. 4 (August 1974): 2-7.

McNeil, Kenneth, "Understanding Organisational Power: Building on the Weberian Legacy", *Administrative Science Quarterly* 23 (June 1978): 254-71.

McQueen, Humphrey, "Keith Murdoch: Hoisted by the Gallows", *Nation-Review*, 24-30 March 1977, pp. 540-41.

"The NBC Listening Post", *RCA Review*, 3 October 1941, pp. 143-44.

Pollard, John A., "Words are Cheaper than Blood", *Public Opinion Quarterly* 9 (Fall 1945): 238-304.

Sawer, Geoffrey, "The Defence Power of the Commonwealth in Time of War", *Australian Law Journal* 20 (December 1946):

Thomas, Alan, "The Politicisation of the ABC in the 1930's: A Case-study of 'The Watchman' ", *Politics* 13, no. 2 (November 1978): 286-95.

Unstead, K., "Commonwealth Government Advertising", *Institute of Public Administration (Australia) Journal* 6 (new series), no. 8 (December 1947):

Walmsley, G.L., and Zald, M.N., "The Political Economy of Public Organizations", *Public Administration Review* 33 (1973): 62-73.

Whetten, David A., "Coping with Incompatible Expectations: An Integrated View of Role Conflict", *Administrative Science Quarterly* 23 (June 1978): 254-71.

White, William, C., "An O.W.I. Outpost in Moscow", *American Review of the Soviet Union* 6 (November 1944): 15-19.

Williams, Francis, "Review: The Government Information Services", *Public Administration* (UK) 43 (Autumn 1965): 331.

Index

Abyssinian crisis, 30
Adelaide News, 42, 89
Advertising Agency Advisory Board, 82
advertising co-ordination, 157; government, 3, 9, 81-82
Advertising Division, 81-82, 86, 91, 103, 119, 157; budget of, 105
Advisory War Council, 65, 73, 78, 80, 81, 143
Age, Melbourne, 57, 144, 180, 190
Air Force, 87, 109, 113-15
Allied Political Warfare Committee, 134
Allied Works Council Public Relations, 109
Amalgamated Wireless (Australasia), 28-29, 84
Anschluss, 30
Anzacs March Again, 28
Argus, Melbourne, 13, 19, 69, 89, 110, 182
Armed Services (American), 145
Armed Services (Australian), 6, 15, 23-24, 81, 86-87, 145. *See also* Army; Navy
Army, 6, 23, 30, 39, 87
Army Directorate of Public Relations, 109-13, 120, 126, 146; criticism of, 110-12
Army Directorate of Research, 124

Ashley, W.P., 96-98, 101-4, 107-8, 111, 117-19, 123-24, 126, 133, 138, 141, 153, 159
Associated Newspapers, 179
Associated Press (New York), 148
Attorney-General's Department, 60-61, 188
Australia First Movement, 45, 154
Australian Associated Press, 22, 37, 38, 79
Australian Broadcasting Commission, 22-23, 28-29, 32, 38, 56-58, 64, 72, 80, 83-84, 100-101, 103, 106-9, 125, 132-33, 136-37, 141, 159-61, 198, 201; news policy of, 106-9
Australian Communisty Party, 48
Australian Federation of Commercial Broadcasters, 80, 117, 148, 191
Australian Information Service, 3, 7
Australian Intelligence Corps, 12
Australian Journalists Association, 9, 89, 144, 177
Australian Labor Party, 19, 192
Australian National Travel Association, 79
Australian News and Information Bureau, 3, 72, 78-79, 91, 166, 170

Index

Australian Newspaper Council, 22, 70
Australian Newspaper Proprietors Association, 107, 110, 147, 177-78
Australian War Memorial, 24

Bailey, David W., 79, 166
Bailey, K.H., 83
Ball, W. MacMahon, 3, 8, 19, 36-39, 57, 72, 83-85, 98, 101, 132-41, 199
Banfield, C. 19
Barry, J.V., 46
Barry, K., 121
Bateson, Charles, 79, 84, 132
Beale, H.E., 170
Bean, C.E.W., 121
Bearup, T.W., 101, 108-9, 133
Beasley, J.A., 100-101
Bell, Roger, 150-51, 189-90
Bissell, W., 110
Blackburn, M., 18, 43, 47-48, 62-63
Blamey, Sir Thomas, 67, 89, 100, 111
Bonney, Edmund G., 3, 8, 89-91, 101-2, 123, 139-50, 156-58, 160-62, 164, 166, 169-70, 175, 177, 179, 185, 187-88, 198
Boyer, R.J.F., 72, 104, 160
British Broadcasting Corporation, 22, 45, 58, 105, 131, 139
British High Commission, 15
Broadcasting Division, 28, 32, 36, 38-39. *See also* Shortwave broadcasting
Brown, Dickson, 149
Burchett, W., 42
Burns, C., 19, 67

Cabinet, 29, 62, 87, 112, 119, 137, 138
cables, 72, 143
Calwell, Arthur A., 3, 5, 98, 153-61, 164-65, 168-69, 174-79, 187-89
Cameron, Archie, 18, 30, 47, 49, 66, 68, 70, 73, 85, 155
Campbell, H.A.M., 144
Canberra Secretariat, 103-4, 112, 126-27, 159, 165

Casey, R.G., 48
Censored!, 3, 191
Censors: as journalists, 5, 42, 140, 148, 157, 198, 200; as military officers, 13-14; diaries, 67-69; women as, 42
Censorship: for morale, 147-50; instructions, 42-44, 67, 85-86, 88, 142, 145, 175, 189; in World War I, 5, 10-15; of cable and wireless messages, 88; of communications, 41; of election broadcasts, 149-50; of films, 69; of parliamentary debates, 89, 91; of references to medical services, 85; of shortwave broadcasts, 140; policy, 3, 4, 8, 23-24, 30, 37, 40-48, 70-71, 86-90, 102, 139-51; regulations, 7, 30-32, 41-44, 57, 61-64; row of 1944, 5, 8, 174-94; rules (Navy), 66; staff, 42, 71; statistics, 4, 191-92, 202. *See also* conference on consorship; Press Censorship Advisory Committee
Censorship Division, 3, 6, 30-32, 39-42, 67, 91, 101-2, 104, 139-51, 170, 199
censorship headquarters, 91
Censorship Liaison Officers, 32, 69
Century, 71
Chifley, Ben, 118, 164, 169-70
Cinema Photographic and Films Branch, 27
Cinematographic Films, 3
Cleary, W., 101, 106-9, 137
Clunies-Ross, I., 121
Code of Censorship Principles, 186-89
Collings, J., 18
Commercial Broadcasting, 7, 8, 21, 28, 32, 56-58, 64-65, 80, 91, 190-91, 201
Commission for Public Relations, 125
Committee on National Morale, 120-26
Common Cause, 41
Communist Press, 45-48
Comrade X, 88
Conference on Censorship, 141-42
Conlon, Alf, 3, 120-21, 124-25

Index

Consolidated Press Ltd, 178
Coombs, H.C., 124, 125
Cooper, Duff, 92
"Cooper's Snoopers", 92, 123
Correspondent Accreditation, 110, 112
Council for Civil Liberties, 45, 46, 63
Country Party, 18, 19, 92
Cowra Japanese POW breakout, 174, 189
Crawford, R.M., 120
Crisp, L.F., 83
Croll, R.H., 88, 89
Curthoys, R.L., 190
Curtin, John, 3, 19, 29, 62, 65, 80, 84, 85, 88, 97, 99, 101, 103, 107-9, 118-25, 134, 141-47, 153-55, 156-61, 175, 189
Customs (Censorship) Policy, 37

Daily Mirror, 179, 180
Daily News, 19
Daily Telegraph, 3, 56, 57, 90, 113, 142, 143, 154, 175, 177, 178-79 185, 189, 190
Davis, Elmer, 121
Deamer, S.H., 120, 125
Defence Act, 30
Defence Power under the Constitution, 183-84
De La Valette, John, 136
Department of Administrative Services, 3
Department of Commerce, 27, 32
Department of Defence, 17, 41
Department of Defence Coordination, 103, 105
Department of Economic Coordination, 54
Department of Education, 89
Department of External Affairs, 18, 32, 134, 137, 138, 160-61, 163-64
Department of Immigration, 169
Department of Information: American division, 72, 103-4; and Army, 112-13; budget of, 3, 32, 73, 97, 105; functions of, 17; "hate" campaign, 115-18, 121; headquarters, 24, 80, 103; media reception of, 20-22; news sessions, 105; organization, 24-32, 79-83, 101-5; overseas publicity policy, 165-70; radio programs, 57, 58-59; staff, 3, 19-20, 170
Department of Information (Malayan), 30
Department of Interior, 77, 79
Department of Labour and National Service, 97
Department of Media, 3
Department of Munitions, 54
Department of Postmaster-General. See Postmaster-General's Department
Department of Postwar Reconstruction, 124, 125, 164, 169
Department of Supply, 32
Department of the Army, 41, 138, 164; Military Board, 82, 110
Department of the Prime Minister, 119
Department of the Special Minister of State, 3
Department of the Treasury, 103, 119, 136-37
Directorate of War Propaganda, 11
Dixon, F., 58, 108
Drakeford, A.S., 19
Dumas, Sir Lloyd, 60
Dunk, William, 49

Editorial Division, 21, 27-28, 79, 91, 199
election, federal, 65
Evatt, H.V., 98, 100-101, 106, 107, 109, 142, 144, 154, 159-60, 180, 182

Fadden, A., 71, 73, 86, 90, 92, 133
Fairfax, Ross, 182
Fairfax, W.O., 144, 176, 179
Farey v Burnett (1916), 183
Federation of Australian Commercial Broadcasters, 64-65
Ferber, Helen, 83, 135
Fewster, Kevin J., 12
film industry, 32
Films Division, 28, 91, 126
Fisher, Andrew, 11
Fisk, Sir Ernest, 29, 54
Fitzgerald, A.A., 169
Fitzpatrick, Brian, 124

Index

Foll, H.S., 77-92, 104, 105, 107, 132, 165-66
Forde, F.M., 110, 155, 177
Fox-Movietone News, 28
Free Presbyterian Church, 54

Gallup (Australian Public Opinion Poll), 63, 92, 99, 118
Gibson, W.G., 132
Gibson Committee (on wireless broadcasting), 103, 107, 131-33, 137, 142, 155
Gone With The Wind, 69
group committees, 25-27, 79, 92
Guardian, 45
Gullett, Sir Henry, 17, 18, 20, 22, 24, 25, 26, 29, 45-47, 48, 49

Hall, H.L., 167
Hamilton, Ian, 98
Hannan, A., 18
Hansard, 44, 71
Hasluck, Paul, 4, 5, 25, 91-92
Hawes, R.E., 101, 102
Heinemann Ltd, 167
Henderson, R.A.G., 53, 178-79
Herald, Melbourne, 17, 36, 56, 70, 79, 89, 120, 144, 180
Herald and Weekly Times, 73
High Court, 5, 174, 181-86
Hoey, Tom, 85, 98, 147-48, 158, 164, 180, 181
Hogbin, R.I., 120, 121
Holmes, Charles, 79, 101-102
Holt, T., 57
Home News, 165
Horne, R.I., 83, 98, 156
Hughes, Richard, 120
Hughes, W.M., 12, 85, 87, 92
Hutcheson, I.B., 81

Inter-Allied Relations Division, 103, 170
Interdepartmental Committee to Co-ordinate Publicity, 168

Jackson, D.G.M., 30
Japanese broadcasts, 135
Japanese monitoring service, 139
Jenkin, Percy, 18, 42, 46, 89
John Fairfax and Sons, 182
Journalists and administrators, 123

Kennedy, E.T., 144, 176
Kerr, John, 124
Kiernan, Colm, 174
Knowles, Sir George, 60-61
Knox, Errol G.G., 70, 89, 107, 110
Kokoda Front-Line, 126

Lang, J.T., 71
Latham, Sir John, 184
Legge, J., 19
Lever Bros. Pty Ltd, 81
Lewis, Essington, 54
Lillicrapp, A.M., 117
"Listening Post", 39, 83-84, 134, 162
London News Chronicle, 149
London Times, 190
Lyons, Joseph, 18, 30, 54

MacArthur, Douglas, 110, 145-46, 98-100
McCauley, Group Captain, 113-15
McCauley, N., 71, 103, 112, 159
McDaniel, Yates, 148-49
McEwen, John, 49
McGuiness, F.V., 67
McLaughlin, A.M., 57
Macquarie Broadcasting Network, 105
Mangrove Mountain Fruitgrowers Association, 117
Mansell, H.H., 144, 178-81, 187
Mant, Gilbert, 180
March of Time, 72
Marr, Sir Charles, 133
Martens, G., 18
Menzies, Robert, 3, 7, 15, 17, 24, 29, 37, 45, 47-49, 53-55, 57, 59, 63-65, 67-68, 72-73, 77, 81, 88, 89, 91, 92, 108, 109, 151, 170
Metro-Goldwyn-Mayer, 69
Military History Section, 112
Military Intelligence, 110
Ministry of Information (British), 6, 15, 27, 29-30, 72, 92, 121, 123, 134
monitors. *See* "Listening Post"
Munitions Public Relations, 109
Murdoch, Sir Keith, 3, 7, 8, 18, 19, 22, 53-66, 69-73, 77, 78, 80, 87, 89, 110, 133, 144, 154-55, 176, 201

Murdoch, Patrick John, 54

Nairn, W.M., 19
National Film Board, 168
National Security Act, 40, 45, 47, 67
Naval Board, 66
Navy, 6, 23, 39, 66, 69, 70, 85, 87, 88
Netherland East Indies Government, 136
Northcliffe, Lord, 54
Norton, Ezra, 179
NSW State Censor, 143-44, 178-81

Office of War Information (USA), 6, 121, 123
Ogilvy, Clive, 117
Order-To-Submit, 31, 45, 67, 175, 178
overseas: broadcasting, 28-30, 163-64; correspondents, 189-90; publicity, 7, 79, 80, 104, 199

Pacific News First Policy, 105-7
Packer, Frank, 178
Paddison, A.C., 107
Palmer, Vance, 124
Paramount Films, 126
Parer, Damien, 3, 27, 91, 126
parliamentary criticism of department, 71, 73; reaction to ABC news policies, 108-9; reception to department, 18-19
Peace Officers, Commonwealth, 179
Penton, Brian, 3, 142, 154, 174, 175-80, 187-88, 191
Philosophy of Anarchism, 88
"Phoney War", 45, 48
Photographic Resources Rationalization, 112
Pinner Review Committee into Civil Staffing, 169-70
Political Warfare Broadcast Policy, 134-36
Postmaster-General's Department, 29-30, 39, 84, 99, 138, 160-61, 164
press, 7, 8, 32, 91, 144-47, 148, 175-76; communist, 66; gallery, 91; metropolitan, 9; reaction to censorship regulations, 61; rural, 9, 21, 82, 91; specialist, 91; suburban, 21, 91
Press Censorship Advisory Committee, 144-47, 148, 175-76
Prime Minister's Committee on National Morale, 120-26, 135
prisoners of war, 99, 135
propaganda policy, 8
public reaction: to censorship regulations, 61-62; to censorship row of 1944, 181
Public Relations Commission, 125
Public Service Board, 24
Publicist, The, 45
publicity, review of government, 112-13

RAAF. *See* Air Force
Radio: 2KY, 30; 2SM, 30; 4BH, 105; Australia, 3; Tokyo, 99
radio listening, 99
Radio Times, 90
Rationing Commission, 109, 112, 124
recruiting: campaigns, 81; statistics, 59
Rich, Sir George, 182
Roper, E.D., 120
Rorke, H.A., 12, 42, 143-44
Royal Commission on the Constitution (1929), 183
Ryan, T.J., 12, 182

Salute the Army Broadcasts, 112
Sawer, G., 83, 98, 156, 164, 182, 183
Sayers, C.E., 56, 79
Scullen, J.H., 144-47
Scullin-Lazzarini Review of Department, 118-20, 123, 153
Shaw, A.G.L., 83
shortwave broadcasting: American reactions to, 84; from the enemy, 142-43; monitors, 83; policy, 83-84, 134
Shortwave Broadcasting Division, 3, 6, 39, 72, 80, 83-85, 91, 102-3, 104, 131-41, 151, 156, 170, 198, 199, 200; academic approach, 85; budget of, 72, 84, 105, 136-37,

138, 164; policy, 139-41; staff, 72, 84, 162, 164
shortwave commercial broadcasting, 29
shortwave service, transfer to department, 157-62
Slessor, Kenneth, 79
Smith, C.P., 18, 26
Smith's Weekly, 99, 119, 120
South Australia State Censor, 180
Soviets Today, 46
Sparrow, G.H., 144
Spender, Percy, 87, 166
Spooner, W., 92
Sportsman, 179
Stanley, Massey, 19
Stanner, W.E.H., 120
Starke, Sir Hayden, 181, 182
State Publicity Censors, 42, 67
Stone, Julius, 120, 121
Stout, A.K., 120
Stutterheim, Kurt von, 176
Sun, Melbourne, 79, 89
Sun, Sydney, 19, 71, 110, 144, 179, 180
Sunday Telegraph, 178-79
Sydney Morning Herald, 53, 57, 89, 143, 144, 178, 179

Think or Be Damned, 176
This Week of War, 83
Thorby, H., 62
Treloar, J., 19, 24-25, 54, 60, 89, 112

Truth, 67, 111, 179

United Australia Party, 54, 192
University of Melbourne teaching staff, 46-47
U.S. War Department's Bureau of Information, 99

Victorian Book Censorship League, 37
Victorian State Censor, 84, 164, 180

Walkabout, 79
Wally and the Major, 88
War Book, 14, 15, 30, 41, 110
War Cabinet, 57, 59-60, 78, 89
War Loan Campaign, 66-67, 81-82
War Organization of Industry Public Relations, 109
War Precautions Act, 11
Ward, E., 18, 71, 177
Weber, Max, 197
White, T.H., 37
Whitington, D., 96
Wigmore, L., 19, 98, 112, 156, 162-63
Williams, Sir Dudley, 181, 182
Winkler, J., 19
Women's International League Monthly News Sheets, 88
Wright, R.D., 120
Wright, R.D., 120

D 810 .P7 A84 1984